HOMELESS ACROSS AMERICA

HOMELESS ACROSS AMERICA

Kevin E. Lake

iUniverse, Inc.
New York Bloomington Shanghai

HOMELESS ACROSS AMERICA

iUniverse books may be ordered through booksellers or by contacting:

iUniverse
1663 Liberty Drive
Bloomington, IN 47403
www.iuniverse.com
1-800-Authors (1-800-288-4677)

Because of the dynamic nature of the Internet, any Web addresses or links contained in this book may have changed since publication and may no longer be valid.

ISBN: 978-0-595-50397-1 (pbk)
ISBN: 978-0-595-61490-5 (ebk)

Printed in the United States of America

1

At no point in my life had I ever imagined I would find myself homeless. Especially in the years and months leading to its reality in the summer of 2007.

Up until that time I had spent most of the previous years as a successful stock broker, a loving father and a good neighbor. I had that cute little ranch starter home on the corner with the well manicured lot that so many young professionals in my age group aspire to start out with just before moving up to the larger, more astute colonial at the end of a cul-de-sac.

I coached my children's sport's teams, volunteered at their school and was active in many civic groups. Unfortunately, I would find out at the hands of life's circumstances filled with surprising twists and turns that what we have today is not always promised for us tomorrow.

I had grown up in the tough, hard working timber town of Richwood, West Virginia, a small, almost village type community where a hard day's work paid off with the ability to meet one's needs and enjoy a good night's sleep. It was a quaint little town nestled around the forks and main body of the Cherry river. Though cut off for many miles from what most would call "society" and trapped within mountains that went as far as the mind could imagine it had the people and the resources to provide for all of our needs.

Made up of a population of roughly 1500 people, many who's families had been in the area for many generations, it was a place where the truly important aspects of living where still a part of every day life; honesty, respect for others, and an appreciation for the simple things.

The town was founded in the late 1800's. It was formed around the timber industry like so many other small, Appalachian communities in those times. It's location at the point where the north and south forks of the Cherry river, a river named for the over abundance of wild black cherry trees that appear there in the most dense population in the United States, is no accident as waterways were the most generally used method of transporting logs to the lumber mills back then. However, at the time of Richwood's founding the railway system was replacing water transportation in the logging industry and no logs were ever actually floated to the big mill in Richwood, but rather hauled by trains.

Though the rivers run so dry in the summer months that we were hard pressed as children to float an inner tube down them without having to get out and walk every 40 yards or so, their waters rage in the spring with the winter's thaw as if a great dam had been released at their head waters.

In the areas throughout West Virginia where logs were floated to the mills via the rivers, loggers would spend months at a time living under the most extreme conditions and often in very undesirable logging camps and would spend the fall and winter working 20 hours a day, felling trees and then muscling them with the help of horses into the frozen rivers. When the snow and ice which always measured many feet would melt away in the spring the flooding waters would carry the logs down stream to the mills in short order.

Men called "rods men" or "pole men" would construct flat boats by tying several logs together with rope and ride down the river with long poles ensuring that no logs got jammed or caught along the river banks or on boulders. They also unclogged any jams that took place within the stream itself along the way.

This was not an easy or even a safe job by any means. My own great grand father on my father's side of the family was drowned doing this very work when he was pinned beneath logs he was floating down the Little Kanawha river in Braxton County West Virginia, about 100 miles north of Richwood.

One must not go too far back in their geneology to find such occurrences if their family had been in the mountain state for many generations and had relied on timber, or coal for that matter as a livelihood. My mother's father had died when a coal mine collapsed on him and several other men when my mother herself was only two years old. I never knew this maternal grand father of mine and she has no memories of him herself.

Perhaps reasons like this is why family is still the most important aspect of life for so many "Appalachian Americans" too often labeled as "hillbillies." The bells and whistles and much of the "bling" of aforementioned "society" has yet to catch on in the mountain state, but fortunately the importance of God, good friends, and family has yet to have been let go.

My father, Ernest Lake, known as "Ernie" to friends, managed the larger of the two lumber mills in Richwood during all of my childhood and still does to this day. His best friend, Bill Glasscock owns the other, smaller mill.

My father's mill was owned by Georgia Pacific for many decades but within the last couple of years was bought out by Collins Lumber, a family owned company out of Oregon for whom my father feels honored to work.

When I look back on my years growing up in Richwood my mind is filled with images of a skinny little boy, me, running along the banks of the Cherry river with a fishing pole in his hand in search of the "big one", which would have been no bigger really than the outstretched hand of a full grown man as this was the average size of a mature native brook trout, a fish that appeared and reproduced in the wild in our mountain streams.

At other times I see images of that same skinny little boy trudging up the side of a very steep mountain, single shot 20 gauge shot gun in hand, tracking flocks of wild turkeys that for some reason never seemed to travel down hill.

When teenagers in other parts of the country were getting out of school and rushing off to the malls to waste time or get into trouble, my childhood best friend, Gene Smithson and I were strapping our compound bows across our backs, jumping on our dirt bikes and screaming to the top of Fork Mountain, the mountain in between the Cherry's two forks, to occupy our deer stands that we had built during and baited all summer.

As I entered high school, I discovered the sport of cross country. To no surprise all those years of hiking through mountains nearly as straight up and down as the trees that grew in them paid off as I seemed to be a natural at the sport.

I spent my winters during those high school years praying for snow and cold weather in which to train. Not that I was a sadomasochist by any means, but the way I saw it most of my competition around the state probably would not go out and run in several feet of snow and sub zero temperatures but I would, figuring that was one more day of training or so many more miles of running I would have over them by the start of track season in the spring.

My method of madness worked as I won the 1600 meter (1 mile) state championship in 1991 with a time of 4:33, which still stands as Richwood High's school record these nearly 20 years later. Though I did not win states or break our school's record in the 3200 (2 mile) I am just as proud of my 9:56 best time in that event.

The work ethic I put into my running and practically every endeavor before or since then is one that I do not believe would have been instilled in me had I grown up in so many other places or in so many other ways. The example my three sisters Carrie (older), Martha and Elizabeth (both younger) had set for us by our hard working father and even harder working stay at home mother Peggy is one that for certain has laid out a road plan for success in our lives.

2

After high school I attended Glenville State College in Glenville West Virginia, eerily located along the banks of the very river that had taken my great grandfather's life many years before. It is here that I met a beautiful little red head with big, crazy green eyes named Amanda who would eventually become my wife. Amanda's father was a history professor at our school and I certainly considered her one heck of a catch, as did all of my friends at the time.

Toward the end of my college years I had transferred to and graduated from Fairmont State College, becoming the first in my family to get a degree, but I kept my relationship with Amanda who was back at Glenville State active. Though I deeply loved Amanda for her many attributes there was one thing she brought to the relationship that I loved most; her two year old son Christian.

Christian was a handsome, well mannered, red headed little lad that seems to have jumped right out of the television screen from the Andy Griffith show. Because of this, I quickly started calling him "OP", a nick name that has stuck with him to this day.

After finishing college, Amanda, OP and I left the mountain state and headed for the motherland of Virginia, a state that West Virginia was a part of up until the outbreak of the civil war. Unless I wanted to dig coal or stack lumber for a living I had to look outside of West Virginia for suitable employment. Sadly, unemployment in the mountain state still hovers at 20 % even though the national average is below its historic level of 5% as of the writing of this book. It is unfortunate that so many West Virginian's, myself included, have to leave the state for employment when there is no place on earth we would rather be.

After a quick marriage at the court house in Lexington Virginia and nearly a year living in nearby Buena Vista, myself working for Georgia Pacific, mostly to take advantage of their health insurance plan which we needed due to the upcoming birth of our daughter Emily we headed further toward the coast and took up residence in Ruckersville, Virginia just outside of Charlottesville, home of the University of Virginia.

Charlottesville is a beautiful Piedmont community of about 40,000 people, resting in the foothills of the Blue Ridge Mountains. Anyone interested in history could spend weeks in this area and still not take it all in. Perhaps it is most known for Monticello, Thomas Jefferson's mansion and plantation that sits high above the town, a town much of which Jefferson himself designed.

It is also the starting point and ending point of the great transcontinental journey of Lewis and Clark. This journey was sanctioned by Mr. Jefferson in an attempt to find a waterway that would link the east coast to that of the west. The fact that I was relocating to the starting point of such a journey would later prove to be quite ironic in my own life in the summer of 2007.

The University is the hub and life's blood of the community. It has been attended by many of the great men in our nations history including Woodrow Wilson, who himself was from Staunton Virginia only 40 miles west of Charlottesville. One of the most notorious students in the University's past was the great writer of macabre, Edgar Allen Poe. Today, his dorm room is glassed off and can be viewed as it was then by the public. It is located in one of the long corridors beneath the Rotunda, the beautiful building of constructional magnificence designed by Mr. Jefferson.

Peering through the glass into Poe's room one will notice its simplicity, consisting of only a single bed, a desk, a fire place and a change of clothes hanging on the wall. Oh yes, and a black raven perched in the window seal.

After settling in the Charlottesville area I went to work as a stock broker for Edward Jones Investments. This profession was a far cry from those of my ancestors and professional as it seemed, my main joy in it was knowing that, if successful at it, I would be able to provide for my family, which would grow even more as our third child Olivia was born only 20 months after her big sister Emily.

Life seemed full of long days and sleepless nights in the days after settling outside of Charlottesville. My day's work involved trying to build a book of business by meeting people daily, mostly by simply knocking on their doors, and trying to convince them to trust me with their savings. At night I often lay awake praying it would work out, and when I did fall to sleep I was too often woken up sporadically by babies. Amanda breast fed all of our children but it was my job to transport them to and from their crib for this ritual.

In spite of often being tired and stressed those days were happy and life was passing by quickly. Somehow, over time I had convinced nearly 400 people in our area to entrust me with nearly $20,000,000.00 worth of their savings and our family's needs were being more than met by the commissions I was generating. Then, only weeks away from Olivia's first birthday which was on September 20'th of that year, 2001, the world stopped, turned upside down and changed forever.

Terrorists had hijacked U.S. airliners and flown two of them into the world trade center towers in New York city. Another flew into the Pentagon in Washington D.C. and yet another had gone down in a Pennsylvania field when its crew, realizing by this point that they were being used as human bombs took matters into their own hands and attempted to regain control of the plane from the terrorists and in so doing plummeted to their deaths.

These events, and those that followed, including U.S. military operations in Afghanistan and later in Iraq would affect the lives of every American in some way. I would have never imagined it, but these events, and the never really before felt since of patriotism they inspired in me would eventually lead to the break down of my marriage and attribute to my state of homelessness.

When I fell in love with Amanda I guess it was for many of the same reasons young, early twenty something year olds fall in love with each other. Reasons unfortunately that are mostly physical. Amanda had a pretty face and a great body, and at 23 that seems to be all that matters. Only later in life when more important issues would rear their heads did I really realize how important so many other things like view points and core values are.

Like so many other Americans following the attacks of September 11'th I felt a strong need for retribution; a need to see that those responsible were held to account. Amanda on the other hand, along with her ivory tower college professor father seemed very bluesy about the whole situation. They would get on tirades about how, "America had this coming," due to our, "Arrogance and treatment of others around the world." At one point, Amanda stated that she had more respect for Osama Bin Laden than she did George Bush because, "Bin Laden was smart enough to mastermind the attacks and Bush is a bumbling idiot from Texas."

Before the attacks, I had always considered myself to be a moderate, non-political type, but certainly pro America in every way. I could not believe the ideology that I was seeing in my wife. I guess it had always been there, it just took an event like 9/11 to bring it out.

As time went by the differences in nearly every aspect of life between Amanda and I seemed to grow until finally, in August of 2004 she decided to leave me and seek a divorce. Though I pushed for reconciliation as much as I could, mostly because I did not want our three children to have to go through a divorce, Amanda would have no part in it. She had made her mind up to get out, and get out she did.

3

To this day I do not fault Amanda for the ending of our marriage. Just as it takes two people to make a marriage work it also takes two to bring about its demise. Nor do I resent her for any of her ill behaviors during the legal process of our divorce which lasted for more than two years. I am sure I was no saint at that time either.

Amanda and I could most often times sit down and hash out what we were going to do, which was generally centered around the best interests of our children, but when the lawyers got involved it was a completely different story. Neither of our attorneys were representing our best interests but were simply representing the best interests of their own bank accounts. The more they could get us to disagree and go to court the more hours they could bill us at the rate of $200.00.

In the end Amanda and I ended up getting that to which we had originally agreed. I would keep the house, since she was the one who wanted to leave, but I would give her half of the equity. We split any debt incurred jointly during our marriage and we divided all of our assets equally. Most importantly we agreed to joint custody of the children and I agreed to pay child support based upon Virginia code. Since I had performed a step parent adoption in regard to OP once he entered grade school I was entitled to the same legal rights over him as I was the girls. Fortunately Amanda was able to find a rental house only 3 miles away so the kids could come and go to either house at any time they liked which we always allowed.

Amanda had mostly stayed at home with our children while we were married except for occasionally when she would seek part time employment, mostly as a substitute teacher, in order to get out of the house and have a bit of extra spending money. Having been raised in a stay at home parent household myself, I greatly valued its benefits and wanted those benefits to continue for my children.

Now that Amanda was no longer married to a stock broker making a decent income she would have to work. The idea of her being at home for the kids at the end of the school day was out of the question.

Fortunately I was in an industry that offered the flexibility to allow me to work from home. Unfortunately it would mean leaving my firm Edward Jones, who I had been with for six years. To work from home I would have to go the route of an independent financial advisor.

Under the independent financial planning platform offered by many companies like Raymond James and Linsco Private Ledger (LPL) investment counselors could work from where ever they desired because they were not employees of the company but independent contractors.

After doing quite a bit of research I left Edward Jones for LPL so I could work from home and continue to provide my children with the benefits of having an at home parent. I hated to leave Edward Jones. The company had always been good to me. Three of the six years I worked there Fortune magazine named them "The best company in America to work for" and this is a testament to which I would agree. Most importantly, of all the Wall Street firms out there, I believed Edward Jones was always placing the best interests of their clients ahead of their own more than any other.

The transition to the new way of life went as smoothly as could be imagined considering the circumstances. Most of my best clients at Edward Jones transferred their accounts to me at LPL. However, I now seemed only to have half as much time to work as before because my responsibilities with my children had doubled.

I quickly figured out that having the laundry done at a launderers, though a bit more costly was well worth the elimination of the chore and the addition of the extra time to my day. By going this route I soon became good friends with Regina Hju, the owner of Sunshine Laundry in Charlottesville. Regina had come to America from Taiwan nearly twenty years ago with the shirt on her back, and now, through years of hard work was a successful small business owner. Regina could always come up with the perfect Chinese proverb to fit my mood or situation of the day. Her friendship has meant more to me than clean clothes ever could.

Also, I had great neighbors. Emily and Olivia's best friend was the little girl next door, Kiki, who's mother Maria was an at home mom and was always more than willing to lend a hand when I was in need. It helped too that when she had worked Maria was a nurse because Emily is one of the craziest, dare devils of a little child I have ever known. Where most people seem to have an innate sense of fear when they know they are doing something that is borderline dangerous, Emily seems to get an adrenaline rush when engaged in dangerous behaviors. We have had family trips to the emergency room on more than one occasion due to Emily's antics, whether it was the time she head butted the thorn of a Bradford pear tree while running head first through the neighbor's bushes or the time she dove face first into a pile of fire wood trying to save a basketball that had gone out of bounds.

One thing that continued to stir my emotions however on a larger front during these times was our war on terror. By now the Taliban had been pretty much disbanded in Afghanistan though they were always trying to regroup. However, in Iraq the situation was a bit more grim.

We had toppled Saddam Hussein's bathist regime pretty quickly but we seemed to be facing an ever growing presence of terrorist insurgents sneaking their way into Iraq from places like Iran, Syria, Saudi Arabia and other mid-east countries, to take crack shots at U.S. soldiers and to disrupt the reconstruction efforts being made on behalf of the Iraqi people. Many at home were tired of the war effort and seemed to be calling for an early, premature withdraw.

Through out the day, in between calls to clients or face to face appointments I would read the news on the internet and rarely did things seem good. I knew that this was not because good things were not happening but it was because the general media seemed only to want to report the bad. You really had to know how to surf the net to find out about all the schools being constructed in Iraq or to find out that there were people now with running water and electricity who had never before had these luxuries, but if you wanted to find out about the latest suicide bomb at a bus or stop or café all you had to do was turn on your computer.

By the end of summer, 2006 we had been in Iraq for more than three years and I was continually hearing and reading about soldiers who were on their third deployment to Iraq.

My ever growing sense of patriotism and belief in our cause against terror had reached a crescendo. I felt I could no longer sit idly by and do nothing. Here I was, nearing my mid 30's, enjoying all the freedoms and luxuries of the American life while men just over half my age were going half a world away, over and over it seemed, to participate in this generation's struggle to preserve those freedoms.

With my family situation I did not feel it would be too wise to just run off and join the army. Nor did I ever at any point before ever consider a military career. Having been more of a non conforming free spirit my whole life, and especially now after thirty some years of pretty much coming and going as I pleased I did not feel I would be able to transition into a life of always being told what to do and when and how to do it.

However, at the risk of doing nothing I had to do something so I began looking into the National Guard. The way I saw it, many of the troops deploying to the middle east were guardsmen who did not serve full time and were able to maintain their family and civilian lives while not active. This was perhaps an option for me. It would allow me to do whatever I could, however small, in taking part in our war on terror yet still allow me to focus on life as a father and a financial planner.

After putting much thought into this, and taking into consideration factors such as my family situation, my age, my level of physical fitness, which I had always tried to maintain since my track days for general health reasons, I discussed the idea of enlisting in the Virginia National Guard with Amanda. To my surprise she was very supportive of the idea. Although her stance on the war was the opposite of mine she knew how important my stance was to me.

"Kevin, I think you would make a great soldier and I know this is something that is really important to you," I remember her saying. "If this is something you want to do I will support you in it!"

Amanda and I agreed that while I was off to basic training and Iraq, if deployed, she would keep the kids full time and I would send her more money than what the Virginia code required. Also, if I were to deploy, we agreed that she and the children would live in my house rent free as I would still need to make mortgage payments on it anyway.

The next day I went straight to the National Guard recruiter's office in Charlottesville. I walked in and was greeted by 26 year old staff sergeant Brad Seay (pronounced See) and informed him I wanted to enlist in the guard.

Sgt. Seay seemed a bit taken back by this thirty something year old in a business suit walking in off the street to enlist. He inquired as to my reasoning behind my desire to enlist and I simply informed him of where I stood in support of the war on terror and how I felt that I could no longer sit by and not play any active role.

"We have a great college payment plan," he said sheepishly, trying to employ his pitch that he had obviously done many times.

"I won't be needing that," I responded. "I already have a bachelor's degree."

"Oh," he said. "Well, we are offering up to $20,000 in enlistment bonuses right now," he stated, almost in a questioning tone.

"That's great," I replied. "I'll take it, but it is not a necessity. I make pretty good money as a stock broker."

At this point the other two recruiters in the room, Sgt.'s Stoner and Vandeveer looked up at me as curiously as Sgt. Seay had when I walked in.

"You're a stock broker and you want to join the Guard?" asked Sgt. Stoner.

"How old are you?" asked Sgt Vandeveer.

"I turn thirty three this fall," I responded. "Is that too old?"

"Not now," Sgt. Seay offered. "There used to be an age cut off at thirty six but it's been raised to forty two now because of the war."

"And because people are living longer and seem to be in better health at older ages," Sgt Stoner added, trying to make sure it did not look as if the military seemed desperate for enlistments, which the media was claiming they were.

"We're giving the ASVAB tonight if you want to come take it," Sgt. Seay informed me.

"What is that?" I asked.

"Oh, that's the entrance exam you have to take so we can determine if you are able to join the military and also to determine what job would be best for you. It is at 7:00 p.m. and you'd need to take it anyway if you really want to do this so can you just come back tonight?"

"Sure," I told him. "I'll go run some errands and have dinner and come back then."

"See you then," Sgt. Seay said and I was off.

Later that evening I returned and took the ASVAB. It was a general exam covering many subjects such as math, literature, science, mechanics, etc. The exam itself only took about two hours. I could have been done much sooner as I seemed to need only a fourth of the time allotted for each of the different timed sections, but there were about half a dozen other folks, all much younger than me taking the test and many of them needed all of the time given. I had not taken a standardized test like this since high school but it seemed not to be a big deal.

After the exam, it was quickly graded by the administrator, a gruff sixty something year old lady like most test administrators I could ever remember for some reason, and the results were handed over to our recruiters.

When I went into Sgt. Seay's office to get my results he seemed somewhat flabbergasted.

"You got a 92!" he exclaimed.

"Is that good?" I asked.

"The highest score you can get on it is a 99! You scored in the top eight percentile in the nation!"

"Wow!" I said. "I guess that is good then huh?"

"You can do any job in the army you want to do!" he stated. "MOS's are determined by your score results. You scored high enough to take your pick!"

"What is an MOS?" I asked.

"Oh," he said, realizing he was using shop talk that I did not yet understand. "MOS stands for 'military occupational specialty.' It simply means job description. There are several in the army, like mechanic, medic, intelligence so on and so forth. You have to score so high on the ASVAB to be eligible to train for each different one and with your score you can take your pick."

"Oh," I said.

"You should look at being a medic," he stated. "Then, in the civilian world you could get into medicine, maybe go on and become a doctor."

"Naw," I groaned. "I'll probably just go back to being a mild mannered stock broker once all this is over."

"Well," he went farther, "Maybe you should look at intelligence. You could do cool stuff like fly predator drones and kill the enemy from hundreds of miles away."

"I always hated video games," I said, "And that sounds like sitting around playing video games."

"What would you like to do then," asked Sgt. Stoner who had come into the office just a minute or two before.

"Well," I began in a matter of fact way, "Without sounding too morbid or sadistic, I would like to do whatever MOS would put me in the best position to get my hands around the neck of some fundamental extremist who would dare to tell me that my little girls can't go to school and learn because they are females, or who would try to come to this land and hijack one of our planes and knock down another of our buildings and in so doing hurt our neighbors, and squeeze the life out of him!"

Sgt.'s Seay and Stoner looked at each other, expressionless at first, and then smiled and in unison said, "Eleven Bravo!"

"What is eleven bravo?" I asked curiously.

"Oh, that's infantry," said Sgt Seay. "Do you have time to watch a 20 minute DVD?"

"Sure," I said. Amanda had the kids that night and I had nowhere else I had to be so I pulled up a chair and watched a DVD on the infantry.

What I saw in that DVD gave me goose bumps. It was filled with footage of soldiers wearing Kevlar helmets and bullet proof vests, wielding M-4 assault rifles kicking in doors in Iraq and dragging insurgents out of darkened rooms by the towels on their heads. It showed men as brave as I had ever seen running in front of the cannon and mortar fire to take the fight to the enemy who was safely covered where the mortar and artillery shells hadn't reached and exterminating them at close range.

"That's what I want to do!" I exclaimed in a convinced voice. "Sign me up tonight!"

They did.

4

A few days later, I received a call from Sgt. Seay explaining that there where several more forms that I needed to fill out to complete my enlistment process. It turned out that Sgt. Seay had actually not been recruiting that long and was still learning a lot of the ins and outs of his position and he had over looked these forms the night I was at his office.

At any rate, he drove out to my house in Ruckersville and we sat down at the kitchen table and finished the few forms we had originally neglected. At the bottom of the first form, when I had to sign and date it, I got goose bumps again as I looked at my watch for the date, out of habit more than anything because I, like the entire nation, knew the date. It was September 11'th. It was the fifth anniversary of the terrorist attacks that had brought me to embark on this endeavor in the first place.

"This is so ironic," I commented to Sgt. Seay, who by this point had given me permission to call him Brad.

"What is that?" he asked.

"I am commemorating the fifth anniversary of the attacks by enlisting in the Guard," I said.

"Spooky isn't it?" he said, sitting back in his chair.

"Yeah," I replied, sitting back in mine and running my fingers through hair just beginning to gray above the temples.

I leaned back over and continued to sign. "Not as spooky for us as for them though," I murmured. "It seems as if a lot of people over here have short term memories but I am not one of them."

After finishing the paper work Brad and I moved to the living room to talk for a bit. I found out that Brad had served four years in the navy and at the end of his enlistment switched over to the Army National Guard to work as a recruiter. He had married a girl he met while stationed in Italy and they had two young sons, several years younger than my children.

"You play guitar?" Brad said, gesturing to my acoustic guitar in the corner that he had been staring at for a while.

"Yes," I responded.

"So do I," he said as he moved over to pick it up. "Do you mind?" he asked as he pulled the pick out of the strings at the top of the neck and sat back down.

"Not at all," I told him.

Brad and I sat in my living room and took turns trading licks and playing songs for over an hour. He was actually much better at playing guitar than I was. It turned out that he was the lead singer in a local country band but also, like myself preferred some 80's rock too.

After we played and talked for a while longer Brad told me he would come pick me up at 4:30 a.m. the following Tuesday. We would be going to the processing station, known as MEPS, at Fort Lee, just outside of Richmond Virginia. Here I would take a drug test, have blood work done, go through an eye exam and other physical informalities and most importantly be sworn into the military and receive my date to ship off for basic training at Fort Benning Georgia, the home of the infantry, which was located about an hour and a half south of Atlanta on the Alabama line.

The following week he did as he said, and way too early in the morning for me, something I guess I would eventually have to get used to, we were off for Fort Lee.

I remember getting to Fort Lee and standing outside with a couple hundred other recent enlistments waiting for the place to open at 6:00 a.m. When it did, a big (and I mean big, like 220 pounds) black lady in her early thirties came out and started yelling at us like dogs! She was explaining to us the process we would go through once entering the M.E.P.S. station, which involved sitting around for long periods of time in silence, waiting to be told, in the same yelling fashion it would turn out, where to go and what to do. I guess I was starting the Army's practices of being yelled at and waiting around for long periods of time early.

Once inside, I spent the day filling out more forms and being poked and prodded in various places, some quite uncomfortable, and being yelled at. At one point I was able to have a brief conversation with a couple other new recruits, an 18 year old black guy from Richmond and a really attractive 19 year old girl from Hampton who was of Puerto Rican descent.

"So why are you joining the army?" I asked the young man.

"I got my girl pregnant and I aint tryin' to be around here for that dawg," he replied.

"Oh," I said. "So you are going to take advantage of the great health insurance offered by the military so you can start raising your family right huh?" I asked.

"Naw dawg!" he said shaking his head and rolling his eyes like I was an idiot. "I aint ready for no kid and I'm getting' outta here yo! The Army is my way outta this thang."

"Oh," I said with no follow up.

"How about you young lady?" I asked, turning toward the girl. "Why are you joining the Army?"

"I aint joining the army," she said. "I'm joining the Navy."

This was the processing MEPS for all branches of the military, not just the Army, it was just located on an Army base.

"So why are you joining the Navy then?" I prodded.

"Because I am gonna find me a real man," she said in a sultry tone. "Can you imagine?" she continued with dreamy eyes, "being out there in the middle of the ocean for six months at a time with hundreds of guys on a boat and only a hand full of women? The odds are gonna be in my favor."

"Oh," I said as I turned back to face the front and mind my own business.

Seeing that I obviously was somewhat unapproving of her reasoning she asked, "So why are you joining?" in a challenging way.

"I have been watching this war for the past few years now," I began, "and I can no longer sit by and do nothing."

"What?" they both asked with weird, crunched up, questioning faces.

"A lot of people think this war on terror is no big deal," I continued. "It seems as if too many people think 9/11 was a one hit wonder on the part of our enemy but I don't think it was. I am somewhat of a history buff and I know full well what our forefathers have gone through to preserve our freedoms after they had won them and we stand to lose all of those freedoms and in so doing state that all of their efforts were in vain if we don't squelch this threat as every generation before us has squelched the threat of their time."

"You're crazy!" the young guy said.

"Yeah!" the girl agreed. "You'll never make it through the psychological exam!"

We all turned back to face forward, leafing through our respective two year old magazines and did not talk again.

After a long day at MEPS I headed home with Brad and spent the next several weeks and months getting my affairs in order to prepare to leave for basic training on January 17'th of the following year, 2007 which was now only three and a half months away.

I transferred my client's accounts to Ed Good, a fellow planner at LPL and somewhat of a mentor for me at the firm. Ed was in his late 50's and had himself spent several years during his childhood growing up in West Virginia. Ed had lived in Pocahontas county, only two counties away from my native Nicholas county. I had spent much time hunting and fishing in Pocahontas county in my youth and had spent a week at the Green Bank National Radio Observatory studying Astronomy while in college. Green bank is located in the center of Pocahontas county.

I also wanted to make sure I had ample time to spend with my kids during those months because I would not see them for several months straight once I shipped off for training. I knew this was going to be the hardest part of this military experience for me. I could get used to getting up at zero dark thirty in the morning and I was banking on the idea that my previous years as an athlete, though many years in the past, would allow my body to hold up through the vigorous training I would be doing with men nearly half my age, but I had never been away from my children for more than a week at a time since any of them were born.

One of the greatest things I loved about being a broker, even while at Edward Jones was the fact that, as long as I was at my production level, which was not really an issue for me after the first couple of years, I could make my own schedule and be out of the office whenever I wanted. I used this to my advantage as a parent and had volunteered in my kid's classrooms several of the past years.

Every Friday I would spend an hour in Olivia's class and then cross the hall and spend an hour in Emily's class. Christian was at the age, now in middle school, where it wasn't too cool to have your dad coming in but I had coached his basket ball team for four years straight while he was in the minor leagues. Now that he played in middle school and the system was much more organized, my coaching assistance was no longer needed but I went to all of his games and we spent quite a bit of time playing one on one in the drive way.

Christian had developed into a great basketball player. He was better by sixth grade than I ever was. He had an amazing outside shot. He was not the fastest kid on his team and couldn't rip to the basket like some of the other players, but he always led the league in three point shots. The days of me "letting" him beat me in the drive way were gone as he could now do it on his own.

Time was passing quickly through the fall and early winter working it's way up to my departure for basic training. I had taken exercising more seriously in the past several months and had worked up to where I was running three to five miles a day five days a week and would usually do four sets of twenty five pushups and sit ups after each run. I had lost a few extra pounds I hadn't really known I was carrying and was feeling better than I had in years.

Then, near the end of November, I received an email from Amanda that would change my plans drastically. It stated simply, "Per our separation and settlement agreement, I am informing you of my new address. My address thirty days from this notice will be...." and then some address in Seattle Washington of all places, nearly three thousand miles away was given.

"What!" I said out loud as I rushed to the phone to call her.

"Amanda?" I said when she answered the phone.

"Yes," she said matter of factly.

"I got your email about the address change. What is going on?" I asked.

"Kevin," she responded "All I am required to do by law is to inform you of my address change. I am not required and I refuse to have any further discussion with you about this issue," she finished just before hanging up the phone.

I called her back and when she answered I asked, "So are you intending to take the kids?"

"Yes I am," she replied before hanging up on me again.

I could not believe it. I was floored. Where was this coming from? What was going on? It was evening and I would not be able to call my lawyer until the next morning. Needless to say I lost a night of sleep that night. However, the following morning I was able to reach my attorney and he was more than happy to get an emergency trial before the thirty days expired.

When we made it to court a couple of weeks later, a time frame in which Amanda held true to her word and discussed nothing with me, other than telling me she had gotten a job with the University of Phoenix as a student coordinator in Seattle, a position I was able to find the University of Phoenix also had available in Richmond and Washington DC, both locations less than two hours away from us, things went the way I wanted them to go.

Amanda and her attorney were trying to get me to sign an agreement on the steps of the court house stating that the kids could go with her and that I would have them in the summer months.

"Hell no!" I barked over and over to her attorney. "We are going before the judge!"

"You need to communicate with me through your legal council," her attorney Ms. Grady would say while smiling through her shark teeth. This woman loved to look at me and ask me questions or make statements directly to me, and then tell me to answer through my attorney when I would bark back at her.

Amanda and her attorney acted as if they were not going to cave and we went before the judge. My attorney, who was as much of a shark in his own right stated the simple facts to the judge that Amanda was attempting to move nearly three thousand miles away, on short notice and in the middle of a school year having had no discussion with me about it and that she was attempting to take our children, over whom we had joint custody. He recommended to the judge that the children be left with me and that we all get back to court at a later date to finalize the situation.

Seeing that she was being provided yet another opportunity to make $200 an hour at a later date, and knowing that they were bluffing on the court steps because their case wouldn't hold water, Amanda's attorney rose and stated to the judge, "Why your honor, I don't know why we are wasting your time here today because we are already willing to do this."

"Well then, write the agreement up and bring it to me in my chambers once your done," Judge Brown, a retired judge from Washington DC who was filling in on the circuit that day said as he rose from his chair and began swaggering to his chambers.

The lawyers took their time in drawing up the paper work, making sure to milk the clock while Amanda and I sat across from each other, glaring at each other the same way we always did during these situations. Once the paper work was finished and we both signed, it was taken to and approved by Judge Brown and we all parted ways.

5

The kids were as relieved as I was when they found out they would not be moving to Seattle. They loved their mother and wanted to be with her, but they also had gone to school in Greene County Virginia since Christian started kindergarten. All of their friends were here and it was the only place they had ever called home, except for the first few years of Christian's life that he had few memories of. Also, both my parents and Amanda's parents were close by in neighboring West Virginia.

My attorney told me at the end of our brief encounter at the court house that he doubted Amanda would actually go to Seattle once she found out she could not take the children.

"What kind of mother just walks away from her three children and moves to the other side of the country?" he asked. "If she does that," he continued, "Not only is she a piece of crap but she has sealed her fate with this case. When everything is finalized you'll be awarded full custody and she'll be lucky to get the kids in the summer months. This is nothing short of abandonment."

In the final two weeks before Amanda was scheduled to leave, on Christmas day of all times, I tried to convince her to stay. Knowing we would not be going back to court before she left and that the kids would be safe with me she confided in me that she really did not have a place to stay in Seattle and that she really didn't have a job. She had visited a very distant relative of hers who lives in Seattle a couple of months earlier, and while there, had a met a guy named Seth who she had become romantically involved with and was moving out there to be with. Her true intentions were to move to Seattle and live with Seth and find employment and perhaps her own place to live from there.

"So you were planning on taking our three kids out there with no job and nowhere to stay except for with some guy you barely know and that I've never met and do it in the middle of a school year?" I unbelievably asked.

"Not really," she answered.

"What do you mean not really?" I asked.

"Kevin," she went on. "You were a terrible husband but you are a great father and I knew you would fight to keep the kids."

"Then why didn't we just work this out between us instead of getting our lawyers involved again" I asked. "I just ran up another $1,000 worth of legal fees."

Amanda I am sure incurred the same amount but she never cared as much about the legal fees because her father, who cared for me even less than she did since our separation paid her legal fees for her. Having just recently come across a sizable inheritance when his father died he had let her know that the "war chest" was full and encouraged her to be, "as liberal with court appearances as she pleased."

"Kevin," she said, "what kind of mother would I look like if I just gave you the kids and walked away from them."

"But that is essentially what you are doing," I responded.

"I know," she pleaded. "But I had to make it look like I was trying to keep them."

Amanda stayed at my house that Christmas eve as we wanted the kids to have us both there on Christmas morning. The day would be hard enough for them with her leaving that evening. Had Amanda not been leaving like she was I would have offered her my bed and I would have slept on the couch but under these circumstances I figured the couch was good enough for her.

The kids woke early on Christmas day as kids always do and had a great time ripping through their packages and were happy as always to find that they had gotten everything they wanted and then some.

With everything that was going on I did not prepare a turkey and all the fixings. Instead we all went to the movies and saw Rocky Balboa (my kids and I are all huge Rocky fans and having seen the previous 5 Rocky movies several times were highly anticipating the Christmas release of this movie) and then we all had dinner at the China King Buffet in Charlottesville. After dinner we would be taking Amanda to one of her friend's houses who would take her from there to the airport in the middle of the night after the kids had gone to sleep.

When I came back to our table after helping Emily and Olivia get their food I was broken hearted to see that Christian was crying, pleading with his mother not to go. Having already been abandoned by one biological parent at birth, a fact he was never aware of until I told him when he was eight years old, I could not begin to imagine how he must be feeling seeing it happen again.

Amanda held him and tried to soothe him but she seemed more concerned with the scene he was causing than she did his emotions. I sat and said nothing, only staring at her disapprovingly as the girls tried to eat though they obviously had no appetite. We all finished what we could of our meals and then took

Amanda to her friend's house and dropped her off. We then drove home in the cold rainy night, the kids all crying the whole way there.

That night all four of us slept together on air mattresses in the living room in front of the fire place. All three kids cried themselves to sleep. Once they were asleep I sat up, watching the fire and praying.

I am not a very religious man though I am very spiritual. My mother was a Roman Catholic and my father was an American Baptist. At times throughout my childhood I would attend both services trying to make sense of it all but if anything, the whole experience left me confused if not somewhat bipolar.

Because of this I never placed too much stock in organized religion. I refer to myself as a non denominational Christian though I do not belong to the organization that goes by this name. I simply believe in God, I believe in the bible and what it says, and at age 18 I accepted Christ as my savior.

I guess these beliefs may put me more in line with the protestants but I simply cannot stand the bickering that goes on between all the different sects of Christianity so I belong to none of them though my faith in God is quite strong. Fortunately I was able to realize, even as a child that all the bickering between the sects was of man, not of God. As I heard it said once, God gave man spirituality, and then the devil came by and said, "Here, lets get all this stuff organized and we'll call it religion."

That night however, I had a long, one way conversation with God. I prayed that he would see my children through this, the most difficult time of their young lives. This was going to be harder for them than when Amanda and I had originally split up. Then she was only moving three miles away but now she would be nearly a thousand times that distance.

I prayed for myself too. I had managed to make it through the past year and a half since we separated but I did have Amanda right down the road to help with the kids. Now I would have nobody. Though the neighbors were helpful this was going to be an entirely different ball game. My parents were 200 miles away and would be of no help other than emotional support.

Also, I prayed for Amanda. I was sure all of this would hit her once the newness of her relationship with Seth wore off. Ever since Amanda left me all I wanted for her was her happiness. I knew she was not happy with me and I don't want anyone to be miserable at my expense. I prayed that God would bring her back to the area for the children's sake, though I would find out in time that was not part or his plan because once she got to Seattle she stayed there.

This was going to be extremely hard on us financially as well. I had a little money in savings but certainly not enough to last us the six months or so it would now be before I was to ship for basic training at Fort Benning. I had to figure out a way to make ends meet until the summer months came and I had no idea how difficult this was going to be.

6

Charlottesville boasts an unemployment rate of only two percent, half that of the national average. This is good for professionals already employed but unfortunate for everyone else. It seems that most of the positions open in the area are low paying service positions and certainly ones that would not allow me to meet the budget of our household. I had inquired with several brokerage firms about the possibility of working as a licensed assistance but none of them felt comfortable bringing me on board since they knew I would be leaving in six months to perform my military training.

A G Edwards, one of the largest firms in the country was actually very interested with the idea of me coming on board as a full time broker once my military obligation was fulfilled. This opportunity with A G Edwards was flattering but I was still left jobless and the money was still dwindling away.

Throughout the past I had played around with eBay as a way to have some extra money to spend on the kids without my ex wife, and more importantly, her attorney knowing about it. One of my favorite things to do was to go to yard sales on Saturdays and buy things for practically nothing then sell them on eBay for quite a bit more the following week.

I would not go at the crack of dawn like most yard sellers in an attempt to get the very best wares the seller had to offer, but I would wait until eleven o'clock and then go. By this time the sellers had made more money than they had thought they would and were faced with having to repack and store everything that was left over.

My strategy was to approach the sellers, who always seemed more disappointed that I was there, requiring them to keep the yard sale going a bit longer, than they seemed happy to see me thinking they might make a couple more dollars. I would approach and say "Wow, it looks like everybody already got all the good stuff huh?"

"Yes," they would always sluggishly respond.

"So you are gonna have to pack all this crap back up and take up space in your house storing it again huh?" I would ask, intentionally trying to dishearten them even more.

"Yes," they would respond, again just as sluggishly.

"Tell ya what," I would then say, walking toward them while pulling my wallet out of my pocket. "I'll give you $20 for everything you have left. I'll go through and take what I can use of it and I'll give the rest to the Salvation Army and save you the trip."

I was never told no. There was more than one occasion when I would actually get a couple truck loads of stuff for $20. I would keep some of it every now and then but half of it I sold on eBay and the other half I would take to the salvation army and claim my tax deduction at yard sale rates. I could easily turn my $20 investment into several hundreds of dollars the following week, plus take advantage of the tax write off.

People on eBay seem to buy everything and you never know what you are going to find at yard sales. Once I sold a 1970's Polaroid land camera to a guy in California for $55. It turns out he was a camera collector and he needed this one for his collection. My largest gain however was the time I found in my truck load of stuff a first addition hard back copy of a book called "The American Wild Turkey." It was published in 1949 and went on eBay for $395. There were several other old books in that load that sold for $25 to $50 each.

I know that in the financial planning industry the big target market now is the baby boomer generation, who are enjoying the transition of wealth coming to them from their World War II generation parents. The gentleman I bought the books from was a baby boomer who had recently inherited his deceased father's house and was simply selling everything in it so he could sell the house which was going to go for more than a million dollars because it came with several acres of land, all of which had recently been rezoned commercial just outside of Charlottesville. As far as I saw it, this transition of "stuff" that was also going on between the generations was a huge market for eBayers though many people probably were not yet aware of this fact.

Also, I had taken advantage of my knowledge of hard woods, having been raised the son of a lumberman in a timber town and had figured out a way to make money on eBay with scrap wood. It seems that there are still quite a few wood turners out there who make beautiful bowls, vases, lamps, pens and many other items out of wood on wood lathes. Black cherry seems to be the most desirable wood to turn among most of these folks because it is easy to work with and it is so beautiful. Also, since it thrives on high elevations and colder temperatures to grow, it does not grow much further south or west than where I was located in Virginia, and certainly not west of the Mississippi river, making it harder to come by to so many people not living in the north east. This was a case of economics

101, supply versus demand. Because of this cherry sold for more than walnut, maple or any other wood that turners used.

I had figured out that I could simply go along the state's right of ways where they trimmed power and oil lines and take any of the cherry that they had left on the ground simply to rot. I made sure to call the Virginia Department of Transportation to get permission and was told to "take as much as I wanted" because if I did it would keep them from having to come back by and chip it up later.

I could at any given time, drive around until I saw where they were clearing or had recently cleared power lines, park and get out and collect half of a truck load of cherry wood, take it home and cut it down into small turning blocks, called turning blanks, and sell it on eBay and make $300 or $400 a week doing so.

As the kids started back to school after the holidays and I quickly found out that due to my circumstances I could not find suitable employment, and knowing that $9 an hour at Burger King would not cut it, I sank a few bucks into a band saw and another chain saw and began to fervently run a turning blank business out of my back yard. At this juncture I was especially happy that I had such good neighbors because my yard quickly began to look like a commercial log yard yet knowing my circumstances none of them complained.

I knew that I would have to increase my production and sales many times if I had a chance of making ends meet doing this full time and I knew that this would involve hiring someone to help and obtaining much more wood.

I ran an add in the local internet job search and sought out another supplier of cherry trees. I got good responses from the add and over the next several months got several part time helpers. Though none of them worked out for any extended period of time, other than one, forty two year old Jim Hochmuth, who had recently moved to the area from Long Island, New York along with his wife and their two children, I was certainly able to get much more done than if I had gone it alone.

As far as finding a new, larger source of wood there was something I knew about cherry trees that most folks do not, but fortunately most farmers do, that I was able to use to my advantage. Cherry leaves are toxic to livestock. There is a poison in the pit of the cherry that travels to the leaves and only 2 pounds of cherry leaves, if ingested will kill a fully grown cow. Unfortunately for the cows they love to eat cherry leaves. Anyone who grew up on a farm in the northeast can probably remember having to go out after heavy rain storms and pick up and dispose of the cherry branches that were blown down before the cows or even the horses, to whom these leaves are fatal as well got to them.

One afternoon while at the local hardware store buying another chain for my chain saw I ran into another gentleman who was there doing the same. I started talking to him and found out that he was Carlton Spicer, a retired linesman for AT&T who owned an 80 acre cattle farm only one mile from my house. I told Mr. Spicer what I was now doing as a livelihood and asked him if there were any cherry trees along the fences of his pastures that he would like to have removed. I already knew the answer before I asked the question. Birds were immune to the poison in the cherries and loved to eat them, perch themselves on top of fence posts and "poop" out the seeds then fly away. Farmers are so busy with all their other chores that getting around to cutting down these cherry trees was generally the last thing on their list if it ever made the list at all.

Mr. Spicer informed me that he did indeed have several large cherry trees along his fence lines that he would love to have removed. He asked me to come out and look at them and determine if they would be of use to me.

The next afternoon I went to Mr. Spicer's farm while out on my run, and jogged along his fence lines and found that he had enough trees to last me the entire spring. I had a 12 feet by 10 feet trailer I used to pull loads behind my truck and Mr. Spicer was kind enough to help me cut these trees when I went by his place and he would then load them onto my trailer with the use of his big John Deer farm tractor. Because of his work involved and wear and tear on his equipment I offered to give him $50 for each load. He refused to take the money over and over but I always forced him to take it. He was helping me and my family more by allowing me access to the wood than I was him by taking it.

Realizing that if I were to offer more types of wood other than cherry that I would increase my total sales as well, I contacted my good friend and former client Andy Morris. Andy lives in a small house on five acres of wooded land just outside of Ruckersville. For the longest time I could remember Andy complaining about running over walnuts with his mower while cutting his grass. He had several large walnut trees growing in his front yard as well as several other desirable woods for turning growing in his small forest.

I asked Andy if he would like me to take down any of his walnut trees so he would avoid running over the walnuts and he was more than happy for me to do so. Also, he allowed me to take any trees that had fallen, or been blown over by heavy winds in his forest. Here I was able to get my hands on some Sassafras and Cedar that sold, though for not as much as cherry, as quickly as I could cut it and list it on eBay. Andy too would always come outside and help me cut the trees and load the wood. I enjoyed this because we had been friends for years and I loved our conversations.

Andy was 74 years old, though he didn't look a day over 58. He didn't drink or smoke and had a relatively stress free life living by himself. He had been divorced 40 years earlier and had only remarried once. Unfortunately his second wife died of cancer and from then on he had remained single. I would gain so much insight from his wisdom that came from nearly 80 years of living and I felt that with Andy I was always walking away from his place with knowledge much more valuable than the wood I was taking from his land.

7

Though I would love to say that my efforts of finding stable wood supplies and part time employees allowed my turning blank business to work out I unfortunately cannot. There were several unforeseen snags that played to my disadvantage. The biggest was the fact that January and February of 2007 were two of the coldest winter months on record. The temperatures stayed below freezing most of the time during these two months.

The discomfort of working under these conditions was not the problem. I had a shed in the back yard were I did most of my cutting. The problem was the fact that wood, though hard as it is, is made up mostly of water and when the temperatures dropped below freezing the wood would freeze. Cutting it was impossible. The only result if you tried was broken band saw blades, dulled chain saw chains, ruined equipment and a lot of frustration. A double whammy was the fact that people don't hold yard sales in the middle of winter so this second avenue of eBay success was not an option.

It seems that I got myself in a hole early in this endeavor due to the winter's weather that I was not able to get out of. I blew through our savings and really got behind the eight ball. Giving up was not an option though so I did what I could which at times involved carrying logs into the house and setting them in front of the fire place so they could thaw out enough for me to cut them. Still though, it was not enough.

The children were holding up as best as they could. Christian's grades did drop, but fortunately since he had always been a straight A student this only meant that he was now getting some B's. He did develop a bit of anger but who would not under the circumstances through which he was going. Fortunately it was now basketball season and he seemed to funnel his anger into his sport. Once again he led his league in three point shots for the year.

Emily became somewhat withdrawn. She had always been a somewhat loud, at times obnoxious child, though only at home for she was always the best behaved student in her class at school, but now she was eerily quite. She started spending a lot of time reading, something she never really enjoyed, as well as writing her own stories. Her teacher Ms. Mikel and I encourage this form of therapy though and made sure to always read her stories after she had finished them.

She really enjoyed writing about ware wolves. She sort of had a series going about a ware wolf family that lived in the nearby Blue Ridge mountains, a family that she herself belonged to and would, in her stories, join up with in the middle of the night while our family was sleeping.

Olivia seemed to be doing the worst of the three. Olivia, though a daddy's girl through and through really missed her mother. She did not withdraw into writing, or express her emotions through anger or make them apparent through lower school grades. She simply became depressed. The saddest thing I have ever seen to this day is a depressed six year old little girl.

Olivia had always been our most sensitive child. The last six months that Amanda lived in our house before moving out I slept on the couch. When Olivia asked me why (Amanda and I was able to hide our problems from our children for the longest time; they never even saw us argue which was very fortunate) I told her I was camping out in the living room. She would drag her little Barbie doll sleeping bag and her pillow into the living room and sleep on the floor beside me so that I would not have to camp alone. Most of those nights she would end up on the couch with me, then at some point I would end up in the floor.

Also, when Amanda finally did move out, Olivia never wanted me to have to be alone. For the first month that Amanda was gone, Olivia would come over and spend the night with me. We would have so much fun with our one on one time. Olivia has been an angel in my life since her birth and it broke my heart to see her so sad once her mother left for Seattle.

At school, Olivia went to the nurse about every day suffering from a stomach ache. Her teacher, Mrs. Helmuth would always try to encourage her not to go and was finally successful near the end of the school year. Also, Olivia would often walk up to the female teachers during reading time or block sessions and ask to sit on their laps. Knowing what her home situation was, the teachers, though advised not to do so per school policy would always allow her to sit on their laps for a little while.

One of the differences Amanda and I had during our marriage was our children's school situation. Though I am and always have been an adamant supporter of the public schools, Amanda always wanted our children to go to some over priced private school. Any doubts anyone could have about public schools and the quality of their teachers would certainly have been eradicated had they seen the quality of the teachers at Ruckersville Elementary School and the way they were able to help my children cope through their tough times.

I had always believed the public schools could be as good as the parents wanted them to be. By this I do not mean through constant complaining and criticism but through getting involved and becoming active. I know that in my daughter's classes there were several other parents who volunteered regularly and stayed active with the school and their activities. I loved going with my girl's classes on field trips and I could always count on seeing several of the same involved parents who always did the same. The teachers at Ruckersville elementary always held an open door policy and never minded any parent coming in at any time. They always seemed over grateful to get the help.

During spring break my children flew to Seattle with Amanda's father to spend the week with their mother. I took this time alone to sit down and assess our situation. It was not good.

I was behind on the mortgage and a couple credit card payments and I did not see any way out by June. As much as I did not want to accept the facts, the facts were that I was not going to make it to my basic training ship date financially and I would probably have to sell my house to avoid foreclosure. The notices were not coming yet but they would be soon at the rate things were going.

A neighbor of mine, Dave Reid, who's son Hunter was best friends with my son Christian would stop in from time to time. Dave owned his own heating and air conditioning repair business and could relate first hand with the difficulties experienced by small business owners. He was very concerned with our family's situation and he made sure to always check in on me because he knew that aside from my time spent with the children I was often alone.

"Have you thought about maybe getting out of your obligation with the National Guard?" he asked one day when he stopped by, having gotten finished with his day's work early. "I mean, due to your circumstances I am sure you could get out without a dishonorable discharge."

"I know I could," I told him. "My recruiters know what is going on here and they told me I could."

"Then why don't you do it?" he asked. "You could go back to Wall Street and be out of this mess in a couple of months and keep your house."

"I know I could," I responded.

"Then why don't you?" he inquired.

"Because Dave," I began, "This thing is bigger than me and it means more to me than a house. What good is this house and the bit of land it sits on if it is not free?"

"You sound like a politician man, but your not," he responded. "Your just an everyday schmoe like me trying to take care of your kids."

"I know that Dave and that is what makes this so important to me," I told him. "I've never been one to focus so much on the now as I have been the future.

The thoughts I have of doing nothing are thoughts of my son or one of my daughters walking into their office one morning many years from now and not walking out because a plane flies through their building."

"That won't happen man, you know that," Dave argued.

"That's what we all thought on September 10'th of 2001," I followed up.

"Dave, I have two daughters," I continued. "A generation ago I am sure there were fathers in Afghanistan who would have never guessed their daughters would be forced to hide themselves from the world under burkas. I am sure those same fathers would have never guessed that their little girls would not be allowed to attend schools or that they would die of common, easily treatable illnesses because the doctors, who were males, would not be allowed to touch them because they were females, thereby not being able to treat them."

"Well have you thought about going on public assistance?" he asked.

"Absolutely not!" I forcefully responded. "I am not going to attempt that as long as I can stand and walk. As long as I have anything of material value that I can sell, including my home if necessary, I am not going to ask society to pay for a situation they did not cause. I brought these kids into the world and it is my responsibility to care for them."

"Yeah," he went on, "but Amanda just left you guys and hasn't been sending any money back at all to help."

"That's true Dave, but why should my neighbors to the left and right of me have more money taken from their hard earned pay checks to pay for that?" I questioned.

"Hey, I'm just trying to help you out man," Dave said defensively, "Maybe give you some ideas you hadn't thought of."

"I know Dave, and I appreciate the help," I let him know.

The kids returned from Seattle in much higher spirits after having spent some time with their mother. By this time, I knew I would have to put the house on the market but I did not make them aware of this fact yet. I wanted to put off yet another blow to their precious hearts for as long as I could.

My best friend Dean Niarchos had recently gotten his real estate license and was amped up about his new career. I called him one spring afternoon and asked, "Hey Dean?"

"Yeah?" he responded.

"I have a gift for you for finishing your real estate classes," I told him.

"Yeah, what's that?" he inquired.

"Your first listing," I told him.

"What?" he asked in a tone that sounded as if he was more disappointed than happy for the business. "You are going to have to sell your house?"

Dean knew the situation I was in. Dean had proven himself over the past couple of years to be the best friend anyone could ask for. Where as many of my so called friends dropped by the wayside once the times got tough for me, Dean had stood there the entire time.

When he had gone for several days without hearing from me he would call to make sure I was alright. We would often meet for lunch or coffee so he could make sure to get me out of my house and my little wood shed in the back yard.

"Kevin, that is terrible," he lamented.

"I know Dean," I agreed, "But I really am down to no other options. I believe I can make it until the end of the school year but not much longer. Can you help me?'

"Sure I can," he replied. "But what are you going to do? Where are you going to live?" he asked.

"Well," I started, "I figure that the kids will be going to spend the summer with Amanda while I am at basic training. That will give me a few months without bills to save up my Army pay and get a rental when I get back. Plus if I end up in Iraq for a year the kids will stay with her and I can save for a year. Who knows," I continued, trying to keep us both positive about the situation, "Maybe I'll be calling on you then to help me buy a house."

"Well let's hope," he agreed.

A week or so later Dean came over and we did all the necessary work involved to get my house on the market. Fortunately the housing market was just beginning to crash and we were able to get a contract on the house that would be executed in the middle of June. God's hand was really at work for me here too because the dreaded foreclosure notices that I had feared would come finally had. As a matter of fact, foreclosure proceedings were scheduled to start on my house the day after our scheduled closing date. I was really dodging a bullet here.

The kids would go to their mother's at the beginning of June when school let out so they would not have to be part of this process. They would not have to go through yet another hardship by packing all of their belongings and putting them in storage.

Dean let me know that if there was any time in between the time of the sale of my house and when I was to leave for Fort Benning I could stay with him at his place. At the time, that was my plan and I thanked him for the offer. However, that plan would soon change while I was attending yet another field trip with my daughter Emily's class.

8

Virginia's nick name is "The birthplace of Presidents" since there are seven of our past executives who came from the state. One of which, the first, was George Washington. Emily's second grade class was taking a field trip to Mt. Vernon, President Washington's home just south of D.C. and only an hour and a half away from Ruckersville.

I wanted to attend this trip as I did most of them. OP was going to stay after school with his friend Hunter but I was unable to make arraignments for Olivia. Though the school discouraged allowing siblings in different grades to attend field trips, a special case was made for Olivia due to our situation and she was allowed to come with us.

Though I always enjoyed the field trips mostly because I was always put in charge of a small group of kids as a chaperone and we always had a ton of fun wherever we went, this trip was especially enjoyable for me because I had wanted to go to Mt. Vernon for some time. I love US history and had embarked on reading a biography on every president we have ever had. I was not reading them in order of when they served as much as I was in the order in which I was most interested in each.

I had read a biography on Washington the previous summer and could not wait to get to Mt. Vernon. When I did I saw that the mansion and its grounds were just as beautiful as I had imagined. I enjoyed being able to give the kids, teachers and other parents information on President Washington that the guides did not provide.

A bit of information that I am glad I was able to provide to the group was Washington's stance on slavery. The exhibits were good at pointing out that Washington was a slave holder but they did little to point out his stance on the issue.

George Washington hated the institution of slavery, mostly because he knew that it ripped families of slaves apart. He was disheartened that at many of the slave auctions fathers were often purchased by one slave owner while the mother was often purchased by another. This so many times left young black children orphaned at the hands of the institution of slavery.

Washington would often attend slave auctions and purchase entire families simply to keep the family together. He had no use for many of the slaves he did own because he already had plenty to work his plantations but he simply could not stand the idea of a family being broken apart.

At many points during his presidency he visited the idea of eradicating slavery, but his Secretary of State, Charlottesville's Thomas Jefferson would always convince him to spend his political capital in other areas. Where as Jefferson in public decreed that "Slavery is a necessary evil," yet enjoyed its many benefits to him in private, Washington believed it was simply an evil and figured out ways in his private life to ease its burdens on at least some of its victims.

One of the most amazing features at Mt. Vernon in my eyes, being interested in wood and trees, were the gigantic poplar trees that lined the driveway going to the mansion. Washington himself had planted these trees more than 200 years before and they were enormous. They were so big in fact that I could not figure out what kind of tree they were until I read the sign posted by the trunk of one. I even grew up with a huge (or what I thought was huge until now) poplar tree in my front yard back in Richwood West Virginia.

I thought these trees at first perhaps to be redwoods. I know that sounds quite ignorant on my part as the redwoods only grow in a certain part of California but these trees were as big and round as a vehicle is long. I had Emily and Olivia pose for a picture at one of their trunks.

We enjoyed that entire day. I loved speaking with a woman who was dressed as Martha Washington that was sitting on a bench knitting beside one of the many flower gardens surrounding the estate. She was in character and would not break her character, which made many of the folks attempting to talk to her feel quite awkward. They would ask her questions pertaining to the past in the past tense but she spoke in the present tense.

I jumped at this opportunity to have a wonderful conversation with someone who really knew quite a bit about Washington.

"Mrs. Washington I presume?" I asked as I drew close to her.

"Well how did you know?" she responded.

Taking a bow toward her, and kissing her hand I responded, "The stories of your beauty spread far and wide and I would imagine that a lady as attractive as yourself could be no other."

"Well," she began, "From where do you hail?"

"I am from Charlottesville," I informed her.

"You have not brought that rascal Mr. Jefferson up here with you have you?" she scorned.

"Indeed not," I set her to ease. "I would not be known to travel with such a type. I have come to visit the home of the General, the true father of our great nation. I have no desire to spend time with a man who would perhaps rather be President of France as opposed to his own, wonderful United States."

"Oh," she cooed. "Mr. Adams would much enjoy meeting you. If only he were here today."

"Well I would love to meet Mr. Adams myself," I continued. "I know of him to be a true friend of your husbands and a true friend to all of America."

I had a delightful conversation with this lady who seemed to enjoy the rare occurrence of meeting someone on a field trip who knew a little more about Washington other than the simple fact that he was our first president. We spoke of how Washington actually did not chop down a cherry tree nor did he have wooden teeth. We looked back on many of his military exploits when he led men into battles that mostly ended in their defeat.

What amazed people in Washington's day about his battles were not his successes because those were few and far between, but the fact that during all of the fighting he would continuously ride along the front line, constantly encouraging his men. Bullets would fly by his head the whole while just missing him by inches yet it seemed as if he were oblivious to their presence. The man had the bravery of a lion and never sought cover. It was often said that it was as if very hand of God was swatting away the danger because he had great plans for this tall, lanky, red headed officer.

After enjoying a packed lunch with the kids and viewing the inside of the mansion, as well as President Washington's tomb, which had originally been placed closer to the Potomac river which the home oversaw but was later moved to higher ground, the students, teachers, other parents and myself boarded the buses and began heading south for home.

It was during this bus ride back that I figured out what I was going to do with my month or so that I had in between the time I would close on the sale of my home and then ship off for basic training. I was not going to sit around on Dean's couch feeling sorry for myself though I was appreciative of his offer to stay with him. I was going to spend my time getting outside of myself and partake on an adventure bigger than me.

I decided that after selling my house and paying off what debt I could from any proceeds left over, mostly debt that would be legal fees associated with my divorce, I was going to spend my time wisely. I decided that day that I would drive all the way across the United States, going the southern route and then up to Seattle to spend some time with my kids while there, and then return along the northern route, taking most of the same route that Lewis and Clark had taken more than 200 years before.

Knowing I would be strapped for cash and that gas prices were now over three dollars a gallon in most places I would not be able to afford the luxury of hotels and motels so I would take my camping gear and stay at state parks or in the woods. I would be sure to take my kayak so I could explore the beautiful rivers and lakes I would come across and also so I could bathe in their waters.

Like Mt. Vernon, I would visit other places of historical significance, places where events occurred that were vital to the formation of our nation by men who too could see past the end of the nose on their faces and realized that there were some things worth fighting for, in spite of any immediate hardships they would have to face by so doing.

It just so happened that this was the year we were celebrating the 400'th anniversary of Jamestown, also in my current home state of Virginia. All signs seemed to be pointing me in the direction of getting to know my country better. The Jamestown anniversary, my visit to Mt. Vernon, it all made sense. Also, I figured I had enlisted to fight for this country, I may as well go see it. That I would. As soon as the kids were off to Seattle and I had our belongings put in storage and the sale of my home final I would go see this great land, and perhaps discover another part of myself in so doing or at least gain some reassurance that what I was doing, refusing to bail out and save myself at the risk of neglecting my part in a greater cause, was right.

9

How we managed to get through those six months without losing our minds I'll never know. The kids and I were so busy perhaps that we didn't have too much time to sit around and ponder our situation. I could use what I referred to as "terrible Tuesdays" as an example of our schedule.

My day would start at 5:30 a.m. when I would wake up after maybe 5 hours of sleep so that I could go out and run 3 or 4 miles and follow it up with my push-ups and sit ups before waking the kids at 7:00 a.m. to get them fed and ready for school. Once they caught the bus at 7:45 I would begin my work in the wood shop and work until they got back home at 4:00 p.m., often times not even stopping for lunch.

The kids would all then gather around the kitchen table to do their home work while I prepared dinner, helping them with their homework the whole while. Christian, who never seemed to have as much homework as his sisters was a huge help here because he never minded and actually seemed to enjoy helping them with theirs.

We would then rush off to Olivia's soccer practice at 5:00 which lasted until 6:30, giving us just enough time to get to Christian's basketball practice at 7:00. The girls and I would most usually drop him off, then go do any grocery shopping that needed to be done and then go home and make sure they had bathes. We would run back to pick Christian up from basketball practice at 9:00 and then come back home and I would tuck the girls in while Christian showered then he and I would have a sandwich or some other snack together before he went to bed and I would stay up and work on my eBay site until about mid night, when I would go to bed to be ready to start the whole process over the next day.

Saturday's were hectic as well as Olivia would have a soccer game in the morning and Christian had one and sometimes two basketball games later in the day. Emily was in charge of constantly reminding me what we had to do or where we had to be next.

As stressful as these times were I can look back on them as some of the best days of my life in spite of the hardships. My children and I developed a bond going through these times together that I doubt many families develop. Though their young minds could not grasp the entirety of our situation, they knew Dad had his hands full and they rallied to the cause. They were so mature for their ages and never got our situation bogged down by being undisciplined or whiney. We all made the best of it.

Before the kids left for the summer there was one bit of business Amanda and I had to tend to. My attorney and I were able to get her in court just as the school year was ending and the court did decide that day to award me full custody of our three children. It was decided that the kids would remain with me during the school year and that Amanda could have them during the summer and we would alternate Thanksgiving, Christmas, and spring breaks. The Judge also decided that any traveling expenses incurred from transporting our children back and forth across the country would be paid for by Amanda since she was the one who decided to move so far away. Lastly, the court also forced Amanda to begin paying me child support in the amount of nearly $800 a month.

Packing the kids off with Amanda for the summer was not easy for me. Though I needed the break after six months of going it with them alone, I hated the thought of them being gone. When they did load up in her rental car with her to head for the airport I kept on my best poker face and told them how much fun they were going to have though they were crying the whole time. Once they pulled out of the drive I went back inside and shed a few tears myself.

I spent the next two weeks packing everything in our house and moving it into storage. A neighbor just down the road from Mr. Spicer's farm, David Shelton, was kind enough to allow me to store our entire household's worth of belongings in one of his old chicken barns on his land. Mr. Shelton had been a chicken farmer years ago but now spent his time repairing small engines on lawn mowers, chain saws and other power tools and equipment and had a lot of space left over in his shed that was about 100 yards long and 50 yards wide.

Mr. Shelton and I had never known each other until recently. It turns out that he and Mr. Spicer had been friends and neighbors for years, and after Mr. Spicer had made him aware of my situation Mr. Shelton flagged me down while I was on one of my morning runs past his house and offered to help me in any way he could, including allowing me to use the space for storage. What a testament of the good people in my part of Virginia. Here was a man who did not know me and barely knew anything about me but yet was willing to help me because the one thing he did know was that I was a neighbor in need.

My part time employee Jim Hochmuth had by this time become a friend. Jim came by a couple afternoons each week after he got off from his day job and helped me move all of the heavy boxes and furniture that I could not lift by myself to Mr. Shelton's chicken house. I don't know where I would have been through all of this without Jim's help.

With everything packed and stored except the few necessities I would need for the last two weeks before I was to begin my journey across America I had some down time for the first time in quite a while. I used it to get caught up on some well over due rest and just took it easy. My plan was to hang out at my house for the next two weeks while it was still mine before the close of the sale and then hit the road.

One afternoon during this period I decided to grab a quick coffee while I was in Charlottesville. I got my cup of Joe and sat down to drink it. That is when I saw her … again.

The woman who had come in and gotten a coffee just after me and sat across from me at another table was the most beautiful woman I had ever seen in my life. I would estimate her to be close to my age, maybe a year or two older. She was black, but seemed to have some other ethnicity in her, perhaps Asian, as she had very high cheek bones and slightly tightened eyes around the edges. Her hair was shoulder length and straight and I could only fantasize about how soft. It would not be prudent for me to describe her body but let's just say I took notice.

I first saw this beautiful creature about 5 years earlier while I was working out at an athletic club to which I belonged. Yes, I was married at the time, and though I never attempted to stray from my wife at any time throughout our marriage, even married men notice beautiful women who cross their paths.

I was running laps on the indoor track and this beautiful woman was riding one of the many computerized exercise bikes. I would either almost fly off of the track or come close to running someone over every time I passed her because I could not quit staring at her. She never looked up from her book she was reading while exercising.

Then I saw her again about a year ago. I had gone to Lowe's to purchase some grape vines to run along the picket fence in my yard and it turned out that she was a cashier at Lowe's at the time. That is when we had a brief, awkward, almost one way conversation.

"Hi," I said to her as I laid my grape vines on her counter to be checked out.

"Did you find everything you need today sir?" she politely asked with the voice of an angel.

"Hi," I said again.

She looked up at me with a funny face and began ringing up my purchase.

"Your total is (whatever the amount was)," she said, again in that same angelic voice.

"Uh huh," I stuttered back.

"Sir," she said while looking at me puzzled, "Will that be cash or credit?"

"Oh yes," I said, fumbling for my wallet. "I have a debit card," I continued, pulling out the piece of plastic and showing it to her.

After a period of silence she said, "Well, just slide it through the machine there and you can be on your way."

"Oh yeah," I stammered as I slid the card through backward.

"Other way," she smiled.

"Oh yeah," I said, dropping my card to the ground.

This is when I noticed that a line of some not too happy customers was forming behind me and I snapped back to my senses. I stood up, and refused to look at her pretty face again so I could check out with no more hold ups.

"Thank you and come again," she said as she handed me my receipt.

"Ok! I will!" I blurted out with excitement, as if she didn't say this to everyone, only me.

"Have a nice day," she said as she handed me my bag of grape vines, hinting that I should be on my way.

I took my grape vines and headed for the door, almost tripping over my own feet as I turned around to get another look at her before leaving.

Then, about 3 months ago I had seen her again. I was at the Golden Corral Buffet with the kids, piling some over cooked macaroni and cheese on my plate when I happened to glance up, sensing someone was beside me at the bar, and realized it was her. She was gingerly piling some conservatively sauced barbeque ribs on her plate.

I returned to my table and dropped half of my food on my shirt while I ate as I was thinking about her more than what I was doing. I had to go talk to her. This was the third time I had seen this Goddess. I was no longer married and I was going to say something.

I got my nerve up, stood up and began approaching her table. She was eating alone, reading a magazine while she ate. I was only a table away from hers when she looked up … and Olivia began tugging on my shirt.

"Daddy, Daddy, come help me get some desert," my little girl chimed.

"Ok honey," I said in my best Daddy's voice.

This opportunity to say something to this mysterious beauty was gone because when I got back up for another approach I was disheartened to find that she had already left the restaurant.

I was not going to let yet another opportunity to meet this woman pass. I had never been the type to just approach a woman I didn't know and strike up a conversation. After Amanda and I split up I rarely dated. I didn't have time for it and when it did happen it was mostly with the friend of a friend and it never went anywhere. Though I met some really neat people, I was just never interested in any them romantically.

This was different. I am sure I had seen several of the same people over and over in town and didn't even realize it but I could remember every time I ever saw this woman. She haunted my memory.

It just so happened that we both finished our coffee at the same time and walked out to the parking lot together. As she was going to her car I followed her and called her attention.

"Excuse me mam?" I said in a quivering voice.

"Yes," she said as she turned around with a questioning look on her face.

"Hi," I continued. "I just wanted to come over and introduce myself to you. My name is Kevin."

With a puzzled look on her face she said, "Well Kevin, it is nice to meet you. My name is Maia (pronounced my yah). Why did you want to introduce yourself to me?"

"Well," I began, looking down for an uncomfortable second and then glancing back up. "I am sure you are going to think this is weird. I'm also sure that you are either married or have a boyfriend, but I wanted to introduce myself to you because you are the most amazingly beautiful woman I have ever seen."

I know it sounded corny but it was the truth. I was hoping that her appreciation of my honesty would out weigh any thoughts she had that I was a stocker, or worse yet a dork.

"Oh, your so sweet," she said, somewhat embarrassed herself.

"Yeah," I went on. "I've seen you around before and I didn't want to see you again today and not at least try to meet you."

It seemed like an eternity before she spoke again. What would she do? What would she say? Would she say, "Nice meeting you," then get in her car and drive away? I didn't know and it seemed like time froze while I was waiting to find out.

"So if you've seen me before I guess that means you live around here huh?" she finally spoke.

"Yes," I answered. "I live in Ruckersville. "How about you? Do you live in Charlottesville?'

"I live in Gordonsville," she responded.

Gordonsville was another small, bedroom community of Charlottesville.

"Did you used to work at Lowe's?" I asked.

"Yes, I did," she smiled. "But I haven't worked there for a while.

"I saw you there once," I informed her. "I bought some grape vines one day and went through your line, do you remember?"

She looked off to the side, appearing to be deep in thought then responded, "Nope. I don't remember."

"Oh," I said. "Well I saw you once, about 5 years ago at the gym. You were on an exercise bike and I was running on the indoor track. Do you remember that?"

Looking off as if in deep thought again she responded the same as before, "Nope. I don't remember that."

"Oh," I said looking down. I didn't feel the need to point out the time I saw her at the Golden Corral.

"But hey," she began. "I remember the time a really cute guy followed me to my car from the coffee shop and introduced himself to me."

I lit up inside! My head came up and my eyes met hers and we both smiled in unison. I was not being shot down. For some reason this beautiful woman was willing to talk to me for a bit longer.

Maia and I stood in the parking lot that hot Wednesday afternoon and talked for an hour. I found out that she had grown up in Philadelphia and had left when she turned 18 because she didn't like living there. She had spent some time living in Arizona were she worked as a veterinarian's assistant before moving to the Charlottesville area about 8 years ago. She loved the area as so many people who come here from other places do and had decided to make it her home.

At the present time, Maia was not dating anyone. Though no one would guess it from looking at her, she was actually 39 years old. Her exotic appearance stemmed from the fact that her mother was black and her father was a native American Indian, Oglala Sioux. The combination of these two ethnicities were responsible for making her 100% beautiful.

As we decided to go our separate ways, Maia motioned toward my truck.

"Is that your truck with the kayak on top?" she asked.

"Yes, that's mine," I answered.

"I have never been kayaking but I have always wanted to go," she informed me.

"I was planning on going this Sunday, would you like to come along?" I asked.

I really had not been planning on doing anything on Sunday other than laying around and scratching, and perhaps read a little but I saw this as an opportunity to see Maia again.

"I would love to go!" she exclaimed. "Do you have another kayak?"

"No, but all my neighbors have several," I informed her. "I can borrow one of theirs and we can spend the day on the Rivana river."

"That would be wonderful," she said as she began digging through her purse. "Let me give you my phone number," she finished as she began scratching the digits on the back of a Wal mart receipt with a pen.

"When do you want me to call you to make final arraignments?" I asked, hoping I wasn't seeming as excited as I actually was.

"You can call me tomorrow if you want," she answered.

"Great!" I said. "I'll talk to you then."

With that we were both off to our vehicles. I almost tripped over my feet again just like the time at Lowe's when I looked back for another glimpse at her. To my delight she was looking back herself, smiling. What a great day this was.

10

It seemed as if it took an eternity for the following day to come. All I thought about until it did was Maia. When the next day did come, I fought the urge to call her all morning, not wanting to appear over anxious. I figured I might be a bit more cool in her eyes if I could hold off calling her until that evening.

When I did finally call her it was about 6:00 p.m. and I got no answer. I left her a brief message that it was me and gave her a return number to call. She returned my call several hours later, at about 10:30 p.m. after she had gotten off work. She was currently a server as well as a server's trainer at one of the many high end restaurants in Charlottesville.

"I got your message," she started. "I was working."

"Oh," I said. "Are you on your way home?"

"I'm just sitting in the parking lot right now," she informed me. "I hate to drive and talk on my cell phone at the same time so I figured I'd just talk to you for a while and then start toward home."

"Don't you go through Ruckersville to get to Gordonsville?" I asked.

"Yes," she responded. "That is one way you can go."

"Well, I don't want to seem too forward," I offered, "But my house is only a mile off of the main road you have to drive on through here and if you want to come by and hang out so we could talk in person for a while you are more than welcome."

My heart stopped beating while I was awaiting her response. I knew I may have come across too boldly. We had just met the day before and here I was already inviting her to my house? Was I risking our date this coming Sunday by being too brazen?

"I'd love to come by," she said, laying my fears to ease. "I should be there in 10 minutes. Where exactly do I go?"

I gave Maia directions to my house and then got off the phone. Fortunately I always kept a clean house and at this time there was really nothing left in my house other than the living room furniture, a few items in the kitchen, my bed in the bedroom and all my camping equipment I would be using on my up coming trip across the country, that was all in a neat pile in the living room.

True to her word, Maia pulled into my driveway 10 minutes later. I cannot explain the elation I felt as I watched this beautiful creature get out of her car and walk toward my front door. Finally, after a long time, something good was coming my way.

"Welcome to my humble and sparsely furnished abode," I greeted her as she walked through the door.

"Looks like someone is going camping?" she said, motioning toward my pile of camping equipment.

"Yes, I am off for quite an adventure here in a couple of weeks," I informed her.

"Oh yeah?" she said as she slipped off her shoes and moved to the couch to take a seat.

"Yes, I am going on a trip across the country and back. I plan to stay at state parks mostly or in the woods when I can," I let her know as I moved over to the couch and sat on the opposite end.

"Wow," she said with sparkling eyes. "That sounds like quite the adventure. What has brought this about?"

"It's a long story," I told her.

"I have the time," she replied. "I'm a night owl and I did come here to talk so why don't we talk about it?"

"Ok," I said, then started to tell her the whole story.

Maia sat there and listened. I tried to stay as positive as possible about the entire divorce and abandonment situation and never really got into how tough the past six months had been. Maia would interject questions from time to time if I hadn't covered a point fully but other than that she seemed to simply lend me her ear.

"So I guess I've proven to you pretty quickly that I'm dysfunctional and come with a lot of baggage huh?" I asked, realizing myself it probably had not been a good idea to divulge as much information as I had so soon.

"Your not dysfunctional Kevin," she consoled me. "It just sounds like you've been through a lot in the past couple of years and it sounds like you've done more than most people would have been able to do under those circumstances."

We then spent some time talking about her. I learned that she had never been married and had never had kids because basically she had just never wanted to.

"I guess I seem a little selfish huh?" she asked after telling me quite a bit about herself.

"I don't think so," I equally consoled her. "I know a lot of people get married and have kids simply because they think it is the next stage in life or because they get pressured to do so by their parents who want desperately to be grand parents," I continued.

"Actually, I think you are pretty selfless by not having kids if you knew you didn't want them and might not be the best mother because of that fact. I would also say you are quite a strong person for being able to live your life the way you want to and not the way society or someone in it wanted you to."

We continued to talk past mid night. We had begun our conversation both sitting at opposite ends of the couch but by this point we were sitting side by side. I did not know if I had moved or if she had moved but since we were both now sitting in the middle of the couch I guess it would be safe to say that we both had moved.

"Maia?" I asked while staring into her big, beautiful brown eyes when the conversation began to die.

"Yes?" she asked back.

"Can I hold your hand?" I asked sheepishly.

"Yes Kevin, you can hold my hand," she said, taking my right hand with her left.

Her skin was so soft. When I touched her hand, I felt electricity move from my finger tips to my heart and then through the rest of my body. We were sitting so close that I could smell her essence. She did not smell like perfume or body lotion, she simply smelled of her natural scent, which in my opinion smelled better than anything synthetic ever could.

"Maia?" I asked again.

"Yes Kevin?" she asked back with a smile.

"Can I give you a hug?"

"Yes you can give me a hug," she responded, opening her arms to accept.

We embraced each other and I felt that same bolt of electricity, only this time much more powerfully as I pulled her toward me. I pressed the side of my face into that hair of hers and found that it was just as soft as I had imagined. We hugged each other firmly for about a minute, and then as we were pulling back away form each other, our eyes met again, and we fell into the deepest, most passionate kiss I could ever remember.

We alternated kisses and hugs for the next half an hour and said few words. Our bodies were doing all of the talking. It seemed like a dream as I could not believe this beautiful, mysterious woman who had haunted my thoughts and crossed my path occasionally over the past few years was sitting on my couch, and that I was kissing her.

"Kevin," she finally spoke as our lips parted.

"Yes," I asked in a mesmerized tone.

"I have to go," she informed me. "It is late and I still have to drive about 15 miles. Besides, we have to save something for later."

Yes!!! There would be a later!!!

"OK," was my only response.

"Maybe I can come back by tomorrow night for a little bit after I get finished with work," she offered.

"That would be wonderful," I said.

Maia got in her car and drove away. I watched as her tail lights rounded the curve leading out of my subdivision and then just stood there, looking up into the starry night saying "Thank you! Thank you! Thank you!" over and over to the God I knew was looking down on me.

That night I could not get to sleep. This time I was finally losing sleep because of a good thing. Meeting Maia and hitting it off with her so well was proof of the proverbial "light at the end of the tunnel."

The next day, which was a Friday seemed to drag. All I could look forward to was Maia getting off of work around 10:30 p.m. or so. She did call me just before she went in at 5:00 to make sure our plans were still on, which I informed her they were. Of coarse they were! It would have taken an act of God for me to have changed them!

11:00 p.m. finally rolled around and Maia returned to my house. We moved quickly to the couch as we had the night before and picked up our verbal conversation where we had left off. She spent more time getting to know me and I spent more time getting to know her. All in good time, our body's conversation took up where it had left off the night before as well. We were soon embracing each other again with sensual hugs and passionate kisses.

Just like the previous night, before things went too far, Maia again left for her drive home.

"What are you doing tomorrow?" I asked.

"I have to work again tomorrow night," she informed me.

"Well," I began, "I know we are going kayaking on Sunday but there is a Lewis and Clark Keel boat exhibit at Darden Towe Park on Saturdays and I was gonna go check it out tomorrow. If you'd like to go I would love your company."

"What is a keel boat exhibit?" she asked.

"Oh, it is a replica of the boat that the Lewis and Clark exhibition used to float up the Missouri river when they crossed the country 200 years ago," I informed her. "One of the Lewis and Clark groups in the area have built it and you can go by and see it on Saturdays between 10:00 a.m. and 2:00 p.m. I figured I'd go down at noon."

Maia didn't seem too interested in the exhibit itself but she obviously wanted to spend more time with me because she agreed to go.

The next day she was at my house around 11:00 and we soon afterward jumped in my truck and went to the exhibit. I probably would have taken much more of the exhibit in had Maia not been with me but since she was she seemed to be all I could think about. It gets excruciatingly hot in Virginia in the summers and she was dressed appropriately, wearing some very low cut denim shorts and an athletic top that only covered the bare essentials to make her legal in public. Come to think of it, I don't think I can even say what the keel boat looked like.

After the trip to see the boat, or should I say the trip I took to the boat to see Maia, we headed back to my house. We had a bit of time to kill before she had to dress and leave for work and we spent it talking, hugging and kissing. At the risk of sounding boyish, I felt as if I were falling in love with a woman I had only known a few days.

Maia changed into her work clothes in the privacy of my bathroom and then headed into town to go to work. I walked her to her car for one last embrace and another of her sweet kisses.

"I'll see you tomorrow at noon," she said as she slipped into her car.

"I can't wait," I responded.

And with that she was off.

My next door neighbor Greg Livingood had allowed me to borrow one of his kayaks for Maia. By the time she got to my house at noon I already had both boats loaded in my truck and had packed plenty of water and some snacks for our adventure. I had everything ready to go a couple of hours ahead of time and had spent the remaining time before Maia's arrival pacing the floor with anticipation.

Maia finally arrived just before noon and we were off to the Rivana River, the main water source for Charlottesville. We got there and I unloaded the kayaks and we dragged them down to the river's edge.

"This place is beautiful," Maia observed.

"Yes it is," I agreed. "I come here quite a bit. I have caught catfish as long as my leg out of this river."

"Really!" she said with excitement. "I have never been cat fishing before! I want to do that too!"

"Maia," I began, "I will take you!"

"Really!" she asked, again with the excitement of a child.

"Really!" I promised her in an almost mocking tone. "I will take you hiking, camping or anything else outdoorsy you want to do."

We floated down stream, passing grazing cows along the banks. I pointed out beaver huts and geese nests to her and showed her where all the best fishing spots were. About a mile down stream we pulled our kayaks together and started talking.

"I bet you are pretty excited about your trip that's coming up huh?" she asked.

"Yes I am," I agreed. "There is only one down fall to it though."

"What is that?" she asked.

"I'll have to be away from you and we've just met."

"Oh Kevin," she said in an insuring tone, "I'll be here when you get back. I'm not going anywhere.'

After a few moments in thought I exclaimed, "Hey! I have an idea!"

"What is that?" she questioned.

"Why don't you go with me?" I recommended.

"What?" she asked. "I have to work."

"Well maybe you could take a few days off and you could go on part of the trip with me," I suggested. "Maybe you could go to New Orleans or so and then you could fly back. I'll pay for the ticket!"

"Something like that might work," she agreed.

"I would love your company," I informed her.

"I would love yours," she agreed.

"So are you having fun kayaking?" I asked her, changing the subject.

"I'm having a blast," she told me. "How about you?"

"Oh, I'm having fun too," I agreed. "There is just one part about it that I don't like."

"What is that!" She asked with a puzzled look on her face.

"Well," I began, "I am over here in my boat and you are all the way over there in your boat."

"Your right," she agreed. "Let's go back to your house where we can hang out without space in between us."

"Now your talking!" I said. "Let's race!"

We turned upstream and paddled as hard as we could to get back to the truck. Though Maia had never been kayaking before she seemed to be a natural at it. She was very fit as well and had no problem keeping up with me. Once there I tied the boats back to the truck in record fashion and we were off to my house.

When we had arrived we raced into the house. We took off our shoes and Maia got a drink of water as I put the snacks we never touched away and stored the cooler under the sink. We turned at the same time and came face to face. I embraced her around the waste and looked deep into those big beautiful brown eyes in which I always found myself lost.

"Maia?" I asked.

"Yes," she cooed.

"Will you be my girl friend?" I asked.

Smiling from ear to ear she responded, "Yes Kevin, I'll be your girl friend."

We sealed our new relationship with our most passionate kiss yet. We fumbled our way into the bedroom and in the middle of the afternoon that Sunday we made the sweetest love I had ever known. It was better than I had fantasized it would be. Our bodies responded to each other as if they had been two missing pieces from the same puzzle since creation. Call it love, infatuation or whatever you like. I just call it ecstasy. I had met this woman, more beautiful than any I had ever known and she was now my girl friend and we were now making love. Life was good. It was better than good. It was great!

11

The next 10 days or so leading up to my departure for my trip across America were some of the sweetest days I had ever known. Other than when she was working, Maia and I were constantly together. We went out to eat, caught movies, went for long walks and at night we rose the heat index of the hot Virginia summer.

Maia's company had made me almost oblivious to the hardships I had recently gone through. That was until June 27'th, the last night I would spend in my home of the past seven years.

With the help of my friend Jim I had stored the rest of my belongings in Mr. Shelton's chicken barn. All that remained was my camping gear in my living room and my single person inflatable air mattress that I would sleep on tonight along with my light weight felt sleeping bag.

It had always been my way to stay positive. I figured the only thing one stood to gain from focusing on one's hardships was a case of depression and a couple of prescriptions. However, on this evening I found it hard not to focus on my misfortunes.

All I had ever wanted to do since getting married and becoming a father was provide for my family. I had not done that. I had not been able to keep my marriage intact and I had to choose between voluntarily selling my home or going through foreclosure.

To sum it up, I felt like a failure. Here I was, getting ready to embark on God only knew what kind of a journey across a land so vast that it spanned four time zones. Then I would go off for several months worth of grueling military training at a time in my life when I knew I was well past my physical prime. All the while my children would be spending who really knew how long in a city they had only visited once and then start school in a place where they had not a single friend because I would not yet be back from my military training before the start of the new school year. In my original plans I was to do my training over the children's summer break but those plans were changed due to Amanda's sudden departure for Seattle.

As positive as I was trying to remain I could not do it any more on this night. I was hurting so bad that I could feel the pain in my bones. I wanted to cry but the tears would not come.

I was laying there with seven years worth of wonderful memories in this house racing through my head when Maia's car pulled into the driveway. Her headlights cast lonely shadows of the skeleton of the curtainless window frame on the wall above my head.

I met her at the door with a somewhat depressing, "Hello," then walked with her to the air mattress and sat beside her. At 5'4" and no more than 105 pounds Maia was a petite little thing, and with myself only being 5'10 and 160 pounds the two of us would have no problem sharing the single air mattress on the living room floor.

"I was afraid you might not be in the best of spirits tonight," she said in a comforting voice.

"Yeah," I agreed. "I never really thought about how hard this night would be."

We laid down and she wrapped her arms around me.

"Kevin?" she began.

"Yes," I answered.

"How about I just hold you tonight until you fall to sleep?" she said.

"Ok," I agreed, resting my head against her chest as she wrapped her arms around me in a nurturing way.

I did not speak again that night, nor did she. I closed my eyes though it would be a while before I fell to sleep. I don't know what I would have done had Maia not been there for me that night. The smell of her skin and the feel of her warmth did so much to comfort me. I eventually fell to sleep and did not dream at all.

The next morning I was awakened by the sun shining through the front window. Maia had already gotten up and gotten dressed and was about to leave to run errands. It was her day off, and only having one day off each week her schedule was full. We agreed to meet in town for dinner that night after she took care of all of her responsibilities and I took care of the close of my house.

I spent the morning with my attorney, the same man that had represented me through my divorce then spent much of the afternoon with my friend Dean, who had mixed feelings about helping me become "homeless." He was happy to close his first sale but he knew what that was doing to me.

That evening Maia and I met for dinner and then returned to her house to spend the night. The following morning I would embark on my great journey.

Maia rented a simple abode on a 60 acre farm in Orange county Virginia. Waking up here was so peaceful, with the windows open allowing both the cool morning summer breeze and the songs of many different types of birds to float into the window and fill the bedroom with nature's natural alarms.

Maia and I had coffee together and then she walked me out to my truck which was gassed up and loaded down with my camping gear in the back, under the protection of my topper and my big orange kayak strapped firmly to the top. Oh how cruel fate could sometimes be. Here I had met the woman of my dreams yet I was too soon leaving her for a six week cross country journey and then would only be able to spend a few days with her before shipping off for several months worth of military training.

Though Maia and I had visited the idea of her going part of the way with me on the trip, she had actually recommended that I go it alone. She felt that after what I had gone through, especially during the last six months, I should use the time to defuse and focus on the aspects of the trip itself instead of her, and those little shorts she loved to wear. As much as I would have loved to have her with me I agreed with her.

Just before climbing into the drivers seat of my old, 1994 Dodge Dakota extended cab that already had 180,000 miles on it, I held her around the waste as I loved to do and we locked our lips in one last kiss.

"I'll wait for you," were the only words she whispered in a caring tone.

"I'll return," was my only reply.

With that I was off.

I had to stop by Sunshine Laundry to pick up a load of clean clothes that I had dropped off to Regina the day before. When I got there I was surprised to see that Regina had prepared a goody bag for me. In it, there were several bags of chex mix, a few candy bars, a box of Chinese melon cakes and a box of caffeine free ginger tea. She also handed me my bag of laundry and did not charge me for her services. She wished me a safe trip, gave me a comforting hug, then sent me on my way.

I didn't pay too much attention to the too often before seen scenery of Charlottesville as I headed for interstate 64 west which would connect me to 81 south, the road I would take into Tennessee. As I left the area I was filled with bitter sweet memories. So many wonderful things had taken place in my life in this town, yet there had also been some unpleasant ones as well.

I bore down interstate 81 once I had reached it and felt my heart go out to the community of Blacksburg, just south of Roanoke when I passed it. Just a couple of months before a deranged student had stormed the campus and taken the lives of more than 30 students before turning his gun on himself and taking his own. Virginia Tech and the University of Virginia had been big in state rivals since the time both schools had existed in unison, but after this event, all of us were Virginia Tech fans. I can remember all of the bumper stickers around Charlottesville that said, "Hoos (UVA's nickname) for Hokies (Tech's mascot)."

It took about five hours for me to cross the state line into Tennessee. There were still several hours of day light left but I wanted to go ahead and stop for several reasons. For one, I had not run yet and I wanted to get a quick workout in before dark, and secondly, I had told myself that if at all possible I would avoid driving at night. I could not see this great land of ours in the dark.

I was able to find a campsite at Baileyton RV Park off of exit 36 in northern Tennessee. It cost me $17 for a tent site and hot showers were provided. I pulled up to my tent site, pitched my smaller of two tents I had taken, a two man pup in which I would store my equipment. I then put off putting up my larger of the two tents until after I had run and gotten everything else situated.

I changed into a skimpy pair of running shorts, laced up my running shoes and having decided to run shirtless do to the heat hit the road. There was not much burm along this back country road to protect me from all the large jacked up pick up trucks that were flying by me so when I came upon a golf coarse only half a mile up the road I decided to run on the safety of its coarse.

I had not run on a golf coarse since my days of college cross country. Back then we would run up to 70 miles a week and running on the softer terrains, like that provided by a golf coarse was essential to avoid many of the injuries one could incur from all the pounding associated with such high mileage.

I finished my run of about four miles and was walking around the edge of the woods at the RV park picking and eating black berries that were growing in the wild when the wind began to pick up and I looked above me to notice the quickly approaching dark clouds of what was going to be one heck of a rain storm.

I ran back to the truck and began to construct my larger tent when I thought better of the idea, realizing the storm was coming faster than I had thought. Instead, I simply put all of my equipment in the small tent outside and inflated my air mattress which fit perfectly snug inside the eight foot bed of my truck. I climbed in just as the rain began and realized sleeping in my truck would probably be a better arraignment during this trip anyway. It would take me less time to arraign my gear and it might be safer as well.

As I was climbing into the back of my truck, a fifty something year old Korean American man who was staying in a nice RV just off to my left approached and offered for me to stay with him in his RV for the night. The coming storm did appear to be quite ominous.

I thanked him for his invitation but declined as since this was the first night of my trip I wanted to spend it alone. Also, I imagined there may be many more nights along the way were I was faced with a similar situation and the convenience of a caring fellow camper might not always be available so I may as well get used to it.

I rolled my thick, goose down military sleeping bag that I had gotten at a surplus store years before across the air mattress and propped my pillows up against the back of the truck's cab, facing out over the tail gate through the door of the topper. I grabbed a can of corn and a container of chocolate pudding, both of which I had brought from my pantry from home. As I began eating the corn with a plastic spoon the rain began hammering away at the top of the truck. It was raining so hard that I could not see out of any of the windows that completely surrounded me.

I was a bit down, having had to leave Maia and having just sold my home, and having been away from my kids for so long now but I quickly found myself thinking about our many soldiers who were in Iraq and Afghanistan. Did they have the comfort of a topper to keep them dry? I simply had rain drops pouring down on me. How many of them at this very minute might have bullets or mortars raining down on them?

I had figured out years before that at times when I start to feel sorry for myself, that if I can get out of myself and think of or try to help others I would soon forget about my own problems.

While I ate, water began dripping into the bed of the truck from the sides of the roof of the topper. I guess after 13 years it had begun to dry rot in places and was no longer completely water proof. As I finished my pudding, I laid down, as it was now dark and found myself praying for the safety of our soldiers over sees. I finished my prayers and was put to sleep by the pounding rain above me and the light "plip plopping" of the water coming in beside me. In spite of the storm I got a good night's sleep.

12

The next morning I woke peacefully just after dawn. I quickly repacked my gear from outside into the truck and checked out of the RV park. Before heading further south toward New Orleans, a city I really wanted to get to quickly in order to walk across the battle field were Andrew Jackson and about 1800 US soldiers had decimated nearly 3000 British soldiers in less than 2 hours at the Battle of New Orleans during the War of 1812, there was another place close by that I wanted to visit this day.

Greenville, Tennessee was only half an hour west of where I had stayed the night before and it had been the home for many years of Andrew Johnson, our 17'th president who had succeeded Abraham Lincoln after Lincoln's assassination. It took me no time at all to make to drive over to Greenville.

Greenville was a very quaint and exceptionally clean little town. It reminded me of my native Richwood West Virginia minus the lumber mills. The Andrew Johnson exhibit lay in the heart of the small community.

The exhibit itself was housed in a small stone building that had a stream running underneath it. The building acted as a bridge for the waterway.

The tailoring shop that Johnson had actually worked out of during his many years in that profession was incased inside the building. Though the shop was only 30 feet by 15 feet it provided him with all the space he needed at the time.

Johsonson's shop was the location of much gathering for political discussion during his years there as a tailor. You could say that Johnson started his political career in this small shop. At the end of the work day, many of the local men in the Greenville community would gather at Johnson's shop and participate in long discussions of the issues of the day.

Johnson himself was not an educated man. He had never finished school and actually never knew how to read until his wife, a lovely lady he met once he settled in Greenville, taught him how. However, he was a great public speaker and he was a genuine soul, a true statesman who did what was right for his constituants as opposed to a mere politician who did what was popular, or right for himself. These traits in Johnson would actually lead to his impeachment as president.

After the end of the civil war, it was Lincoln's plan to forgive the southern generals for any part they played against the union and focus more on rehabilitating the war weary nation. When Johnson took over at the helm he wanted to act in this same way, though many members of his congress wanted no less than a pound of flesh from the southerners.

Johnson refused to seek retribution from the southerners and this quickly arose into a great debacle when congress began intentionally putting in place men who would go after the southerners. A rule, known as the "Tenure of Office Act" had been set in place by the congress disallowing the president to remove any leading cabinet member without congress's permission, but when Secretary of War Edwin Stanton began to over step his bounds and sought punishment toward former southern combatants, Johnson removed him without the congress's permission.

This got Johnson a vote of impeachment in the House of Representatives. He was not forced to leave office however as his detractors fell only one vote shy to make him do so in the senate. After Johnson's term as president he would later return to serve in the senate as he had before, becoming the only president to do so and he died shortly thereafter.

Johnson's style of leadership earned him the nickname "Defender of the Constitution." He was able to look beyond what was popular, or what "felt good" to do at the time, and concerned himself more with doing what was right and what would benefit America greater in the long run.

Here I had come to Greenville Tennessee and had walked in the footsteps of a man who might understand some of the actions I had taken recently in my own life, realizing that I myself might suffer in the short run, but knowing that in the long run I was playing a small part on a large stage, the war on terror, which held greater benefits for our masses in the future than any small reward I might selfishly enjoy on my own at the present. I began to feel as if I were not as crazy as my neighbor Dave Reid thought I was for making materialistic sacrifices in my own life to lend a hand toward a greater cause and help benefit the lives of others.

It was interesting walking through the museum and taking note of many of the advertisments of the time. Having just sold my little three bedroom ranch house that sits on only half an acre of land in Ruckersville Virginia for $212,000 (I had bought it seven years before for $118,000) there was one particular ad that leaped out at me. It was an ad for land west of Tennessee.

At the time of the early 1800's Tennessee was about as far west as one could journey in the settled United States and still find fairly civil land though Indian attacks were still common. Westward expansion had made it to the Mississippi River and St. Louis was quite a little hub. The lands west of there, recently acquired through the Louisiana Purchase were being marketed heavily.

The government was encouraging westward expansion, mostly through settlement, and the ad of interest to me was one for land that was selling for only $3 an acre. On top of that, the ad boasted, no principle was required to be put down at the time of purchase and there would be no taxes required to be paid for the first six years of ownership.

After watching a brief video on Johnson were I brushed up on many of the facts of his life that I had already known, like the time he and his brother threw a rock through the window of his tailoring mentor for whom he was an apprentice and therefore had to run away to avoid arrest, I had lunch on the back of my tail gate in the museum parking lot. I was low on cash and I figured that the more I avoided eating at restaurants the more likely I would be able to make this nearly seven thousand mile journey without having money problems.

After lunch I walked across the street to view a replica of the home Johnson and his family had lived in. The house, which would not have been any larger than his tailoring shop had it not been for an upstairs loft, was very simple. It really makes one wonder if we need all of the 3,000 square feet of living space that currently seems to make up the modern home. I remember reading recently that the average sized SUV of today would not even fit in the average sized garage of the houses built in the 1970's.

I always preferred smaller living quarters myself because it seemed to me that the more space people had the more "stuff" they tended to accumulate. One of my house hold practices to avoid accumulating all of this "stuff" was that for anything new I brought into the house, something of equal or greater size had to leave. Also, if I had anything other than collectibles that had not been used in over a year, it was gone too.

It had not rained as of yet today but the clouds from the night before seemed to be moving back in. After walking around the town of Greenville itself for just a bit, enjoying the polite, "Hello's" from its residents that I passed, I jumped back in my truck and made it back to the interstate. I would travel further south on 81 and pick up interstate 75 just south of Knoxville. I would not be heading as far west in Tennessee as Nashville, but if I had been I would have loved to have stopped at Andrew Jackson's home, the Hermitage. However, I would make that trip at some later date I had decided and I was sure to be entertained by much history about the General once I made it to New Orleans.

I spent all afternoon and most of the evening hours driving. I passed through the upper north west corner of Georgia briefly, not desiring to stop anywhere as I knew that in all good time, only six weeks from now, I would be spending several months of my life at Georgia's Fort Benning farther to the south.

As I blew through Alabama I did want to stop but those ominous storm clouds were behind me and I heard repeatedly on the radio of severe thunderstoms that were in all of the areas surrounding me. At one point I passed through a pretty heavy storm myself.

I used this time passing through Alabama as a time of reflection. I thought back on the previous six months and again wondered how I had made it through. I dearly missed my children and found myself thinking of them often. We had been apart for almost a month now and we had never been separated that long. If given the choice of this, relaxing time to myself, or more time spent as a full time single father of three and all of the hecticness that came with it, it would be an easy choice for me to make. I would take the hecticness and my kids over the peace any day.

I had been calling my kids every evening since they left and was able to reach them most days. I always loved talking to them but getting off of the phone was very hard. Though they always knew the answer, they always asked the same questions, "Daddy, when do we get to come back to Virginia? Daddy, when will we get to see you again?"

I found myself thinking of Maia quite a bit too. I still could not believe how everything had worked out between us, or that we had even met just a few weeks before. I often wondered why I had been single for nearly 2 years after Amanda had left me. I always believed that God had a person who was for me and that I would meet them only when the time was right and I knew that while I was going through the turmoil of my divorce and the turbulent times with the kids that the time was not right.

I do not believe it was mere coincidence that Mia and I met when we did. Had I actually met her that day in the restaurant it probably would not have worked out between us because the timing would have been wrong. Here was God working in my life to my benefit yet again. It amazed me how many times things might not always work out how I wanted them to but seemed to always work out the way they were supposed to.

As night began to fall I had made it to the small community of Meridian, Mississippi. I was able to locate the Narrabe Creek Camp Ground here and secure a tent space just before dark.

The camp's office was located inside a very unique and large A frame building. Inside, the place reaked of mildew and dust and had stuffed heads of every large mammal in the southeastern United States hanging from the walls. There were mostly white tailed bucks but also a bear and a large wild turkey.

I approached the fifty some year old lady working the desk, who it turned out was the second generation owner of this fine establishment. I tried to engage her in friendly conversation but seeing that it was nearing 9:00 p.m., her closing hour, she seemed less interested in talking and more interested in simply taking my $18 and pointing me in the direction of the tent sites.

I paid my fee and drove around behind this gaudy A frame and once again set up my small tent. Tonight however, I decided to leave my gear in the truck and inflate my air mattress in this smaller of my two tents and simply sleep in it.

I laid down and went to sleep just after dark and less than an hour later was awakened by the screaming whistles and whinning wheels of a freight train that was rolling through the night on a track located no more than a quarter of a mile away. It must have been one heck of a long train as this disturbance lasted for nearly 10 minutes. After it subsided I was able to get back to sleep pretty quickly. That was until it happened again about an hour later. I would soon find out that about every hour or so this would happen.

After spending a night of sleeping off and on due to the trains I was awakened at 5:30 a.m. by a truck load of screaming rednecks. It turned out there was a small construction crew of some type made up of about six men who where camping in a collection of tents just 30 yards up from me.

"Time to wake up everybody!!!" they yelled as they jumped in their trucks and blew their horns on the way out of the camp ground. I guess they figured if they had to be up then everyone else did too.

I was more than happy to roll out of my tent and get ready to hit the road and be gone from this place. I got up, put my tent and sleeping gear away, and made myself a breakfast that consisted of three fried eggs and some wheat bread. I had brought along my little Coleman camping stove and everything I would need to cook with, again trying to be fiscally conservative while on this trip. I sat there and ate my eggs and bread quickly while the local mosquito population sat there and ate me.

At Meridian I picked up interstate 59 south and followed it all the way into Louisiana. Just past the state line I got on Interstate 10 which ran almost the entire length of the southwestern portion of the United States heading east to west. I would follow this road all the way into New Orleans.

After entering Louisiana it was not long until I hit my destination for this leg of the trip. As I began crossing the long bridge over Lake Ponchartrain that would lead me into New Orleans I became very excited at the thought of seeing the battle field where one of my all time favorite American heroes, Andrew Jackson, had changed the coarse of American history forever.

Up until the time of the war of 1812, though we had defeated the British in the American Revelution, America had not yet proven herself to be a world power militarily. The war of 1812, and Jackson's courageous part in it would change that. However, as I came off of the other side of the bridge into the St. Bernard Parish, I saw a sight I had not expected to see that would lengthen and reprioritize my time spent in the New Orleans area.

I first took notice of the demolished boats, or better yet, pieces of boats that were scattered among the marshes on both sides of the road. It looked as if the place was one huge grave yard for partial boats.

As I drove further into the community I began seeing roof tops in the marshes as well. I was sure that for every roof top I saw there was a house that was in need of one somewhere close by.

As I came into buildings I saw empty store fronts with boarded up windows and the words "Demo," or "Do Not Demo," painted on each one. There were few people out and about. There were heaps of rubbage piled higher than my truck all along the road every so many feet.

It had been almost two years now since our nation's largest natural disaster, Hurricane Katrina had ripped through New Orleans but you could not tell that nearly two years had passed since it happened. I have never been to a war zone but I would imagine that this is how one might appear.

Before I was half way through St. Bernard Parrish, heading toward the state park of that same name to set up camp, I decided that I had to help the people of New Orleans in some way. I turned left onto St. Bernard Parrish road and began heading along the levee, passing huge naval ships along the way toward the state park when I noticed a sign on my left that read, "Camp Hope."

I pulled into Camp Hope and was greated by two young black girls in their early twenties who were manning the check gate.

"How can I help you?" one of them mumbled while not looking up from filing her really long, really fake purple fingernails with many different colored lines racing across them.

"I want to volunteer to help out," I informed her.

"What do you want to do?" asked her partner, looking up at me only slightly interested in my precense.

"Whatever I can," I said. "I roofed houses during the summers in college and had done a little remodeling with my father in our house while growing up. I'm a quick learner and am willing to do anything."

"Come back tomorrow at 9:00 a.m. (it was a Sunday afternoon) and we'll let you go into the office and check in and they'll give you an assignment," the girl with the nails told me, again never looking up.

With that I was off to St. Bernanrd State Park to check in and set up camp.

13

St. Bernard Park State Park was very interesting. It seemed to be a refuge for cotton tail rabbits and the largest grass hoppers I had ever seen in my life, and there were lots of them. After checking in at the office and paying $80 for the next 4 nights because I had decided to stay as long as I could without endangering my trip's time frame, I weaved my way around rabbits and these large, dollar bill sized grasshoppers to my tent site. These grasshoppers, black in color with red wings beneath their wing shells were in such number that I could not avoid running one over every now and then. When I did, it let out a loud crunch as if I had just ran over a goose egg. I counted over twenty rabbits before I made the half mile loop to my tent site.

I pitched the larger of my two tents since I would be staying here for an extended time and then walked around the camp site to investigate its strange insect inhabitants. In so doing I also noticed that the place was overrun with tree frogs, tree lizards, and unfortunately, fire ants.

I caught one of the large grasshoppers, referred to by the locals as "grave yard grasshoppers" and turned him upside down to investigate his under side. Squirming to get away, he latched onto my fingers and I flung him away quickly as his little prickly hands nearly pierced my skin.

I found myself thinking of Emily and how much she would love to be here with me. She was always catching critters in our yard or whenever we went hiking or fishing and she would absolutely love all of the wild life at this park. I would imagine that she would herass them so much though that she would greatly diminish their population and the residents of New Orleans would find that aside from all the debris from the hurricane, they would also have to deal with the homeless grasshoppers and rabbits.

With several hours of day light left and no work for me to do in regard to helping reconstruct New Orleans until tomorrow I decided to go to Chalmette Battfield, the site of the Battle of New Orleans. This site was located only ten minutes from my camp site.

I pulled in and parked beside a trailer that had been set up for use as the park's office since Katrina had evidently taken the original. I walked in the door and was greeted by the only person in the building, the park ranger Harold Songer.

Harold was a man of about 45 years of age and stood about six feet tall. He had peppered hair, wore glasses and a ranger cap and had a good personality for his position. He was welcoming and very friendly.

I told him I had driven down from Virginia and that I was a huge Andrew Jackson fan and was ready to talk about the General. Acting as if he hadn't heard a word I said he reached for a map. I thought at first that he was going to give me an outlay of the battlefield and talk me through the play by play of the battle but I would soon find out I was wrong.

Harold had pulled out a map of the city of New Orleans and he instead began talking me through a play by play of the hurricane.

"It killed 150 people just from St. Bernard Parrish," he informed me.

"That is terrible," I said, wanting to hear about the Battle of New Orleans instead.

Harold continued with his story about the storm and I soon realized that this was some sort of therapy for him. Instead of being too concerned with my own selfish interests of the battle I decided to participate in Harold's discussion of the storm. I had plenty of time left in the day to see the sites and if need be I could swing back by on one of the next four days that I would be in the area.

"My elderly parents still live in the area," he continued. "I decided to go get them and make sure they got out of the city with me. We decided to go to Houston. That is usually a ten hour drive but that day, due to the traffic it took us eighteen."

"Really?" I said, truly astonished.

"Yes," he said. "My best friend tried to head north into Mississippi and the traffic was worse that way. We talked back and forth on the phone the whole time."

Harold went on about Katrina for a good half hour. He told me how high the water was. The battle field, being just on the other side of the levee, was more than twenty feet under water. The more he talked about it the better he seemed to feel and I didn't mind listening. I could not imagine having gone through what the folks down here had gone through.

At some point a couple in their late forties came in and asked to view a film on the battle. I watched it with them and then went outside to walk the battle field.

I was first drawn to the rampart with its many cannons spaced evenly about every twenty yards apart behind its width. I stood behind the largest of the guns, probably a twelve pounder, meaning it fired a twelve pound ball, and looked over the rampart which stood about six feet high and was every bit as thick. The Americans would have been as safe as an egg in an incubator, while the British, marching across the field on the rampart's other side would have been as easy to shoot as fish in a barrel. I marveled at either how ignorant or how arrogant the British must have been to march in formation toward those cannons and the hundreds of muskets firing straight at them.

During this battle, Jackson, just like George Washington in his battles, road along the firing line throughout its coarse and cheered on his men, waving his sword and shouting encouragement. A smaller group of British had tried to over take the rampart on its right flank, but General Jackson had thought ahead and had made sure to man that post heavily as well.

At one point, the British had tried to travel up the Mississippi to launch an attack from behind but they did not recon the might of the water flow and that avenue of approach proved useless as well.

The British army had been bogged down not just fighting us during the war of 1812 but through much of it were still fighting Napoleon. However, by this point in the war the British had already defeated the French, freeing up their troops to cross the ocean and lay the hammer down on the Americans. These very troops in New Orleans were some of the British's best that were responsible for defeating Napoleon at Waterloo.

This was a day that Andrew Jackson had fantasized about since his youth. During the American revolution, when Jackson was only fifteen years old he had been taken as a prisoner of war by the British. When a British officer approached the young boy and demanded he shine his boots, and the boy refused, the officer took his sword out of its sheeth and swung it across his face. Jackson threw his hand up to block the blow and moved away but the sword still cut his face and hand, leaving scars that would remain with him for life.

Jackson's older brother died while in the same prison camp and his mother, who had convinced the British to allow her to care for her ailing son, would later die as a result of catching ill herself while in the camp. In eccense, the British had killed off what remained of young Andrew Jackson's family as his father had died while his mother was still pregnant with him. Jackson was left an orphan at age 15.

This is a fact that perhaps led to Jackson's decision to raise an orphaned Indian boy that was taken after his parents were killed during the Indian wars that Jackson would play a major role in several years after the war of 1812. However, he would show no mercy to the British on this fateful January day in 1815 in Chalmette.

After viewing the cannons I crossed the rampart and walked through the field the British had used for their approach. After they had been blown away and the firing had stopped the ground was covered with bright red coats and crimson red blood. A witness of the battle said that once the firing had stopped, wounded British soldiers and others who had simply laid down and played dead began to rise and it appeared, with the gun smoke, that the dead were rising from their graves.

The british suffered an estimated 1200 casualties that day and the American side suffered less than a dozen. It was the largest lop sided victory against the greatest army in the world in recorded history.

These events made Jackson a national hero and no doubt played a major role in catapulting him into the white house when he ran in 1828. He had actually won the popular vote in 1824, but at the time he did not win a majority in the electorate, though he had more electorate votes than the other two candidates. The vote went to the house of representatives where he was robbed at the hands of dirty politics. John Quincy Adams of Massachusetts, the eventual winner had promised House Speaker Henry Clay that if he voted for him, thereby giving him the presidency that he would make him his secretary of state, which he did only a few days later after Clay had followed his directive. This was the first presidential election in history in which the eventual winner had not received the majority of the popular vote.

Though Jackson stood six feet tall, he never weighed more than 145 pounds at any point during his life except for in his later years when he put on weight due to illnesses that would eventually take his life at 78 years old. However, he seemed to have a very angry temperment if challenged and packed the punch of any many twice his size. He once participated in a duel with a man who had slandered his wife Rachael in which a bullet was lodged within an inch of his heart. When Jackson died, not from this wound but many years later of illness and old age, the bullet still remained.

Though Jackson is perhaps remembered most for his triumph at New Orleans and his performance as a military leader, he actually made a very good president. Though he had his problems with the British in two wars, it was he who finally got trading with the British flowing smoothly again while he was in office. Also, he opened trade for the first time for America with several Asian countries such as Japan and Syngapore.

There were several nations too who had owned America quite a bit of money due to their impressment of American vessels during the Napoleonic wars, an act that eventually led to the war of 1812 with the British. Whereas no president before Jackson could get these countries, particulary France, to pay up even though it had been decided in international courts that the money was owed the

Americans, Jackson was able to get these nations to cough up the money. In so doing, he was able to eliminate the national debt by the end of his second term. Teddy Roosevelt would say years later to "Walk softly but carry a big stick." Andrew Jackson rarely walked softly but he certainly carried a big stick and the world knew he was not afraid to use it.

Jackson was actually the first president on whom an assassination attempt was made. His attempted assassin waited for him on one of the porches of the White House one day in the rain and fired two shots from two separate pistols at him at close range. Due to the dampness in the air the guns never went off because the powder had gotten damp and it was all his guards could do to hold Jackson back and keep him from beating his assailant to death.

The British took into account many things when they attempted to storm the city of New Orleans. They took into account the best way to approach the city through the swamps and they took into account the man power they would need. They did not however, take into account Andrew Jackson.

14

With a couple of hours of daylight left I decided to roll into New Orleans itself after viewing the battlefield. I drove across old rail road bridges, through the infamous ninth ward and into the French quarter where a local R&B radio station was holding a live music event. I could hear the music from my truck and there were hundreds of people everywhere, all of which seemed to be having a good time. I decided to park my truck and check out the party.

I could not find parking close to the show so I had to park on the outter edge of the ninth ward. I pulled my old pickup truck with the big orange kayak on top into the lot of a run down gas station and prepared to walk the several blocks to the event.

After getting out of my truck, locking the door, and beginning my walk, it occurred to me what I was doing. Was this safe for me? Here I was, an out of town white guy walking through the middle of the ninth ward by myself.

All I had seen on the news in the past couple of years were angry blacks in New Orleans who were constantly lashing out at the establishment. Would I be viewed as one of the establishment's members and thereby be placed in harms way?

As I started down the side walk I said to myself over and over, "Just don't look at or speak to anyone."

As I approached the first person I would pass, a black man appearing to be in his late 30's, I tensed up and continued to look straight ahead.

"Hey buddy?" he said. "You goin' down to the show?"

"Yes," I said nervously, trying not to make eye contact.

"It's a good one man. Have a good time!" he said as he went by.

He must have been a tourist. All the local blacks here are pissed off and are blaming the government instead of nature over Katrina, at least according to the media. There is no way a black man that friendly could be from New Orleans, especially this part of town.

As I got closer to the show I began passing even more people, all of whom were black.

"What's up man?" they would ask as we would pass each other.

"How ya doin' buddy?" asked others with a big smiles.

Ok, something was wrong here. Was this town filled with nothing but tourists? I thought these people were not friendly and happy. These people were mad and this was not a safe part of town for me to be in. What was going on?

I made it into the show after passing many more people and after having been given many more friendly greetings. Inside the barriers where the show was being held in a big courtyard of what appeared to be a hotel, there were probably four or five hundred people gathered to listen to the music and have a good time. I was one of less than a handful of whites yet nobody seemed to even notice.

The band on stage was amazing. It was made up of a bass player, a drummer, a keyboardist, a man on trumpet and a trombone player. The trumpet and trombone players took turns singing lead.

I am always quick to point out to folks that I was a state champion miler in high school, but I'm not always as quick to point out that I was also the drum major in my high school's band. I played several brass instruments including the trumpet, the French horn and the mellaphone.

The reason I point this out here is to let it be known that I know quite a bit about music and have been around it a lot, but I had never heard music coming from brass instruments like this before.

The trombone player in this R&B band was astonishing! He was playing notes on the trombone so quickly that you would think it had the rapid fire key capability of a trumpet, not the long flowing slide that it did possess. This guy was unbelievable! At one point, toward the end of one of their songs, he actually held a note for what had to be two minutes! Back when I went through a triathlon phase many years ago and was doing quite a bit of swimming, I held my breath once for two minutes, though it damn near killed me, but this guy was not holding his breath, he was exhaling! He was by far the best brass instrument player I had ever heard in my life.

All of the people at the party were dancing and talking to each other. Any time I made eye contact with any of them they were just as happy to talk to me as they were any of their own friends that they were there with.

This is when I realized the people of New Orleans were survivors. They were not the hateful, bitter cermudgeons the media had been portraying them to be. I have no clue were the news people were finding all of the angry people they were showing on TV because of the hundreds of people I had seen so far I did not see anyone who was not happy. The news people probably had to look long and hard to find the unhappy ones themselves.

I sat back for some time and took in the music that was flowing from the band and the happiness that was flowing from the people. The people of New Orleans had not decided to give up. Here it was only two years after the storm, much of their town still in tatters, and they were driving on, continuing to move forward with their lives. I found myself drawing inspiration from them for my own life.

After the show I headed back for the camp. But first I stopped at Main's Market on the way to get some bread and fruit were I struck up a conversation with a gentlman in the parking lot.

Eddie Montz, a friendly gentleman appearing to be in his early forties was parked at the side of the store with his bass boat hooked behind his truck.

"Where ya been kayakin'?" he asked me as I got out of my truck.

"Oh, nowhere yet," I replied. "I am down from Virginia and am traveling across the country and back and I guess will just put it in the water whenever the spirit moves me."

"That sounds like quite a trip," he responded. "Why are you doing that?"

I walked over to him so that we would not have to yell at each other. I explained to him, with the thirty seconds or less version, that I had recently had to sell my house due to complications of a divorce and that I was out to see this great nation for which I had recently enlisted to fight.

"I understand being homeless," he said, as his wife Dianne and their two daughters, Sage (6) and Samantha (4), came over to join us after just coming out of the store.

"Yeah, we lost everything during the Hurricane and were homeless ourselves for a while," he went on.

"What did you do?" I asked, feeling kind of ignorant about what questions to ask someone like this and exactly how to ask them.

"We actually ended up staying at a church shelter up in Tennessee for more than a year," Dianne chimmed in. "We went up there with my father and step mother."

"All the way to Tennessee?" I asked.

"Oh yes," she said. "Hurricane victims were everywhere, not just in Texas and Mississippi."

"I work for the docks down here," Eddie informed me. "Once the docks got back to running again I came back and started working while my family stayed in Tennessee. The house we had been renting was demolished and it took us over a year to be able to find another."

"Wow!" I said. "You had to be away from your family for over a year?"

"I went up to see them every other weekend," he replied. "It was hard but we had to do what we had to do."

"When we did come back," Dianne spoke again, "The church we were staying at gave us an entire household worth of furniture and a car."

"Wow!" I said again. "That was awful nice of them."

"People helping people man," Eddie said. "That's how we've all gotten through this thing. Just people helping people."

Sage and Samantha crawled into the back of the bass boat and played while their parents and I talked for a good hour. They continued telling me about their experience with the hurricane and Eddie talked quite a bit about the local fishing scene.

"We saw an alligator while out on the boat today," he said.

"Really!" I exclaimed.

"Yeah, one of the girls were swimming about six feet away from it so we had her get in the boat and we moved to a different spot," he said without a care in the world.

During the length of our conversation neither Eddie nor Dianne said one bad thing about the government's role after the storm nor did they bad mouth, or even mention President Bush. They stayed completely positive about their experience and smiled the whole time.

"I do have one question for you though," I said toward the end of our conversation.

"What is that?" smiled Eddie.

"Knowing that this could happen again at any time, are you still planning on staying here?" I asked.

"Absolutely!" he said without hesitation.

"Home is home huh?" I responded.

"When you leave here, which way are you going?" he asked.

Not knowing why he was concerned with my direction of travel I answered, "I'm heading west on Interstate 10 into Texas."

"Ok," he started. "When you get to the other side of the bridge crossing Lake Pontchartrain you'll see a sign that says 'Montz' with an arrow pointing in the town's direction."

"Yes," I said curiously.

"My great, great, great grandfather founded that town," he told me. "So the answer to your question is yes, home is home."

The Montz family and I talked a while longer but since it was growing dark we eventually parted ways. I went into the small convenient store and bought my bread and about half a dozen plumbs. I absolutely love plumbs and the only time

I can find them is in the summer. I spend half of my summers it seems eating plumbs as ridiculous as that sounds.

After getting back in the truck I made the short drive back to camp. I pulled back into my site, running over several more gigantic grasshoppers in doing so, scared the rabbits out of my path, knocked a few tree frogs off of my tent, climbed inside and went to sleep for the night.

15

The next morning I rose at 6:00 a.m. local time, taking advantage of the time change to central thereby enjoying the extra hour of sleep, and prepared for my morning run. Already it was more humid than any day I could recently remember.

I put on my skimpy running shorts, laced up my shoes and headed out of the camp site, again counting more than twenty rabbits and playing hop scotch over giant grasshoppers.

I went to the main road and took a left, heading down along the levee. At one point I saw a trail heading to the levee so I took its route and ran along the levee itself. It was quite an eery feeling, being able to look to my right at the waters of the Mississippi and then to my left and see that the community of St Bernard's Parrish sat so much lower than their levels. Anyone willing to live here was a braver soul than me.

I ran out about a mile and a half, and after running through and scattering a flock of what appeared to be some type of gulls, watermellon sized white birds that stood on long yellow legs, I turned around and headed back for my tent site. Though I was running at a slow, comfortable pace, as I seemed only to do these days, I was drenched with sweet due to the outrageous humidity.

I got back to my camp and showered then prepared a breakfast of three eggs and wheat bread and followed it down with several of the plumbs I had bought the night before. I then sat in my truck, with the doors open and the windows down and began filling out post cards I had purchased at the battlefield the day before that I would be sending off to my kids, parents and Maia. A small brown wren of some type lit on my door frame in the open window and watched me as if it hadn't a care in the world or a concern for its safety.

After finishing my post cards I laid in my portable hammock I had set up beside my tent and continued reading David McCullough's "1776" that I had started just before leaving Virginia. By 8:00 a.m. the heat index had gotten to where it was quite uncomfortable so I decided to head to Camp Hope a bit early.

After getting through the gate, having talked to two diferrent, yet equally apathetic guards as the day before I made my way to the office. Here I was met by a young blond haired lady, and I use the term "lady" loosely, who was in charge of handing out the day's assignments. She cussed as much as I would imagine any of my soon to be drill sergeants at Fort Benning would.

"What kind of f——g work do you do?" she asked in a not so pleasant tone.

"I'm a stock broker," I answered.

"How the h—l is that gonna do any good?" she asked, glaring at me with piercing eyes.

"Well," I continued, "I have done roofing and remodeling and though its been a few years, I'm sure I could pick it back up pretty quickly."

"Ok!" she huffed. "I'm sending you a few blocks down to help with a couple of houses we're working on. Do you think you can find your way if I just tell you how to get there?

"I hope," I said naively.

"Ugh!" she moaned heavily. "I'll print you off a f——g map!"

"Great!" I exclaimed. "My father is in the wood industry and the more trees we can kill the better my chances of an inheritance!"

The look she gave me made it obvious that she did not think my ill attempt at humor was funny.

I got in my truck and followed her little map to my destination with no problem. When I got to my arrival point, I found about a dozen young people, ranging in ages from sixteen to twenty five, save for a man in his late fifties who was obviously the crew chief, sitting around on the steps of and beside one of two houses that were under construction.

"So what do we have to do guys?" I asked.

"Just sit here for a while," a young man, no more then eighteen years old told me. "We are waiting on the truck to get here with the roof trussels."

"Oh," I said. "Well I'm only here for four days and I don't want to spend my time here sittiing so I am going to walk up the street and see if there are any locals doing any work that I can help out with," I informed them. "I'll come back when I see the truck drive by."

I began walking up the street when I heard a voice call me from behind.

"Wait up!" it said.

The voice was coming from a sixteen year old girl named Allison Poirier. Allison it turned out was from Medfield, Massachusetts and she was down here volunteering for the summer with a group from her area known as 'Rustic Pathways.'

"There is actually some siding that can be done on one of our houses but it takes two people and I can't get any of those lazy kids to help me. Do want to do it with me?" she asked.

"Sure!" I said, turning around and walking back.

Allison had been siding quiet a bit this summer it seemed and she had to teach me how to do it. Mostly we took turns holding the opposite ends of pieces of siding in place while we would then take turns securing them in place with nails. Then we would place a nail through the siding and into every stud going down the siding's length to secure it to the house.

We were working on the house further away from the group that was assembled at the other and we spent quite a bit of time talking while we worked. I learned that Allison's father was a college professor in Rhode island. Though only sixteen, Allison was mature beyond her years. I could have as much of an intellectual conversation with her as I could anyone my age or older.

"Yeah, I was afraid to come this far south," she offered at one oint.

"Why is that," I asked, assuming she was not accustomed to the heat and humidy of the deep south.

"Because I'm Jewish," she said.

"What does that have to do with anything?" I asked.

"All these southerners are so racist and ignorant I actually feared for my safety," she continued. "Didn't you see the way all of those ignorant Texans acted in the movie Borat?"

"Wow!" I exclaimed. What must have been pumped into her head growing up?

"We're not all that way," I said. "And I'm sure you'll find ignorant people in all parts of the country."

"You're from here?" she asked, acting surprised.

"I'm from Virginia," I told her.

"Well," she probed, "Wouldn't you admit that your partially racist then?"

"So much so that I'm dating a black girl," I laughed.

"You are?" she said, again just as surprised.

"Yes," I told her. "It has been my experience from the few places I've been that people are pretty much the same wherever you go. They generally too are simply a reflection of you. If you have a good attitude you'll find that most people will feed off of it and they will too."

I then told her a story that I had heard years ago. It was about an old man who was standing on a street corner when he was approached by a younger man. The young man asked, "What are the people in this town like? I am new here."

The older man then asked, "What were the people like where you came from?"

The younger man went on to say that the people where he had come from were the salt of the earth and that he hated to leave his town. "Yes," he added, "Anytime I needed anything there was always somebody I could find who was willing to help me out."

"Well," smiled the old man. "I am happy to tell you that you'll find the people of this community to be the same way."

With that, the younger man was off with a smile.

Then the old man was approached by another young man. "What are the people around here like?" he asked. "I'm new in town."

"What were the people like where you came from?" asked the old man, the same question he had posed to the other gentleman.

"They were terrible!" the young man groaned. "I couldn't trust any of them. They would all stab you in the back the minute you turned around. I am happy to be gone from that place."

"Well then," the old man began in a solumn tone, "I am sorry to inform you that you'll find the people here to be much the same."

With that the young man left, kicking the curb and cursing.

Allison seemed to take this fable in for a minute and then responded, "You still don't strike me as the average dumb southerner."

We continued to talk about many things as we kept siding. It turned out that Allison and I had a lot of things in common in spite of our geological differences. She ran cross country for her high school and enjoyed reading about US history.

"I'm reading a biography on John Adams right now," she informed me.

"Is it the one written by David Mccullogh?" I asked.

"You know who David Mccullogh is?" she asked with astonishment.

"Of coarse," I responded. "He is only the single best biographer of our time. I read his book "Truman" and am currently reading his "1776. I've already bought a copy of 'John Adams' and can't wait to get to it."

"You continue to amaze me," she said.

"You'd be even more amazed that "Truman" was recommended to me by my best friend Dean who is from Massachusetts (again, trying to prove to her not all of us southerners hated northeasterners) and that "1776" was recommended to me by my father who like myself is a southerner."

"I bet you stick out where you live," she replied. It seemed that she had her mind made up about everyone south of the Mason Dixon line and there would be nothing I could do to change her impression.

Later in the morning the truck carrying roof trussels showd up and Allison and I made our way to the others and helped unload them. There were so many of us in our group that it didn't take long and we were soon carrying the trussels up ladders in groups of three and handing them off to others who would then secure them to the roof.

After finishing with the trussels Allison and I made out way back to siding. We continued to talk and though it was excruciatingly hot, with the eat index hitting 110 at one point, the work was enjoyable. I picked on Allison quite a bit, mocking her from time to time using an over exaggerated southern drawl to answer her questions. At one point, she was laughing so hard she accidentally smacked her finger with the hammer, drawing blood. Viewing this mishap as my fault, she beemed me in the face with a siding nail.

Because of the excessive heat and humidity our crew knocked off at 3:00 p.m. and agreed to regroup at the same place the next morning at 8:00 a.m. I drove back to the camp site and took a luke warm shower. The rabbits and reptiles had sought refuge from the heat of the day within the woods but I still had to play hop scotch around the giant grass hoppers that sat baking in the sun.

At 4:00 p.m. I decided to seek air conditioning to get in out of the heat so I headed back into St. Bernard Parish to have an early dinner. As I pulled into "Charlie's," one of just a few local diners close by it began to rain quite heavily. A storm had rolled in so quickly I had not even noticed it was coming. Instead of jumping out into the rain I decided to sit in my truck and call Maia.

"Hello boyfriend," she said as she answered the phone.

"Hellow beautiful Maia," I said, like I always did when I greated her at any time.

"So where are you now and how is it going?" she asked.

"I'm in New Orleans," I told her. "It is hot and humid as can be but other than that I am doing fine."

"How long are you staying there?" she asked.

"I am actually going to stay here for a total of four days," I informed her.

"Wow!" she said, knowing I had not planned on staying in any single area for too long. "It must be a pretty fun place to be huh?"

"Well," I began, "It is a neat place. I went to the battlefield last night and saw an amazing band at the French Quarter but the reason I'm staying is to help a group of volunteers work on rebuilding some of these houses down here."

"Oh yeah," she said, as if remembering a point forgotten. "What does that place look like now?"

I explained what I had viewed of New Orleans. I told her about the ruined boats that had greeted me when I entered the city and of all the homes. I went on and told her of all the R.V. parks that were scattered everywhere that many of the displaced locals were still living in. I told her about meeting the Montz's the night before and how enjoyable it was talking to them.

Maia and I talked as long as we could but she had to get off the phone and be inside her restaurant for work at 5:30.

"I miss you," she let me know in her soft angelic voice.

"I miss you too and I think of you constantly," I told her. "I am really enjoying this trip so far but I can't wait to get back and see you."

"Like I told you before you left," she insured me, "I'm not going anywhere and I'll be here waiting for you when you get back."

With that we said our goodbyes and I headed into Charlies. I was overwhelmed by their menu that featured over three hundred items. When my server Gary asked me what I was ordering I said, "I don't know, you tell me. I'm overwhelmed by all the choices."

He smiled, as if he had heard this before, and recommended I have the red beans and rice. "It is kind of a tradition in Louisianna to eat red beans and rice on Monday's" he told me.

"Well then red beans and rice it is," I said.

I don't recall ever having eaten red beans and rice before but if they were all as good as they were here at Charlie's I would soon be eating them every day! The seasonings were perfect, strong but not too bold. I ate my entire bowl and complimented the owner, Terry Blanchard, a lovely woman in her early 60's, and she showed her appreciation of my kind words by having Gary bring me another bowl free of charge.

When my second helping came I moved from the table I had been sitting at and ate at the bar so I could talk to Terry while I ate. Terry had quite an interesting story of her own about the storm.

"I woke up in the middle of the night at the end of June for some reason and just felt like something terrible was going to happen," she said. "As long as we've owned this place, my husband and I had never had flood insurance on the building."

"Really!" I said, shocked at the idea.

"Yeah," she continued. "It is really expensive. But after having that feeling that night I felt as if I had to do something so I began getting all of my affairs in order which included insuring this building even though my husband didn't think I should. Just over a month later Katrina hit and it all made sense."

I had an enjoyable conversation with Terry as I continued eating. I found out that she had a son in the National Guard and her daughter was married to a Guardsman. Ironically, both her daughter's husband and her son were in the Virginia National Guard like myself. They were living in Fredericksburg which was only an hour north of Ruckersville and less than an hour south of Washington D.C.

"I could tell I liked you for some reason," Terry told me.

After finishing my dinner and my lovely conversation with Terry I returned to my camp site to continue reading in my hammock. However, I had not put the rain flap on my tent so I had to scoop several gallons worth of water out of my tent before I could begin reading. I read for just a few minutes before I was out like a light, having been completely drained by the day's work and the heat. I was awakened about half an hour later by some distant, rolling thunder.

Nearing 9:00 p.m. I decided to call my father and check in with him and then I called my children in Seattle. After talking with all three I crawled in my tent and went back to sleep and slept soundly until the next morning.

Having a better idea of what was in store for me later in the day, I decided not to run this morning knowing I should conserve my body fluids and avoid becoming dehydrated and running the risk of some sort of heat casualty. Instead, I enjoyed a hot cup of Regina's ginger tea and took a lazy walk around the camp ground counting rabbits. This morning I counted 35, I guess seeing more because I was walking instead of running.

By 8:00 a.m. I was back at the work site and spent the day much as the day before, siding with Allison and acting like a "dumb southerner" whenever the opportunity presented itself to get on her nerves.

Like the day before we knocked off at 3:00 in the afternoon. Having not run though this morning I still felt like working so I drove through the neighborhood simply asking people that I saw doing anything if they could use an extra hand. By the third time I asked I received a "yes" so I parked my truck and got out to help.

I had stopped at the home of a black lady in her mid forties named Michelle. Michelle had a teenaged son and a daughter that would soon be a teen herself. They were living in an R.V. parked on the street in front of their house that had been partially destroyed during the storm.

I went inside and was greated by a crew of contractors who were working on the master bathroom. They delegated the job of grouting tile to me. I had never done this before but it was an easy job to learn. I simply took this sandy gooey stuff and smeared it into tile cracks. After I had completed all the tiles and the goo dried, I then went over it with a wet sponge to remove all of the excess from the top of the tiles themselves.

Jessie, the contractor who had moved to the area from Baton Rougue just over a year before to claim his share of all the business to be had in the town in his profession worked along beside me measuring off the size of the tiles that needed to be cut and placed like pieces of a puzzle. We talked the entire time we worked though I had a hard time understanding much of what he said due to a combination of his strong Cajun and deep southern accents. Allison would have a field day listening to this guy I thought. Jessie informed me that he and his crew had been working from 8:00 a.m. until 9:00 p.m. seven days a week since they had arrived in New Orleans.

After finishing up around 6:00 p.m. I swung back by Charlie's for another bowl of rice and beans, this time with catfish as opposed to the saausage I had the last time, and talked again with Terry. After finishing my dinner I returned to the camp ground, showered and then was asleep before dark.

At some point in the middle of the night I was awakened by the hooting of an owl that was perched on a tree only twenty yards from my tent. Along with the hooting I heard the screaming of what sounded like an army of frogs.

I walked out of my tent to see if I could get a view of the night life. Across the road from my tent there was a huge puddle of water that had collected from the rain the day before. Since the elevation here was below that of the nearby Mississippi river the ground remained supersaturated at all times and any water left behind from rain was slow to dry up.

What I saw at this puddle, which was the size of a green on a golf coarse was well worth getting up for. I could indeed see the large owl perched on a limb above the water peering down on the dozens of frogs that were sitting at the water's edge. There were two really big racoons walking around the puddle picking up the frogs, who didn't even seem to try to get away, and devouring them head first for a tasty midnight snack. At one point one of the racoons glanced over at me and then simply went back to dining as if I were not standing there at all. I watched this show for about ten minutes then went back to the tent where I was able to finally fall back to sleep in spite of all the noise.

When I awoke the next morning it was the 4'th of July, the day we celebrate our great nation's independence. I opened my eyes slowly and began to stretch as I suddenly realized that my feet were on fire, or at least felt like it. I sat up quickly and looked down at my feet which appeared to have poison ivy all over them. I quickly realized it was not poison ivy though as I saw something small and red, a fire ant, crawl across my big toe and then take a bite into the one beside it.

"OUCH!" I yelled as I bent down and slapped it off.

This is when I realized that I had been invaded! There was an army of ants marching in formation from the opening of the tent to my cooler that I had accidentally left the lid loose on in the back of the tent. So much for insect screening.

I got out of the tent as quickly as I could and ran to the water hook up provided at my site and turned it on full blast and stood under it, allowing the cool water to ease the burning of my feet to some degree.

Fortunately I had come prepared and I had a tube of ointment cream in my truck. After standing in the water for about five minutes I hopped over to the truck and sat in the passenger's seat with the door open and rubbed the cream all over my feet. As I was doing so a large hoot owl, perhaps the one I had seen the night before swooped down and lit in the branch of a tree no more than ten yards away from me. He sat there and turned his head in a questioning way as he watched me perform my strange act from my truck.

"Thanks for keeping me up half the night!" I said to him as he simply continued to stare at me like I was an idiot.

I finished creaming up my feet and then tried to figure out how I was going to get to my cooler and prepare my breakfast. I knew it would have to be a quick mission in which I would suffer more bites so I wasted no time in getting it over with. I ran into the tent, pulled my cooler over to the water tap outside, sustaining bites the whole way, and turned the water on full blast to knock off the ants. Though it was a messy act it worked and I was soon able to have my eggs, bread and what remained of my plums.

Since it was the 4'th of July, our crew was taking the day off. I had thought about going into New Orleans to celebrate the 4'th, but by 10:00 a.m. it was already too miserable to be outside so my plans quickly changed.

Though I was to be in New Orleans for another day I decided to pack my belongings and continue to head west into Texas. The air conditioned truck cab would be a more pleasant place to spend the day. It was still early enough to where I could make it to Houston by dark. I figured they would be celebrating the 4'th in style there as well so that became the new plan for the day.

I took down my tent, having to pick several sticky handed tree frogs off the top in doing so, loaded my gear into the back of the truck then drove out of St. Bernard State Park, trying to keep all grass hopper casualties to a minimum.

As I left New Orleans I crossed the bridge again over Lake Pontchartrain and I did notice the sign for "Montz" once on the other side. I had taken a lot from this city. Though I helped in a small way while here, being here and meeting the people I had helped me more.

I had been feeling sorry for myself for my state of homelessness, yet my time here had put the real meaning in the word "homeless." I lost my home perhaps to some ill planning on my part and by the help of a deceitful former spouse, again, a fact that I myself contributed to in so choosing her as a spouse in the first place. The people of New Orleans however, had made no bad choices. They had not planned poorly. They say hell has not wrath like a woman scorned and Katrina was a winch that made my often times angry ex-wife seem like a saint.

If the people of the city of New Orleans could be as accepting of their situation and continue to fight in life in spite of what they had been through, then so could I. I drew so much strength from having come here and this would be an experience I would draw upon many times later in life at times that I would be in need of strength, hope and faith.

16

I continued driving west on Intersate 10 past the rest of New Orleans and then through the Louissianna country side. This was a land unlike any that I was used to. At times I would cross bridges that went for miles over swamps and bogs. I had gotten to where, in spite of my knowledge of trees and vegitation within the Appalachian mountains, which boasts more species than the entire continent of Europe, I could not identify many of the trees, plants and shrubs I now passed.

I caught myself peering off of these long bridges into the bogs many times in the hopes of spotting an aligator. I never saw any but I saw an amazing array of many different water birds, most of which had really long legs and bills in spite of smaller bodies and several people rushing through the bogs on various types of boats.

I stopped at LaPlace Louisianna to fill up with gas and have lunch on my tail gate. I ate a cold can of Chef Boyarde spaghetti and meatballs, some salt and vinegar potato chips, and longed for some more plumbs. At 92 degrees and much less humidity than in New Orleans it almost felt cold.

Several hours later I found myself crossing the Texas state line. I stopped at a road side welcome center and took a picture of the state's welcome sign that read, "Welcome to Texas, Pround Home of President George W. Bush." I wanted that picture not only for myself but also to show my ex-wife once I made it to Seattle. I doubted there were any signs anywhere in the middle east claiming to be the proud home of Osama Bin Laden.

At this rest stop I walked on a nature trail located on the property and saw cactus in the wild for the first time in my life. I almost took a picture of this prickly little plant too but decided I would appear too much like the tourist I was so I did not.

I got back in the truck and continued heading west. After being on the road for only a few minutes I saw another sign. This one read "Elpaso 857 miles." Great God! Texas was not a state! It was a freaking country!

To kill time on the road I decided to call my father and make him aware of my wereabouts. I wished he could have come on this trip with me. I remember him often talking of the desire to take such a trip while I was a child but he was such a workaholic he would never take the time off to do so. Even when we did take vacations when I was a child he would spend much of his time in the hotel room calling back to the mill to make sure everything was running smoothly. You would have thought he owned the place instead of managed it. But I guess that is one of the reasons he was so successful as a manager and Collins Lumber was more than willing to keep him on board once they had bought the mill from Georgia Pacific.

"How's it going so far?" my asked when he answered the phone.

"So far so good," I told him. "But my butt is getting numb from sitting in the truck so much. The camping fees are starting to add up too."

"You should just spend the nights in Wal Mart parking lots," he told me.

"What?" I asked, as if it was a crazy idea.

"Sure!" he said. "Every time I go to Wal Mart over in Summersville I see a whole caravan of R.V.s and campers where people traveling spend the night there."

"No way," I said.

"Yeah," he went on. "Just park off in the far side away from the front and I doubt they'd say anything to you. They probably make money off the campers who go in there and buy their supplies anyway."

I thought of this idea as I continued driving through Texas toward Houston. I would save quite a bit of money, hundreds of dollars as a matter of fact over the next several weeks. My experience with the fire ants in New Orleans had not been too pleasurable any way and I doubt I would run into this problem in Wal Mart parking lots.

I continued through Texas marveling at the ever changing landscape. Everything now had become flat. There were no mountains to be seen in any direction and the luscious green scenery of the east coast had given way to dimmer greens and ever darkening browns.

I made it to Houston with an hour of day light left and noticed a park of some sort off of the interstate to my right where hundreds of people were gathered, I was assuming to watch a fire works show. I took the next exit, turned around and began heading back in the opposite direction and sought a way to join them.

While waiting at a red light getting off of the exit there was an S.U.V. in front of me with about six young Mexican men inside. Sitting on the curb to the left side of the road was what appeared to be a homeless guy minding his own business with a dog sitting beside him. He had a leash that appeared to be nothing more than an old rope tied to the dog's neck.

I noticed the guys in the S.U.V. with obnoxious rims on the wheels motioning toward the guy from inside and laughing amongst themselves.

"Those b———s!," I thought to myself. He wasn't bothering anyone and he could probably pay a months rent and eat for as long somewhere with what they had spent on those rims.

One of the guys in the back seat opened the door, got out and approached the man. He said something I could not hear and pointed at the dog. I saw the man pull the dog toward him with a look of fear in his eyes.

I honked on the horn to get this thug's attention. He looked back at me and I pointed toward his big S.U.V. that now had really loud Mexican music blaring through the open door and motioned for him to get back inside. He snarled at me and then did as I had suggested just as the light turned green. As I went through the light I smiled and waved at the homeless man and he did the same to me.

I followed this carload of hooligans in front of me to the entrance of the park. They looked back at me and talked amongst themselves the whole time. After the adreneline rush of doing something somewhat heroic wore off I began to realize my unfavorable odds here. Instead of following them all the way into the park I took another direction and looked for another place to park.

This proved not to be a good idea because I could not find parking and when I got back to the main park entrance I was waved away by security guards. The park had filled with parking and they were not allowing any more cars in. I had no other choice but to get back on the interstate. I continued heading west as it became dark, disheartened realizing I was going to miss the fire works on the fouth of July.

I was proven wrong however, as when it became fully dark fire works started lighting up the night's sky on both sides and directly ahead of me. It seemed that every citizen of Houston was celebrating and they were attempting to out do each other with their pyromania.

I tuned into a radio station that was playing all patriotic songs like Toby Keith's "Coutesy of the Red White and Blue," and Lee Greenwood's "God Bless the USA." Later it played the instrumentals of the Army song, the Navy song, the Marine song and the Star Spangled Banner. Though I was driving and had been to many fire work shows in the past on this holiday I had never seen a show like this before. I watched fire works for miles and miles before realizing I had better get off the road for the night. Fortunately I came upon a Wal Mart sitting off to the right of the interstate. I took the exit and pulled around into the parking lot.

I ran inside and bought some plums from the grocery section then came out and began driving around the parking lot looking for the camper caravan. I could not find it. Instead, what I found where signs stating that over night parking was not allowed. There was a parking lot cop driving around in a little white golf cart with a flashing yellow light on top making sure that the signs were obeyed.

"Great!" I thought. "So much for this idea."

I got back on the interstate and continued heading west. It was now 10:00 p.m. and even if I could find a state park its office would be closed and I would not be able to check in. A motel room would cost me three times as much as a camp site. Then, to make things worse, it started to rain. I cannot see very well at night and the rain was not helping.

I came upon a truck stop and figured it was my only option so I pulled off and went around to where all the semi's were parked for the night. I pulled off to the side of the lot so as not to get run over by one of these bohemuths and parked. I made my way to the back of the truck and pulled out my light weight felt sleeping bag for comfort more so than for warmth as it was a hot night.

I got back in the cab, reclined my seat all the way back and slept for the night. In spite of the rain coming through my slightly downed window and the uncomfortableness of sleeping in the reclined bucket seat, I actually slept fairly well, waking up only from time to time when another large truck pulled into the lot.

After waking up around 6:00 a.m. local time I walked into the store at the truck stop, used the restroom and bought a bottle of orange juice and a pack of cheese crackers for breakfast. The attendant glared at me as if she knew I had spent the night in the truck lot, but she said nothing of it.

With that I was back in my truck and continuing West. I remember crossing many streams with strange names like "Woman Hollering Creek" and wondering what God awful act must have happened here at some point in the past for the stream to get its name.

Just before making it into San Antonio I decided to stop at an I.H.O.P to have a real breakfast. Due to where I had stayed the night before I did not have the luxury this morning of being able to cook on my small camp stove and the pack of crackers I had eaten did not do the job.

I was greeted with a friendly Texas welcome by my pleasant server and was enjoying my breakfast of eggs, bacon, sausage and pancakes until a couple of women in their fifties with distinctive New York accents came in and sat beside me, complaining about every aspect of Texas and the south. "Were these some of Allison's long lost relatives?" I chuckled to myself.

"Howdy ya'll," the same pleasant server I had said as she greeted them.

"Look," one of the two women began in a curt tone. "Can we just skip all of this pleasant crap and just put in our orders! We have to catch a plain!"

"Well, if that's how ya want to do it," the server said in a pleasant tone.

"We're from New York!" the other lady said, confirming my suspicion based upon their accents, "And that is how we do it there!"

"OK then, that's how we'll do it here," the server responded, keeping a smile on her face the whole time. I don't know how she did it except for that maybe this was not new to her.

As I finished my breakfast I began to get indigestion as I overheard these two bitter curmudgeons gripe and complain. "That does it," I thought to myself. "I am getting off of the interstate as soon as it is feasible and taking the back roads where there are no major airports so I can avoid this type of stuff."

I went back to the truck after I paid for my meal and complimented the manager on the service I had received and broke out my road atlas. I saw that I could take state highway 285 north once I got to Fort Stockton and head into New Mexico from there. I had originally thought of taking interstate 10 all the way to California's west coast but I would now change that plan and head straight up through the guts of America, crossing the deserts of New Mexico, Utah and Idaho and pass through the southern portion of the Rocky mountains in Colorado. I would now be seeing the eastern side of Oregon and the heart of Washington state as I made my way to Seattle.

I drove on through San Antonio where I saw a sign for the Alamo. "Oh, the Alamo," I thought out loud. "That would be nice to see some time."

As I kept driving I thought again. "When might there ever be a next time!" I immediately turned back and headed to see this great fort.

Once I made it into the town's center where the Alamo was located I actually drove right past it. I had expected something big, being as this was the site of a great battle during the war for Texas' independence from Mexico. However, the city had grown up so much around the Alamo that it was hard to notice even if you were looking for it. Well, at least if I was looking for it.

After making my way back to the town's center I saw it on my second pass and was able to find a place to park within walking distance of this historic fortress.

There seemed to be people form all over the world here visiting the Alamo. I stood in a long line and was finally able to make my way through the gate. The court yard inside was beautiful. It boasted the greenest grass and shrubbery I had seen for many miles.

Inside the corridors of the Alamo itself were several interesting exhibits. I saw many of the weapons that were used by the soldiers who had fought off Santa Anna's forces for nearly two weeks before being stormed. These weapons included rifles, pistols, swords and knives.

The Mexican side during this battle boasted between 3,000 and 4,000 forces while the Texans, led by William B. Travis and Jim Bowie had mearly 187 troops. In spite of these difficult odds the Texans held their ground for 13 days before the Mexican forces stormed the fort, which had started out originally as a catholic mission, and killed all inhabitants except for the women and children and one black slave. The legendary frontiersman Davey Crockett was among those that lost their lives that day in March of 1836.

Though the Texans would lose the battle of the Alamo they would not lose the war. The events that took place here galvanized Texans and Sam Houston's forces would later defeat those of Santa Anna's at the Battle of San Jacinto, allowing Texas to win her independence.

The spirit of America could be summed up by the spirit of those brave men at the Alamo. This was simply one time, such as the Battle of New Orleans in the war of 1812 where Americans stood at long odds yet met those odds with unbelievable results. Though the battle at the Alamo would not end in the same successful way as the Battle of New Orleans it was awe inspring none the less.

This is why I never understand what people mean when they say things in America are "hopeless" during the tough times that we occasionally go through. We need not focus on the direness of the current situation as much as draw on situations in the past where we have come together as Americans in spite of our differences and rallied for a great cause. Along these lines I am reminded of what President Ronald Reagan often said during the recession of the early 1980's. "I believe America's best days are still ahead of her."

As I drove out of San Antonio and away from the Alamo I thought of my own situation and the forces stacked against me; homelessness, separation from my children and the uncertainty of whether or not I would end up in Iraq, a place to which I was more than willing to go though I would not imagine it to be too pleasurable. Whether I went or not, what would my gainful employment be once back in the civilian world? I found myself drawing strength from the spirit of the men of the Alamo and from my faith in God, knowing that as it says in the good book that when we are faced with difficulties and trials it is only because God has greater things in store for us. I knew not what these greater things might be but I knew that I had not been walking alone. Just as in the anonymously written "Footprints in the Sand," I was being carried by a power much greater than myself who had not forsaken me. This trip was really panning out as an experience that was giving me hope in spite of my difficulties. The great men and women of our past had prevailed in the face of adversity and I was more and more, with each passing mile and with every historic site seen believing without a doubt that I would do the same.

17

About 150 miles past San Antonio, still traveling on intrestate 10 I realized that I had just crossed over 3,000 miles since my last oil change. Knowing that taking care of my truck was of the eccense on this trip to avoid breakdown I quickly looked for the next exit which I could pull off of and seek an oil change. This brought me to the small community of Junction, Texas.

I pulled off onto one of the many beautiful Texas bi-ways and rolled into Junction, crossing over the North Llano river via a bridge that for some reason was only half painted. Just on the other side of the bridge I pulled into Roy's gas station and garage, parked my truck and sought an oil change.

I was greated by a gentleman, Louis Britto, who I assumed worked there as he approached me and asked how he could be of assistance.

"I need and oil change," I informed him.

"Ok," he said with a big Texas smile. "Roy can hook you up. I'll go in and get him."

Louis went into the shop and told one of the two Mexican American brothers that owned the place what I was in need of and he walked out and took my keys.

"We'll have you ready to go in about an hour," he informed me.

"Great!" I said. "I'll walk up the street and get a hair cut while I wait. Where is the closest barber?"

"You can go to Oscar's," Louis said. "It is about a mile up the road on the left. I can take you there."

"Wow!" I said appreciatively. "Now that is service. Do you treat all of your customers this way?"

"Oh, I don't work here," Louis said. "I just hang out here with these guys when I'm done with work. I work for a gas line company."

"OK," I continued. "Well I really appreciate the lift."

With that Louis and I got into his big four door diesel pick up and headed up the road to Oscar's barber shop. Louis walked in with me and introduced me to Oscar, another Mexican American man in his late fifties, and told him that he would be back to pick me up when my oil change was complete. I could not believe the service I was receiving from the citizens of this little town of maybe 1,000 inhabitants but I was enjoying it.

I sat and waited my turn at Oscar's and took part in the drifting conversation with the other couple of gentleman who were waiting as well. I told them about my trip and they recommended that I spend the night there at South Llano River State Park.

"It is a beautiful place," chimmed a gentleman also in his late fifties who was a retired school teacher from Junction. "They have set up bird blinds around the park where you can sit behind a glass window and view the birds that they bait in with seed and water fountains. There is an elusive bird called the "painted bunting" that I have been able to see a couple times that would make it worth the stay if you are fortunate enough to see one."

As much of an outdoorsman as I was I had never been much of a bird watcher. However, I was really enjoying the treatment I was receiving in this community. Though I had several hours of daylight left that I could use driving, I had made my mind up to stay in Junction.

My turn to sit in the chair eventually came and I was elated that the cost for a cut was only $9.00. I had to pay at least twice that in my super suburbia community of Charlottesville. Oscar's work on my hair was just as good or better than any I had received by the much higher priced "stylists" back in Charlottesville, Virginia.

True to his word Louis pulled in to pick me up just as I was paying Oscar for his services. We rode back to Roy's with Louis complimenting me on my truck the entire time. Though it was 13 years old and had 180,000 miles on it, the truck had been well maintained by its original owner I had purchased it from the summer before. I had decided years ago, when I had to finance a car from a dealer due to my lack of cash, that I would never buy and finance a car from a dealer again, but wait until I had the cash to pay for one in full and then buy a used one from its original owner only after a dutiful inspection.

One of the tricks I would employ while inspecting used vehicles was to request to use the seller's bathroom while at their house. In so doing, I could get a glimpse of the inside of their home. If their house was a wreck and their bathroom, the room most people generally cleaned last, was in shambles I would know that they probably had not taken care of their vehicle and had simply cleaned it up nicely in an attempt to sell it. However, if on the other hand their home was neat and the bathroom clean I knew that they were the type who took care of their belongings and the vehicle was probably safe. When I employed this scheme with the gentleman I had purchased the truck from, a retired fireman who lived only 2 miles up the road from me in Ruckersville, I was happy to see that his home appeared as if a maid had just left, though he did not have a maid, and it appeared as if you could eat off of the bathroom floor. When he told me that he had washed the truck nearly every weekend and had always wiped down the motor when he did, I knew I could believe him.

This gentleman had also modified the big V8 engine with some really neat hardware I did not really understand and also had put a dual exhaust on it, making it more fuel efficient and giving it that loud, baffling, red neck truck sound that I'll admit always made me feel powerful every time I started the engine. He had recently bought himself a brand new diesel powered four door Ford F350 to help him in his retired part time profession as a landscaper and claimed that he hated to part with this Dodge Dakota. I could tell he was sincere in telling me this and it made me even more confidant to purchase this truck for the below Blue Book value of $4900 in cash.

On the way back to Roy's I told Louis about my trip when he inquired as to what brought me this way from Virginia (he had obviously noticed my tags). When he asked where I would be spending the night, I told him that upon the recommendation of the folks at the barber shop I had decided to stay at South Llano River State Park.

"Great!" he said. "I can drive you out there and show you were it is!"

Knowing I had plenty of time left in the day as it was only two o'clock in the afternoon I took him up on and thanked him for his offer. After stopping by Roy's to pay my bill, again one that was much less than that I was used to in Charlottesville, and receiving compliments on my truck from the two brothers, Louis and I left my truck at the shop and we rode in his truck out to the park.

Louis took me back across the half painted bridge I had crossed coming into town. He explained to me that the contractor who had painted the bridge kept allowing debris and paint to fall into the North Llano River while he was performing his work so the town's people paid him the original amount they had promised him for his services then sent him on his way with the work only half completed. It was more important to them to have a clean, healthy waterway than to have a pretty bridge.

After crossing the bridge we took a right and drove past Junction's community branch of Texas Tech college. We wound our way up the country road until we came to a low water bridge crossing of the South Llano river at a place known by the locals as "flat rock." Here, there were several children and a couple of adults swimming and inner tubing in the river's warm, flowing waters. The waters were beginning to rise from a heavy rain storm many miles upstream and Louis wanted to check their levels to give the report once back in town. It seems that doing this was one of the activities participated in by this sleepy Texas community. There was always a sense of pride within the individual fortunate enough to get back with the first report.

We crossed this low water bridge and kept heading upstream, this time on the same side we had been on before crossing the half painted bridge to leave town. Louis and I talked the entire time we drove.

"I am originally from Odessa," he told me. "I moved down here a couple of years ago to take over the responsibility of overseeing our pipeline that runs through here. We pump diesel from Houston to El Paso and my line's worth of responsibility is about 150 miles long."

The vegetation here was much greener than that of most that I had seen through Texas. Louis informed me that it was due to all of the rain that they had been receiving this year. Actually, several hundreds of miles north of here, Oklahoma was currently experiencing the worst flooding in state history as I was making my journey. I had made sure to stay far enough south to avoid this danger.

I noticed that there were small, scrubby cedar thickets everywhere. When I pointed this out Louis informed me that one of the ways many of the locals made their money was by clearing this cedar and selling it to a company close by that extracted the sap and used it to make deck stain.

"They get about $50 per ton," he informed me. "Most people can haul in a couple truck loads a day giving them about $100 a day. The economy here is week so a lot of people do it."

As we continued driving we saw a Rio Grande turkey cross the road. Being the turkey hunter back east that I was I got excited at seeing this bird. Though it appeared to be the same size as the eastern wild turkeys I was so used to, its coloring was much different. Whereas the eastern birds were mostly black, this Rio Grande sported a lot of brown, especially at the ends of its wings.

"Oh you'll love the park if you like Turkeys," Louis informed me when he noticed my excitement. "The river banks at the park are lined with pecan trees and the turkeys love to roost in them at night."

We did not have pecan trees where I lived in Virginia but during my time as a turning blank provider online I noticed that pecan wood was a very popular and pricey species that turners loved to work with.

"Can you get your hands on any pecan wood around here?" I asked Louis.

"Of course," he said. "I have a bunch of it in my fire wood pile in the back yard."

I told him about what I had done with wood and explained the process of cutting blanks to him. He was familiar with eBay and had some power tools and I told him how to perform the work. He seemed interested enough in doing it himself.

"Could you use a table saw instead of a bandsaw!" he asked.

"Oh heck no!" I told him. "You'll cut your finger off doing it that way. Just go to the closest Sears and buy a twelve inch band saw for $250. It's not much money and the safety factor is greatly increased. A table saw will rip the wood right out of your hands and probably take part of your hand in the process."

"I don't know," he said. "I bet it would work."

"Dude," I said, "Don't try it!"

As we got closer to the park's entrance Louis slowed as a terrantula slowly made its way across the road in front of us.

"It is going to rain," Louis said as he watched it cross.

"How do you know?" I asked.

"Every time before it rains the terrantulas come out," he said. "They live in holes just under the surface and they can sense the difference in the air's moisture levels and they come out to seek higher ground."

"That is the first terrantula I have ever seen in the wild," I informed Louis with an excited tone. "I had never seen a cactus in the wild either before getting to Texas."

"Let me guess," Louis said while throwing his head back laughing. "I bet you got out and took a picture of it didn't you."

"I wanted to take a picture but I didn't," I said somewhat defensively.

"Everyone always takes pictures of the cactuses," he continued laughing.

"Oh yeah?" I said, "Then pull over here and I'm gonna take a picture of you standing in front of that big cactus right there," I said, pointing in the direction of one of these large prickly plants, one of a different type than I had seen at the rest stop.

We pulled to the side of the road and Louis posed with a smile in front of the cactus as I took his picture. He then showed me a fruit that grows on the plant where it branches out from the forks of the trunk.

"Later in the summer," he began, "these fruits will turn purple and you can eat them."

"Really?" I said.

"Oh yes," he stated. "Actually, farmers walk around with small torches through their cattle pastures and burn the thorns off so their cows can come by and eat the entire plant."

After taking Louis' picture in front of the cactus like the tourist that I was, we got back in his big truck and continued on to the park. I was marveling at the landscape when Louis explained to me that this was the point in Texas where the prairies meet the hills and form the foothills. This was by far the most beautiful point of my journey I had seen so far. There were giant rock out croppings on the tops of all the hills that were gray and brown in collor and looked as if they would be impossible to climb.

We made it to another low water bridge crossing that we went over and then we came to the park's office about a half a mile later.

"Here it is," Louis said. "All you'll have to do is come back up and check in once you get your truck."

Louis and I made our way back to town, seeing several more terrantulas and several white tailed deer along the way. He explained to me that much of the land in the area was being purchased by wealthy Californians who were turning much of it into hunting reserves, the type you see on the outdoor channels where they bring celebrities in and put them on a stand that has been baited for years, allowing them to kill a big buck that has basically become tame and let them think they are some kind of great white tail hunter.

When we got back to Roy's Louis gave the water level report. The two brothers and a couple of customers hung on his every word. I would be sure to check the level tomorrow before coming into town to head on my way so I could be the hero of the day and give the first report.

After the water report was taken care of I asked if there was a local library close by so that I could use a computer to get on the internet and email my friends and family as to my whereabouts.

"Just use ours," one of the two brothers who owned the shop said as he sat at his desk and got online. This treatment I was receiving continued to blow me away.

I took them up on their offer and fired off a few quick emails and deleted several dozen spams. I then wished them all a good evening and got in my truck and headed back to South Llano River State park to check in for the evening.

Once at my site, I threw up my small tent and spread the large one across a close line that was provided at the site. It was still damp from a combination of the rain and humidity in New Orleans. As I was doing this a dastardly little fire ant that had caught a free ride to Texas took a bite out of my calf. Too bad for him that he would never be leaving Texas. Instead he would become part of the dirt here as his carcass decomposed.

After eating a couple of peanut butter and jelly sandwiches I decided to brew a cup of Regina's tea and call my dad. After dialing the number I took my tea and began walking up a trail to one of the bird blinds the gentleman in the barber shop had told me about.

"This place is great!" I told my father when he inquired about the area I was now in. "This guy that lives here gave me a ride to the barber shop and then drove me all around the area for a couple of hours and told me all about the place!"

"You'd better be careful just jumping in the car with some stranger out there!" my dad scolded. "You never know what kind of crazy people there are in this world.

Having spent 8 years in sales I had become a pretty good judge of character and was able to read people fairly quickly. I had never at any point felt nervous or threatened while around Louis and I told my father as much.

"Yeah," he said, "Well that's what everyone thought about Ted Bundy too. Some of these guys are good and can fool anyone!"

"You're right," I said more to make him feel as if I was taking his good fatherly advice to heart than to be in agreement with him.

"Why aren't you staying at Wal Mart," my father then asked.

"Oh, I tried that last night," I said. "It didn't go too well."

I explained to him the situation with the signs and the lot cop and how I had spent the night at a truck stop. He encouraged me not to give up on the idea just because it had not worked the first time. I told him I wouldn't and I intended to try it again the next night.

After making my way to the bird blind I got off the phone and sat in a small shack that had three sides made out of wood and the fourth out of plexiglass. I sat drinking my tea and waiting.

It wasn't long before some cardinals and a yellow finch came to drink from the small fountain and feed on the seed provided from many small feeders. Just as I was growing board watching birds of a type that I had seen several times before back east, I was given a treat as an ellusive painted bunting indeed showed up.

The man at the barber shop had been correct. Seeing this small bird did make it worth the stay at the park. I had never seen anything like it. It had a green head and a mostly blue body but it had patches of red, yellow, orange and green scattered about itself in no particular pattern. It looked as if it had found a painters easle and rolled around in it to dust mites. It was a fascinating little creature.

After this bird had its fill of seed and water and flew away I made my way back down to the camp. I took a much welcomed shower and then sat and played my acoustic guitar I had brought along on the trip until dark. Once it got dark I looked up at the stars in that big Texas sky. I wondered if my kids were looking at them too in Seattle or if Maia had noticed them back in Virginia. After my short period of star gazing I climbed into my little tent and went to sleep.

I awoke the next morning at 6:00 a.m. and decided to make another cup of Regina's tea and go back up to the bird blind. I saw a couple of more cardinals and a clay colored sparrow but no painted bunting this time.

After finishing my tea I walked back down to the tent and put on my skimpy running shorts, laced up my running shoes and went for a three mile run.

There were several trails in this park for me to run on. I took the first I saw and once winding my way into the woods and out of site of all the campers I jumped a small flock of seven toms, or young male turkeys. Upon seeing me they trotted at a quick pace, but not really a run for about 50 yards then stopped and looked back at me. It was obvious that these birds had seen people before and had gotten used to them. I felt sorry for them when this years big Nascar winner or the quarter back of the next super bowl championship team came out here to turkey hunt.

I continued running through the trail, which was now following the South Llano river down stream. I saw several more turkeys and a few deer before turning around to come back. The run felt great and I actually ran the middle mile at about a five minute and twenty second pace, a pace that is quite quick for me these days.

When I got back to the road and off of the trail I walked for a bit to do a cool down since I had run so hard in the middle of the run. I noticed a sign about the Rio Grande turkey so I went over to read it. I found out from reading this sign that the park actually shuts down during the winter months because at that time there are as many as 800 turkeys roosting in the park's pecan trees. The park is shut down so that the birds are not scared away and forced to face more dangers than they need to during the winter.

As I made my way back to my tent I noticed a brown object that appeard to be a piece of drift wood sitting in the grass only 10 yards away from the tent. I thought that to be strange as I had not noticed it before and also because the river was on the other side of the road and at least 100 yards away. Just then this piece of drift wood moved. It was then that I was able to notice the really long ears and goofy looking body of a jack rabbit. As it noticed me it turned and hopped away in the most awkward fashion. It looked as if it was jumping about a foot and a half into the air, springing off of its long back legs, yet only moving about a foot forward with each leap. This was also a first sighting for me as I had never seen a jack rabbit in the wild. It was certainly much different than the eastern cotton tails I was used to 1500 miles away. It made its way to the wood's edge and was gone.

After showering from my run I made myself a few eggs and this time ate a bowl of ceral as well. I was joined by what appeared to be the local stray cat. I gave him some eggs and let him drink the milk from my cereal and then he crawled under my truck and stayed with me until I left later in the morning.

As I was packing my truck and getting ready to leave a little boy of about 8 years old pulled up on his bike to talk to me and pet the cat. He told me about a mother panther that lives on his farm somewhere in Texas and that it had had kittens, or cubs this spring. He claimed his 200 pound older brother had gotten close to the cubs twice and both times the mother panther had chased him away. Had I heard this story yesterday I might not have ventured up to the bird blind or gone for my morning run.

After talking with this little boy for a while and packing all my belongings in the truck I made my way out of the park and back into Junction. I usually did not refuel unless I was pretty near empty and this morning I had half a tank of gas. However, since the brothers at Roy's had been so nice to me the day before I decided to stop by and top off the tank and tell them goodbye. Also, I wanted to be the first to give the river level report for the day.

After I gassed up and let the folks at the station know that the water level of the South Llano River was not rising at the present I began to drive away. As I was beginning to leave I stopped as I saw Louis pulling in, waving at me with a hand that was almost completely bandaged.

"What did you do to your hand?" I asked him as he got out of his truck and came over to wish me the best on my journey.

"You were right about the table saw," he said. "I went home last night and tried to cut blanks out of some of the pecan in my wood pile and almost cut my finger off," he said as he was pointing at the index finger on his right hand with that of his left. "I had to drive to the emergency room and I got five stitches."

"Oh no," I lamented. "I feel bad about that, like it's my fault for telling you about it."

"Don't feel bad man," he laughed. "Besides, you told me not to use a table saw."

With that we both laughed and I was on my way.

I stopped at the local grocery store and stocked up on food and then swung by the local post office to mail out more post cards before leaving town. As I pulled back onto interstate 10 and away from Junction I couldn't stop thinking about my experience there. The people reminded me of Mr. Spicer and Mr. Shelton back in Virginia. Here were more strangers who knew nothing about me and were willing to help me as if I were their best friend. This is when I realized that nice helpful people are not just in Virginia, or the southeast but everywhere. We really do live in a great country filled with great people.

18

As I drove through Texas I did so with the windows down and the radio off. I wanted to take it all in; the air, the smell, the view. It was hot but not humid and the sun was shining and there were only a few white fluffy clouds in the sky.

The speed limit on the interstate in this part of Texas was 80 m.p.h. but I kept the cruise set on 60 both to save gas and protect my engine. I knew it was a good engine but I also knew I was not even at the half way mark of my journey yet. I would have to go through the heat of the desert and climb the Rocky mountains at some point so I wanted to go as easy on my truck as possible. I would be asking quite a bit of it later.

I drove for hours and marveled at the scenery. At one time I passed huge wind mills that were set up to be used for wind energy. They stood high upon the tops of bluffs and and one point they went on for forty miles.

At another time while driving when I had to go to the bathroom really bad I realized that I had not seen a rest stop, nor a sign for one for hours. However, I also realized that I had not seen another car for at least thirty minutes. With this in mind I simply pulled off of the road and did my business while standing beside my truck. No one came by while I was doing this nor did they do so for quite some time later.

As alone as I was in the middle of Texas I did not feel lonely. It did not have that lonesome dove western spaghetti flick feeling that I had always imagined would accompany this barren land. Instead, I had a great feeling of both peace and appreciation toward the creator and his marvelous work. Texas was indeed absolutely beautiful.

At Fort Stockton I took state route 285 and started heading north through Pecos and then about an hour later across the New Mexico state line. I had spent three days driving and still had not made it the entire width of Texas.

Once in New Mexico I saw terrantulas everywhere. At one point I had to swerve to avoid running some over that were traveling in a small group. Fortunately I missed them and they did not end up joining so many of the large grass hoppers from New Orleans who had been less fortunate in that big bug ridden field in the sky. Just like Louis had said, it soon began to rain after I started seeing these large spiders.

As the rains stopped I made it into Carlsbad, New Mexico. With two hours or so before dark I found the local Wal Mart and went in to buy some plumbs (they had not had any at the grocery store in Junction) and then came back out to scope out the parking lot. I saw no R.V.s or campers but I decided I would spend the night here anyway. That was at least until I got back in the truck, looked at the atlas and realized I was only about an hour south of Roswell, the site of the most famous U.F.O. crash in history.

On the summer evening of July 2, 1947 a disc shaped object that could not be identified was seen flying through the night sky over Roswell, a small farming community in southeastern New Mexico. The next day, while tending to the responsibilities of his ranch, William Brazel and his son and daughter came upon some unidentifiable debris. They quickly notified the local sherrif and he intern contacted the authorities at nearby Roswell Army Air Base.

Major Jesse A. Marcel was put in charge of the investigation and the rancher, Mr. Brazel, was incarcerated for a number of days for questioning. In the mean time, the debris was collected and sent on to Wright Patterson Air Force Base in Ohio to be studied. Mr. Brazel was released after questioning but only after being encouraged not to discuss the incident on grounds of national security.

This incident in Roswell was the only time there has ever been a U.F.O. sighting or crash, in which case there was actual evidence collected. A short time after the incident, the government released what they "claimed" was the material they had collected but the material they used was simply that of a weather balloon. Few people then or now believe they released the real material.

To further complicate the government's claims that there had been no U.F.O. in the area, another crash site was soon reported in Socorro, New Mexico where it was claimed a damaged but complete disk as well as dead alien bodies were collected. I could not wait to get to Roswell!

I drove through the streets of Carlsbad that had been flooded by the rains with the water literally coming half way up my tires. My kayak on top of the truck was getting as wet from the splashing as if I were floating it down a river. I soon made it out of town however, and continued north on 285 until coming into Roswell about an hour later.

I could not have planned my trip to Roswell more perfectly if I had tried. When I entered Main Street I was greated by a banner stretched across the street overhead that read, "Welcome to the Annual Roswell Internation U.F.O. Festival."

The streets were lined with street lights that had alien head shaped globes with big black eyes. Many of the town's buildings had either aliens or U.F.O.s painted on them and the streets were filled with people from around the world, many of whom were dressed up as aliens.

I made my way to the local Wal Mart, which had a big U.F.O. mural painted on the front of the building and went inside to walk around and stretch my legs. Inside there was a man dressed up as an alien and wearing a Wal Mart apron. I flagged him down and asked him if he was a legal alien or an illegal alien. He did not respond and I figured he didn't speak my language but that still meant he could be either. A middle aged lady who was in town for the event and I took turns taking pictures of each other with this alien.

I went outside just as it was getting dark and finally was happy to see the campers caravan at the far side of the parking lot. I pulled in with them, got my felt sleeping bag out of the back of the truck and reclined my seat back to sleep for the night. I thought about moving all of my gear to the front of the truck and sleeping in the back on the comfort of my air mattress but I was still a little uneasy about this whole Wal Mart parking lot idea. Until I got used to it I wanted to be able to make a quick get away in the event of being confronted by an angry lot cop enforcing any rules against staying in the lot over night.

I could not get to sleep because of all the artificial lights in the parking lot. I sat up and noticed that in the Sam's parking lot, just the next lot over, there were no lights on the far side. Knowing I would not have the safety in numbers factor working for me that I did in the Wal Mart parking lot I decided to drive over to Sam's anyway. I quickly did so then reclined my seat again and was asleep in no time.

Some time in the middle of the night I was awakened by a loud rumbling noise. As I opened my eyes I realized that there were lights of different colors, red, orange, yellow and white all around me. I could feel the earth shaking so I knew that what ever was projecting the lights was of considerable size. Could this be a lot cop? No! They ride around in small golf carts and sport only a small yellow light.

Without sitting up, taking advantage of the fact that I was hidden in the cab of my truck by laying at a lower level than the windows, I glanced up into the rear view mirror. What ever this thing was it was right behind me! That is when I realized that it was a U.F.O.! It must be. What else could it be?

I laid there, with my heart pounding wondering why I just had to come to Roswell and spend the night in an unprotected parking lot. I should have known that aliens would come to town during the festival that was being held in their honor. I should have checked into a hotel if nothing else.

The shining lights and the shaking ground continued for about five more minutes and then they both simultaneously stopped. At this point I was tempted to either sit up and look out the windows or get out of the truck and investigate but I had seen the movie "Fire in the Sky" about those loggers that were abducted by aliens years ago and thought better of it. I remember seeing that movie as a child and thinking how terrible it was what the aliens did to the guy's eyes. I was not going to voluntarily put myself in a position to have aliens hold my eyes open with sharp metal objects and drop chemicals in them as if I were nothing more than a test bunny for a cosmetic company.

I laid there for quite some time before drifting back to sleep. I slept without being woken up again all night. However, I did awaken abruptly the next morning when I had a dream that I was kissing Maia and the lizard head of an alien tore through the skin of her face and began gobbling me up.

As I sat up with a start, and realized it had only been a dream I turned around to see that a huge semi was parked directly behind me.

"That explains it!" I said to myself. There was my U.F.O. A big red Mack truck with a metal bulldog emblem on the hood. I felt like such an idiot!

I looked down at my watch and saw that it was seven o'clock local time and that the date was 7/07/07. According to the Chinese, this was supposed to be the luckiest day of the year. I wondered what good fortunes lay in store for me today.

I made my way into town and caught the end of a 5k road race. Had I known the event was being held I would have come into town earlier and participated. I asked one of the finishers, a middle aged man who had painted his entier body green and was wearing some corny looking ear muffs that had two balls going straight up from his head for about eight inches what the winning time was. He said he thought it was 17 minutes and some odd seconds.

"Oh," I sighed. My best time back in the day had been 16:20 for this distance but I would be lucky to run 19:20 these days at my age and in my conditioning.

I began walking the streets of Roswell. There was to be a parade in the evening but since it was now so early there was not much going on. I was able to find a blood bank bus however so I decided to go in and donate to both kill time and because it had been about six months since I had given my last donation. My father began donating blood years ago and he kind of got me into it myself within the past couple of years. I always thought that for the small inconvenience of only a little bit of my time it was a good thing to do. What if some day I or one of my children would need a blood transfusion?

I enjoyed talking with the two lovely young ladies who were working as nurses in the bus. They told me about some of the crazy people they had delt with through the week including a man from Canada who swore on his mother's grave that he was actually an alien. There had been many others who told stories of their abductions.

After gulping down my free pack of crackers and can of tomato juice I was given by the nurses, which also served as my breakfast for the day, I left the bus and continued walking the streets of Roswell. It was now nine o'clock and the International U.F.O. Museum and Research Center had opened so I decided to go inside. The gentleman taking admissions saw my military I.D. I had gotten just before leaving Virginia and knocked $2 off of my fee and I was able to get in for $3 instead of $5. I thanked him kindly and began browsing the premises.

Along the walls of the museum were numerous news articles from back in the late 1940's and early 1950's pertaining to the crash and the government's alleged cover up. Further back there were model U.F.O.s and artificial aliens as well as news articles from other sightings from around the world. Further into the exhibit yet there were many authors who had written about these unexplained phoenomenas trying to pawn their books. One was a gentleman who's book claimed most of us have been abducted at one point or another in our lives and that he could prove it through psychological methods.

I made sure not to walk anywhere near his personal space bubble because it seemed that anyone who invaded it was pounced upon and told that they had been abducted at some point in their past, based upon their personal interests or personality traits. I overheard as he tried to convince people that they had been abducted simply because of certain things they liked to eat!

I could not believe this guy! What was even more unbelievable though is that as I glanced back at him during my stay at the museum was that people were actually buying his book. I guess there really are all kinds in this world, and out of it.

I went into the small gift shop in the museum before leaving. I wanted to pick up some memorabilia to add to the small collection of gifts I had been picking up for my kids while crossing the country that I would give to them once I reached Seattle. I was able to find little U.F.O. shaped containers of some type of sticky goo that they loved to play with but that I always hated picking out of the carpet and furniture. What a shame for Amanda.

My best find however, was a can of Vienna sausages that had a customized label around the can claiming it to be "alien meat." During one of our phone conversations when I had asked the kids what they wanted me to buy them Emily had told me that she wanted me to get her some food that was indigenous to the areas I was visiting. That was quite a mature and intelligent request I thought for a girl of seven years old. How convenient to find this can of alien meat that I was certain she would not be able to find anywhere else.

I went outside after paying for my purchases and realized the number of people out and about now had quadrupled. It was time for me to try something I had always wanted to do but had never had the courage to; panhandle.

I made my way back to the truck and put my purchases in it and pulled out my accoustic guitar. I had always marveled at the folks I would see in the streets who were brave enough to just sit down behind their open cases and play and sing. I was always equally amazed at how much money they seemed to make doing it. Not only had this always been something I had wanted to try but I figured if I were successful at it I could add to my dwindling gas money fund.

I found a place on the side walk that seemed to have heavy foot traffic. I sat down, took out my six string, took a dollar bill out of my wallet and threw it in my case and began to play. I first played "Wanted Dead or Alive" by Bon Jovi. I loved Bon Jovi and I figured the opening lead, which is repeated in between all the versus of the song would impress the passers by. I played and sang my heart out but when I looked up I noticed that I had no money other than the lonely dollar bill in my case and that the foot traffic had made its way to the other side of the street.

That song was too old I thought so I played "Slide" by the Goo Goo dolls next. This song too has a pretty impressive picking part and I knew it would do the trick. Again though, after finishing this song I saw that I still had made no money and that no one was paying any attention to me, other than to go out of their way to avoid me.

"Ok!" I said outloud. "It is time for one of my originals!"

I then began playing the opening power chords of "Hillbilly Gangsta Rappa," a song I had written to tie my back woods West Virginia roots to my modern suburbanite slob life style. It had always been popular among my friends.

"I'm a hillbilly rapper from West Virgin-I-A!" I began.

"I aint got no education, but what can I say!"

"I grew up in a trailer on the side of a hill!"

"Ten brothers and sisters 'cause mom never took the pill!"

I pounded that guitar like I hadn't in some time. I blew through the first couple of verses with enthusiasm. I was sure to make a killing with this!

"So I came out of the mountains just to see what I'd find," I went on into the third and final verse.

"I see that life's a whole lot different than the one I left behind."

"People walkin' around with shoes on they feet, killin' cows for they clothes, but not for they meat!" (I figured any true aliens in the crowd would love that line).

"I think I'll go back to the hills until forever after, cause this world it just aint ready for a hillbilly gangsta rapper!" I finished the song strong!

When I looked up, there were about a dozen people staring at me in amazement with their mouths gaped open.

"Yes," I thought. "They loved it!"

I looked down however, to see that there still only sat one lonely dollar bill in my case. At this time a woman who worked in the store behind me informed that I would have to leave. So much for this idea.

In my wilder youth I had kept my guitar in plain site in the living room of whatever dungey apartment I was living in at the time. Whenever I could lure an unsuspecting lady friend back to my place they would always ask me to play and sing. That always proved to be a sure fire way to make sure I would not be spending the night alone. However, on the streets of Roswell I quickly learned that there was a big difference between getting laid and getting paid!

19

I had no desire to stick around for the evening's parade. Besides, after my less than stellar musical performance I thought it best that I get out of town while the getting was good so I made my way back to the truck and continued heading north.

Once I had driven for more than an hour I was in the total seclusion of the New Mexican desert. I decided to pull over at a wide spot at an intersection and have lunch on the tail gate.

I got out and made myself a couple of peanut butter and jelly sandwiches and chased them down with some of the lucsios plumbs I had purchased in Carlsbad. After eating I decided to walk a bit and take in the desert. The radio had reported that it was 110 degrees, but without the humidity I was so use to back in the southeast I found it to be very comfortable.

I had worked with several clients as a stock broker who had retired from this part of the country. I remember often getting into pissing matches over which place was more miserable in the summer; Virginia at 95 degrees with 100 percent humidity or the southwest at 110 degrees and no humidity.

"A hundred and ten degrees is a hundred and ten degrees with or without humidy," I always remember them saying.

Well, I now had proof that they were just playing one-upmanship because frankly I found this weather out here to be much more tolerable than that of the southeast, especially after now having spent time in New Orleans. I was not even breaking a sweat out here but back home by the time you walked from your front door to your car your shirt was sticking to your back because of all the sweet brought on by the humidity.

Standing there looking out across the beautiful desert, viewing more cactuses of yet another type than any I had seen in Texas I noticed the movement from something small and multi-colored at my feet. I bent over to investigate and saw that it was a grass hopper as interesting as the ones I had seen in New Orleans.

Though it was no where as big as the ones in New Orleans, it was just as unique to me just the same, sporting a green underbelly, a black head, an orange body with white dots splattered across its wing casings. It kind of put me in the mind of the painted bunting I had seen in Junction Texas.

I then noticed a beattle nearby that was of similar coloring just in a different pattern. I took notice of the sand grains and pebbles where I was standing and saw if I looked close enough that they were multi colored as well. Nature is absolutely amazing! These small creatures blended in with their surroundings to the point that if they did not move they were practically invisible.

I returned to my truck and continued heading north and east. I soon began to get an excruciating headache. When I entered the town of Vaughn, New Mexico, which was practically a ghost town I figured out why I had the headache. A sign at the town's entrance let me know that I had now climbed to an elevation of over six thousand feet. The thinner air and the change in pressure was the reasoning for my pain.

As I continued driving I saw another first for me; several antelope grazing on some bushes just off the side of the road. I could not believe I was seeing these beautiful, deer like creatures in the wild. Seeing them made me even more happy that I had decided to take this trip.

As I continued on, making my way toward Clien's Corner, New Mexico I began climbing even higher in elevation. At the top of one particularly long hill I saw a sign that read, "Danger, Cross winds."

"Yeah right!" I said outloud.

I was still driving with the windows down and the radio off to take in the entire experience of this new place. When I topped the hill and was no longer protected by the rock outcroppings that had been along both sides of the road during my accent, I saw exactly why those signs I had scoffed at had been put in place.

As I topped the summit my truck was hit with the strongest wind I could imagine existing short of a hurricane or tornado! Dust and debris started coming in the window and pelting me in the face. It took all the strength in my right arm to keep the truck on the road as I rolled the windows up with my left. I drove under these conditions for miles promising the gods of the highway signs that I would never laugh at another of their signs again.

This windy land between Vaugn and Clien's Corner was desolate yet beautiful. I saw several more antelope, some by themselves and others in small herds. Another of nature's beauties I saw were distant storms.

Off many miles away to my east I could see what looked like funnel clouds but that I knew were not. What I was seeing were large storms which appeared small because the open sky was so big. The color scheme went blue, then gray (where the storm was) and then blue again. Inside the grey I witnessed repeated lighning strikes as the storms rolled on.

In this part of the country there were many ravines that looked like dried up creek beds. These seemingly empty beds could be very dangerous however, as these violent and sporadic storms could appear at any time and cause these beds to gush with flooding waters.

I watched at one point to my left as a long train screamed its way through the desert on lonely rails. Later, there would be one to my right doing the same.

I eventually reached Clien's Corner which sat at 7200 feet in elevation. I stopped to use the restroom and to buy some more ice for my cooler. When I got out of the truck I realized that it was now very cool due to the higher elevation and complete lack of humidity.

The convenient store at Clien's Corner was out of ice. A building next door claimed to house a "World Famous Gift Shop," so I decided to go investigate.

Inside there were thousands of trinkets being sold. Most of the wares were cheap western toys made in China, native American Indian garb made in India, and desert nick nacks such as replicas of the area's cactuses that were made in Taiwan. I decided not to purchase anything for the kids or anyone else on this stop.

I got back into the truck and continued on my way, making it to Albuquerque before long. Coming into Albuquerque provided a beautiful view. I had topped and was now rolling over the southern most portion of the Manzano Mountains. The city of Albuquerque lay many miles below but could be viewed almost in its entirety from my vantage point. Off to the west now I could witness more of those beautiful, distant storms.

I stopped for gas in Albuqurque as well as to put air in my tires and decided to have dinner out of the back of my truck on the tail gate. I had been driving for hours since last eating and didn't want to take the time to go to nor spend the money at a restaurant. It appeared by viewing my atlas that I could make it to Durrango Colorado by nightfall and that was my plan.

After eating a large can of Campbell's Chunky Beef Stew I got back in my truck and continued heading north. During the drive I called my kids and talked to all three. I told them what I had gotten them in Roswell and they sounded very excited.

"When are you going to get here Daddy?" they all asked at one point when I talked to them separately.

"I'll be there in about a week or so," I informed them.

It was killing me to be away from them. I could only imagine how much harder it would have been had I stayed with Dean instead of having taken this trip to help keep my mind off of the enormity of my circumstances. Sure, I could have been with Maia more had I stayed, but as much as I was in love with her my emotions for her paled in comparison to those that I had for my children. Since the birth of my kids they had become the center of my universe.

I was also able to talk to both Maia and my father while driving through the northern part of New Mexico.

"Your lucky you didn't get arrested!" my father said when I told him about my panhandling experience. "You need to watch what you are doing out there!" he added.

"I know, your right," I told him, again as with the time in Texas when I was agreeing with him that Louis could have been a serial killer I was flattering him more so than agreeing with him.

When I talked to Maia she was excited about a customer who had tipped her $10 on his way out the door the night before. She had not waited on this gentleman but had noticed that he was sitting at his table being neglected by his server who had not even made her way over to greet him after he had been sitting there for some time.

Maia went over to check on him and once gaining knowledge of his situation took his order and put it in and then transferred the ticket to the other server who she made sure made her way over to greet this man. On his way out, he handed her a ten dollar bill and thanked her for her help. She was giddy about the whole situation.

This was just one of the many reasons I had fallen in love with Maia. She was genuine! There was not an artificial air about her. She was able to enjoy the simple things in life and did not require extravagance to be brought to excitement. Where had she been my whole life?

I had gotten onto state route 550 in Albuquerque and at some point in the evening traveled on it across the continental divide. I also had gone through the Zia Indian Reservation, viewed huge white Messas and driven through the near ghost town of Cuba, a town so small that its grocery store, hardware store, and lumber store were all the same store.

Just north of Cuba the terrain changed drastically, almost immediately. What was desert now gave way to green grass and pine forests. I continued driving through Aztec, where at 88 degrees and no humidity it felt cold and I rolled the windows up again. I witnessed one of the largest flocks of sparrows I'd ever seen fly across the road here and had I not known it was summer I would have guessed they were migrating south for the winter.

Shortly after leaving Aztec I crossed into Colorado and saw a sign that read, "Durango 20 miles." I had planned the timing perfectly as it would not be day light for more than another half an hour. This part of the country was so beautiful that I didn't want to miss any of it by passing through in the dark.

I began climbing a long, windy, narrow hill that went for several miles. When I came to the top I saw grass that was greener than any I had seen since leaving Virginia. There were sprinkler systems in place in the fields and there were many cows feeding on the turf. The place reminded me of Virginia's Shenandoah valley, with its equally green grass and herds of grazing beef and dairy cattle.

After going for no more than three miles on top of this mountain I began to descend the other side. The steep road here was equally narrow and windy. Half way down I could see the lights of Durango that were starting to kick on automatically as it was now dusk.

I got to the bottom of the hill, took a left at the T intersection, made my way into Durango and felt over joyed to see the Wal Mart.

I pulled into the Wal Mart along side the nomadic caravan at the far end. The parking lot was well land scaped and had trees every here and there and they were actually blocking the view of the front door from where I was. I guessed that if I couldn't see the front door, anyone at the front door couldn't see me so I decided I would sleep in comfort this night. I quickly put all of my gear in the cab of the truck and locked it up for the night. I then unrolled and inflated my air mattress with the electric pump I used to do so with, rolled my heavy military sleeping bag across it as it was now quite cold, and turned in for the night. It felt great to lay down completely after not having done so since Texas. I slept like a baby. My goose down sleeping bag kept me warm throughout the night even though the temperature at one point dropped into the thirties. Ah, the comforts of homelessness.

Before drifting completely to sleep I took a relaxing mental inventory of my day. Had I been lucky like the Chinese claim I would due to the date? I hadn't made any money panhandling but I had not been arrested for doing so either. I had not had any vehicle problems. I had not been abducted by aliens in Roswell. I had gotten to talk to all of the most important people in my life, minus my mother who had been out when I called my father. I saw antelope in the wild for the first time. Yes, I had been lucky today.

20

I woke up in Durango the next morning just after seven o'clock and was astonished to see that the caravan of campers was gone. I was the only one left. I had not even heard them as they pulled away.

No wonder the people at Wal Mart didn't seem to say much to these nomads about their odd practice. It seemed as if they pulled into the lot only at dark or just before and were gone as mysteriously as the sun rose the next morning.

I decided to get started slowly however, as I was beginning to feel a bit tired from all the traveling. I was actually gutsy enough to make a hot cup of Regina's tea on the tail gate and drink it slowly while I sat in the back of the truck and filled out post cards from Roswell that I would be sending off to friends and family members.

"I didn't need to come to Roswell to see Aliens," I wrote on Maia's. "I already have a girl friend that is out of this world!"

After eating a bowl of cereal, rolling up my sleeping gear and putting away my Coleman stove, I drove slowly by the front of the Wal Mart and dropped my post cards into the mail box outside. I then proceeded out of Durango heading toward Utah.

As I began to leave Durango I did so climbing higher into the southern most portion of the Rocky Mountains. I thought that I had seen mountains having grown up in West Virginia but these Rocky Mountains were something else!

The scenery was exquisite. All of the brown I had seen since Texas had now disappeared and everything was as green as could be. Most of the land was wooded, except for the occasional rock outcroppings on the tops of the mountains.

Just a few miles out of Durango I passed a flock of wild turkeys feeding in a field off to the right of the road. I passed more cyclists trudging their way up the mountainside in the bike lane provided for them than I had ever seen in any one area unless there had been a tour passing through. Occasionally I saw huge mountain estates that I would say cost in the millions of dollars each to have built. Colorado was beautiful.

On this part of the journey I would not be seeing much of Colorado though as I was simply cutting through the southwestern corner of the state. It was not long before I crossed into Utah and everything went back to brown as I reentered the desert.

I stopped for lunch and gas at a small business that provided both in Monticello, Utah, I'll admit feeling somewhat homesick due to this communities name reminding me of the home of Thomas Jefferson back in Charlottesville. I then got back in the truck and headed on my way feeling somewhat disappointed because the scenery was seeming lack luster. That was until I made it just around the next bend in the road.

As I came out of the next turn, witnessing another first, a large grey wolf that unfortunately was dead beside the road, the landscape gave way to the great canyons of Utah. It appeared as if I were driving through one of those beautiful pictures on the calendars that the Disabled Veterans of America sent me every year in appreciation of the small donations I always gave them.

These canyons were so beautiful that I was inspired to stop at the next rest area just to get out and walk through them. When I did, it was over 100 degrees, but again without the humidity it was very comfortable.

I plugged my cell phone into an electrical socket in the bathroom then went for a walk on a trail that headed straight through the middle of one of these canyons. The rocks appeared just like the artificial walls that were present in so many indoor rock climbing facilities back east. I climbed a little way up the side of one of the deep canyon walls just to see what it felt like. The rock seemed almost sticky and though I thought I could go farther safely I decided not to.

I quickly noticed that every thirty yards or so that I walked up the trail I had to stop and catch my breath. I was walking at a very slow, lackadaisical pace but the elevation was now over 8,000 feet and the oxygen was much thinner than I was used to. This would explain my being out of breath.

I began climbing another part of the canyon when for some reason I remembered the story of the mountain lion the little boy back in Texas had told me. I decided I had walked out into the canyon alone far enough, and after witnessing a lizard of some type race across the rock's ledge just above me, I decided to climb down and head back.

I laid on the grass at the rest stop for about half an hour, giving my phone time to charge completely. I then went back into the bathroom to retrieve it, where I found the ground's keeper standing, staring at my phone.

"Is that yours?" he asked.

"Yes," I said. "I am traveling all across the country and I plugged it in to let it recharge."

"Oh," he said in a friendly tone. "I was just keeping an eye on it to make sure no one stole it."

"Thank you very much," I said as I unplugged it and headed on my way.

Heading north on state route 191 I soon entered the tourist community of Moab, Utah and crossed over the Colorado River. As I peered at this river while crossing the bridge, and saw how it flowed right out of the canyons I said to myself out loud, "That is the most beautiful river I have ever seen."

As I got to the other side of the bridge, I then said out loud, "What are you doing?! That is the most beautiful river you have ever seen!"

I quickly turned around at a wide spot beside the road and headed back for the river. I had not used my kayak as of yet on this trip and I was going to take advantage of this beautiful river and have this be the first.

I was fortunate enough to find that there was a small public park, more like a picnic area, just under the bridge and it had river access. After pulling into this park and parking my truck I untied my kayak, took my shaving bag with me as I had not bathed or shaved in three days, and hit the river.

I paddled about a mile upstream, taking in the beauty that surrounded me the whole while. The water about three feet under the surface was flowing quite rapidly but on its surface it was very calm. This made for both easy upstream paddling and provided a natural mirror that reflected the canyon. It looked as if I were paddling on land due to the reflection.

As I went upstream, hugging the bank to take advantage of the reverse current, just as Lewis and Clark had done on the Missouri so many years ago, I ran off schools of carp and other types of fish. I saw lots of frogs and turtles and several different types of water fowl.

Once about a mile upstream and around a bend, out of sight of the road, I pulled over to the side and banked my boat. I rested the shaving bag on the end of the kayak and began shaving my grizzled face while standing about waste deep in the warm water. The bank gave way rapidly here and if I were to step out only a few more feet I knew the water would be over my head.

When I finished shaving, I swam around to get wet, wearing only my sandals and my running shorts I had slipped into in the privacy of my truck before hitting the water. After enjoying the relaxing water for a few minutes I returned to the shaving bag, pulled out a bar of Ivory soap and lathered up from head to toe, making sure to scrub my shorts good as well since they had not been cleaned in days either. I then returned to the deeper water to rinse off all of the soap.

I completely submerged myself, rubbed my hands violently through my hair to get all of the soap out, and then rose up out of the water. As I stood there and wiped the water from my face, opened my eyes and stared up into the canyon I felt an unexplained spiritual cleansing come over my body; a baptism of sorts. I stood and stared, marveling at God's creation all around me.

I believe God reveals himself to us at different points in our life through different ways. I remember when Amanda was pregnant with Emily and we had just gotten married I was scared to death. Only months before I had been barely taking care of myself and I would now be responsible for taking care of a family of four. I remember praying several times a day that God would guide my paths and allow me to accomplish this mission.

Emily was not due until the second week of December, but when she was born on November 29'th, my birthday, I took this as a sign from God that everything was going to be alright. I found out over the years leading up to my divorce that everything had been alright.

I couldn't count the number of times I had prayed during a bad selling month during my career as a broker when it looked as if I might not even make enough money to make ends meet and on the last day of the month an existing or new client would walk into the office without an appointment with a considerable amount of money to invest, allowing me to make it through another cycle of bills.

As I stood there in the water, looking up into the canyon I felt as if God were talking to me again. It occurred to me that I had spent the past couple of years falling down but now was the time for me to start getting back up. I had lost all I could lose except for my health. My house was gone, I was separated from my children and I no longer was married to the woman that I had vowed to be with until we parted at death. All I possessed was a truck with way too many miles on it and my sparse belongings in the back.

I bowed my head and prayed as I stood there in the warm waters of the Colorado River.

"God," I began. "Please allow me to find your strength in my time of weakness and begin rebuilding my life. Please allow me not to focus on the destruction of the past but allow me to continue moving forward with my future. I know that as lonely as I have been at times these past couple of years I have not been alone because you have been there beside me, carrying me at times through these turmoil's. I ask that you will continue to be with me and see me through this great hallway I seem to be walking through until you reveal to me the next door to be opened in my life. Amen."

After sitting beside the river for a few minutes and allowing this feeling that had come over me to run its coarse, I got back in my kayak and took some pictures from the water, being very careful not to drop my digital camera in the river. As I began to head back downstream around the bend I heard a loud, curious pounding noise. When I came around the bend I saw that there was a small group of about half a dozen people hanging out on the bank on the opposite side of the river from my truck looking up. I glanced up to see what they were looking at just in time to see a mad man jump off of a boulder that had to be every bit of forty feet high and into the water below.

"Those people are freakin' crazy," I said to myself. "I have to get pictures of this."

As I made my way back down stream I did so crossing to the river's other side. The river was wide but the distance I had to travel downstream was so far that it took no effort on my part to cross it. I simply gave a row every here and there as I made my way both downstream and across the stream at the same time.

When I came upon this group of people, both male and female ranging in ages from sixteen to almost thirty, I sat far enough away from the bank to stay out of their path and took pictures as they jumped.

"You guys are crazy!" I said to them when they noticed I was marveling at their bravery, or should I say insanity.

"We do this all the time," a local sixteen year old kid told me. "You should come try it."

"No way," I said, paddling just enough to hold my position.

After a couple of more guys jumped off of the rock, a sixteen year old local girl in a little bikini made her way to the top of the rock. She looked down hesitantly, smiled at her friends, then leaped off the rock, closing her eyes and holding her nose. Several seconds later she made a loud thud as she entered the water.

"Come on man," the kid who had spoken to me originally mocked. "If a girl can do it you can do it."

With this I felt challenged. Besides, I would soon be going to basic training and I had heard that if you performed exceptionally well in certain areas you could win a spot to Airborne School. I had never before thought about jumping out of air planes but when I signed my enlistment papers I viewed it as a promise I was making to three hundred million Americans that I would do my best in all military aspects to best prepare myself to keep them safe. I wasn't sure what exactly I would have to excel at to win one of the coveted spots to Airborne but I knew that when I did find out what it was I would put all of my heart into it. I supposed that if there was even a slight possibility that I would be jumping out of a plane from 1200 feet six months from now maybe I should get warmed up to the idea by scaling this boulder and jumping from 40 feet into the water below.

"OK," I said to this challenging teenager as I began paddling toward the shore. "You've convinced me."

"Its not as bad as it looks," a British gentleman in his mid twenties who was in the states visiting his sister who was going to college over here said to me as he helped pull the nose of my kayak on the bank. "You just don't think about it. Just jump," he continued in that British accent that for some reason seemed to drive so many American women crazy.

"You can do it," an attractive girl in her early twenties, scantly clad in a bright pink bikini said as I got out of the boat. There was no doubting that this was the gentleman's sister due to the British accent she spoke with as well. I could finally understand what it was about this accent that drove people of the opposite sex crazy.

I made my way up a narrow foot trail that ran up the bank to the top of the boulder. I got on top of the giant rock and eased my way out to the edge, taking only six inch steps and looking down the whole time.

When I got to the edge I felt my stomach sink as it looked even higher from here.

"Oh my God," I said in a queasy tone.

"Don't be scared," the sixteen year old local boy said as he was laughing from below. "Just jump out as far as you can and keep your legs together so you don't smack your nuts!"

I had never thought of that! That gave a whole new since of danger to this crazy idea.

I stood there on top of the boulder and began contemplating the idea of getting back down. I could claim that I got a cramp in my calf and maybe they would buy it.

"Hurry up," I heard a girlish voice say from behind me. "I want to do it again."

I turned around and saw that it was the sixteen year old girl that I had seen jump before. Ok, I was going to do this.

With that I took a three step run and pushed off with my right foot as hard as I could. It seemed as if I was falling forever. I took a deep breath, made sure to keep my legs together, and looked down. This is when I realized I was only half way down so I let my breath out and took in another just as I hit the surface.

What an adrenaline rush! They were right! It wasn't that bad!

I swam back over to the bank to the applause of all the other jumpers.

"You did it old man!" the sixteen year old boy mocked.

"Yeah," said the Brit. "But anyone can do it once just off of adrenaline. The true test of courage is to see if you can do it again."

Who did this guy think he was? Winston Churchill?

He was right though. Now that I had done it, mostly off of nerve, it did seem somewhat more foreboding because I now knew how long the fall actually was. However, giving in to the peer pressure coming heavily from the mocking sixteen year old, and witnessing his equally young female friend do it again, I climbed back up and took another try.

I didn't think about it this time, I just jumped. I wished I had thought about it a little more though because this time I did not keep my legs completely together. Let's just say that I got the feeling that it was a good idea that I already had three kids because I may have greatly decreased my ability to father more children after hitting the water on this second jump.

"I bet that hurt like a mother f——r, didn't it?" the sixteen year old boy laughed.

"Yeah," I agreed. "You could say that."

"We all do it from time to time," he said. "Sometimes you just don't think about it."

As encouraging as his words were they did nothing to ease my pain.

The British guy had taken my picture with my camera when I was on top of the rock, while I was in mid air, and as I was entering the water. I sat on the rocks of the bank of the river and viewed the pictures while I watched the others jump and slowly was relieved of my sickening pain. I never understood why when you got hit or kicked in the testicles you felt the pain in your stomach.

After hanging out on the river bank for about another twenty minutes everyone began parting ways so I crawled back into my kayak to cross the river and do the same. Once I got to the other side of the river, I secured my boat to the top of the truck, ate a peanut butter and jelly sandwich and then got back on the road and headed on my way, marveling again at the beautiful Colorado River as I crossed over it on the bridge again and feeling very satisfied that I had stopped. I got to kayak, bathe and jump off of a huge boulder sustaining only minor pain which was now completely gone.

21

I continued heading north on state route 191, passing almost chartreuse green cliffs that looked much like soil that had been sprayed with grass seed and fertilizer after a stripping operation though this was actually the rock's natural color. These green rocks gave way to ivory white ones as I entered Cardova County.

As I drove through Cardova county I began to see the smoke from distant forest fires. It seemed that this summer the entire western portion of the United States was on fire. Just as I had stayed far enough south through the center of the country to avoid the flooding rains in Oklahoma I was now going out of my way to avoid these forest fires as much as possible.

However, the closer I got to Crescent Junction, Utah where I would pick up Interstate 70 and head west, I began to get ever closer to the smoke and the fires. I eventually drew close enough to where I could see flames. To make this experience more nerve wracking the radio station I was now listening to as I had rolled the windows up to protect myself from some more cross winds was suddenly interrupted by a public service announcement.

The announcer warned of the dangerous fires that had made their way to route 191 through Cardova County and warned all travelers to get out of the canyon as quickly as possible and that the fire departments and state police where going to be shutting the road off within the next couple of hours.

Realizing I was directly in harms way I picked up the pace in an attempt to make it out of the canyon and to the interstate before the road was shut off. As I continued on my way I saw several danger seekers in old four wheel drive pick ups and several on A.T.V.s actually racing off of the main road and onto the back roads to get even closer to the forest fires. I thought these people were just as crazy as the cliff jumpers I had just met, but this was one adrenaline rushing activity in which I was not going to participate in with the locals. I continued driving, actually going a few miles over the speed limit, something I rarely did.

I finally reached the interstate and immediately began heading west to put as much distance between myself and the forest fires as possible. I was now driving directly into the powerful winds, making them go from cross winds to head winds. They were so powerful that the hatch on my topper was sticking straight out behind my truck due to their force and it was taking all of my strength using both arms to keep my truck on the road.

I drove for several hours before finally stopping at Soldier's Summit just before I would reach Interstate 15 heading north. There was a rest stop here and I got out to stretch my legs and eat dinner, which consisted of a 20 ounce can of hash with potato squares.

As I walked to the rest room after eating my hash I noticed several small children kneeling on the ground at the wood's edge behind the restrooms. I took a closer look and saw that they were feeding a small group of prairie dogs out of their hands. I had never seen prairie dogs in the wild, as there were none back east so I walked over for a closer view.

The children were holding sun flower seeds in the outstretched palms of their hands and these small rodents would sneak up, grab a seed with their mouth, then retreat about ten yards and sit on their back haunches and eat their treat with both hands, much like the gray squirrels in over whelming abundance back east would do with nuts. I bummed some seeds off of a little boy and fed the prairie dogs with them.

After doing this for a few minutes and then using the restroom, I made my way back to the truck, crossing over a small foot bridge. Here I stopped to witness several children who where playing in the small creek that flowed underneath the bridge. I noticed that they had a small brook trout surrounded and where trying to catch it with their bare hands.

Each time one of the children made a move the trout would dart to the other side of the creek, or slightly up or down stream and then hug the bank or slide under a rock for protection. Having tried to catch these lightning fast creatures with my hands back east I chuckled as I knew in spite of their best efforts, all of these children's efforts would be in vain. This small trout never at any point attempted to head any great distance up or down stream which made me think it had obviously been through this routine before.

After witnessing a few more failed attempts on the part of these children to catch this fish I got back into my truck and continued heading north on Interstate 15. Every now and then I could see more smoke from more distant forest fires. This was a disheartening site. I wondered why the many scientists and government officials could not come up with some sort of way to better prevent these incidences, but I guess the answer lied in the fact that no one can be every where at once and there was always going to be the human factor of irresponsibility playing its part.

I entered the city of American Forks, Utah with a couple of hours of day light left. I was only half an hour south of Salt Lake City, a destination I had planned on easily reaching by dark, but I couldn't help noticing all of the "help wanted" signs everywhere. I had pretty much decided that I would try to find some sort of short term work somewhere on my trip to help add to my gasoline fund, which was still stable but that I knew would be threatened once I crossed the Mississippi River again heading east.

Seeing all of this apparent opportunity I decided to cut my travels a little short for the day and seek out the local Wal Mart. I found the store and its beautiful parking lot with ease as it sat just off of the interstate and I pulled in to investigate. I quickly located the part of the lot furthest away from the entrance of the store and vowed to return at dark to spend the night. I then began driving around the community to stake out businesses that I would visit the following morning in an attempt to find employment.

I was able to find several places with "help wanted" signs posted within just a couple of miles of the Wal Mart so with still more day light left I made my way to Lake Utah. At the gate a gentleman asked me if I intended to fish or kayak and I informed him that since it was so close to dark I had just intended to walk around the water's edge. After telling him this he waved my entrance fee of $6 and allowed me to roll in and park for free.

I got out of my truck and walked out on one of several boat docks at the head of the lake. I watched as half drunken and some completely drunken boaters came in from the day's boating trips and tried to load their big motor powered toys onto the trailers connected to the back of their trucks.

As the sun began setting over the water I watched as sparrows dive bombed the top of the water to catch lots of unsuspecting insects. I wondered how these small birds would react to seeing those large grave digger grass hoppers back in New Orleans. Would they approach with the excitement of seeing the largest meal of their lives or would they turn and fly away in fear? Since the grass hoppers were bigger than these small birds themselves, I figured they would do the latter.

At dark I made my way back to Wal Mart and parked in my desired spot, this time within the safety of some campers that had shown up while I was gone. I then went inside to buy some groceries. I came out and ate a bowl of cereal and then tried calling my kids without success. I was able to get in touch with Mia since I was now two hours behind her time wise and though it was only ten o'clock in Utah it was mid-night back east and she had just gotten home from work.

We talked for about half an hour. I told her about my experience of jumping off of the boulder into the river and about the forest fires I had seen that almost trapped me inside their burning canyon. Maia told me about how well her evening had gone at work and then we ended our conversation. I inflated my air mattress in the back of the truck again and slept in the felt sleeping bag as it was much warmer here in American Forks, Utah than it had been in the Rocky Mountains of Colorado.

I woke up the next morning with an excruciating head ache and a soar throat. My sinuses were clogged as well and when I blew my nose to clear them I was shocked to see that my mucus was full of blood. I got out of the truck to find that the air was full of smoke as more forest fires had made their way into the area over night.

In spite of the smoke the sun rise over the Uinta Mountains, which housed King's Peak, Utah's highest elevation at 13,528 feet was astonishing. I stared at it as I sat and ate a bowl of cereal and several plumbs for breakfast. After eating, I packed my belongings into my truck and headed off to find work.

I first went to Gerber Construction, where I found that no one was in yet. I then drove on to a cabinet business called "The Cabinet Barn," where I talked to a friendly young foreman for about fifteen minutes but was informed by him that the work there required skilled labor that took a month to learn how to perform via their training program.

After leaving here I headed to a local flour mill that had been locally owned by the same family for three generations. Though their offices were open and I waited at the receptionist's desk for some time, reading framed news articles about the company posted on the walls, no one ever came in so I decided to head elsewhere.

I stopped at a couple of more business and was turned down before finally making my way to Tempest Enterprises. This was some sort of excavation company and I found out here too that working here would be a no go due to an extended training period that I would not be around long enough to complete. I did however enjoy taking to the foreman, Thoral Wardle.

"So you're in the National Guard huh?" Thoral asked when he noticed my guard sticker on the tail gate of my truck. We had been standing at the back of the truck, both of us resting a foot on the bumper while we talked.

"Yeah," I said. "In Virginia."

"My son is in the guard," he informed me.

"Really?" I said, surprised. "Out of here in Utah?"

"Yes," he said. "But he is actually deployed in Afghanistan right now."

"So I guess you are a Bush supporter then huh? I stated assumingly, only to find out that I was wrong.

"I hate Bush and his entire administration," he told me. "Especially Dick Cheney."

"Really?" I said surprised, figuring that since his son was in the military he might be supportive of the administration.

"Yes," he continued. "I don't trust any of them and I don't agree with their reasoning behind going into Iraq."

"That must be tough on you knowing your son is deployed," I said.

"Not really," he said. "Though I don't support the administration I do support the war on terror and I am glad that Sadam Hussein is gone."

"Really?" I said again, somewhat confused.

"Yes," Thoral continued. "I think the Bush administration could have taken a different avenue to get us into Iraq other than lie to the American people about weapons of mass destruction that we've yet to find, but I do believe that if we were wrong to go after Sadam then we owe Adolph Hitler an apology."

"I know we are making a difference in the lives of the people in the middle east," he continued. "My son stays in contact with me and he tells me that the people of Afghanistan are happy that we are there. He tells me that it is common for them to come out of their houses and show their praise and support when US soldiers go through the area."

What Thoral was telling me was something I had heard from many people. It seemed that Bush was not very popular in much of the country, though many people did like him and still supported him, but many people I had talked to across the country did seem to understand our threat from the terrorists when the topic came up.

Thoral and I continued talking about current events and he eventually asked what had brought me this way from Virginia. I told him about my trip and he said it sounded very interesting, which I confirmed to him through telling him of some of my experiences so far that it was.

"If I were you," Thoral said, changing the subject back to my work situation, "I would wait until you got into Montana and try to find a farmer to help out up there. I used to work for farmers up there in the summers when I was a kid. It seems as if they always need some kind of help."

"Besides," he told me, "The fires are moving their way into the area and there is talk that they might shut the interstate down. If you are on your way north from here you might get trapped."

Feeling the same sense of doom I had felt when I almost got trapped in the canyon lands south of here the day before I agreed that his idea to continue moving was a good one. We talked for a few more minutes and then parted ways with a hand shake. Thoral went back to his responsibilities at Tempest and I got back in my truck and continued heading north after filling up with gas at $3.09 a gallon at a local gas station. I was keeping a log of my miles and what I paid for gas on the trip and this price was lower than the $3.39 I had paid the last time I had stopped. I had watched as the gas prices continued to move up to this point from the $2.76 they had started at when I left Virginia.

As I traveled toward Idaho the smoke from the fires grew thicker with each passing mile, actually blocking the view of the mountain tops. I heard on the radio that they had indeed shut the interstate off in the American Forks area. I had avoided being trapped by less than an hour.

Just before I crossed the state line into Idaho I noticed an old abandoned building to my right just off of the highway. This building had been spray painted heavily with graffiti and the message that stood out the most was one of big words that read, "Happy Birthday Amanda!"

"Wow!" I said out loud. "That is my ex wife's name. "Wow!" I said again, realizing today's date. "Today IS my ex wife's birthday!" How weird was that?

I never believed in coincidences and viewed seeing this message as representing an opportunity. It was time I believed for Amanda and I to truly move past our differences and become friends as opposed to enemies. This would only benefit our children. I immediately picked up my phone and called Amanda to wish her a happy birthday.

"Hello," she said in a not too pleasant tone when she answered the phone, I am assuming because she recognized my number.

I sang her the happy birthday song which seemed to throw her for a loop.

"What was that for?" she asked defensively.

"Because it is your birthday and I wanted to wish you a happy birthday," I said in my most pleasant tone.

"Where are you at?" she asked again in that same unpleasant voice.

"I am just going to cross into Idaho from Utah," I informed her. "You wouldn't believe what I just saw painted in big letters on an old building on the side of the road."

"I give up," she said un-amused.

"In big letters someone had painted 'happy birthday Amanda,'" I told her.

"That is weird," she said, seeming to soften up some. "So has that old truck of yours broken down beside the highway yet?"

"Not yet," I said, tapping on the artificial inlaid wood on the dash. "I did almost get trapped in the canyons of southern Utah yesterday though due to all the forest fires down here. I wouldn't have like that I would imagine."

"I would rather be trapped with fires than all those Mormons down there," she said sarcastically.

"What is wrong with the Mormons?" I asked her.

"What do you mean what is wrong with them?" she asked sarcastically. "They are a bunch of sexists, cultish freaks! They still practice polygamy!"

I don't think I had ever personally met a Mormon but I would imagine them to be just like other folks. As far as polygamy goes, I do feel sorry for them for that practice I suppose. Heck, I only had one wife and it was more than I could handle. Who really was the victim of polygamy then, the women who had to share a husband or the husband that had to deal with more than one wife?

I continued talking to Amanda about birthdays and Mormons as I drove through southeastern Idaho's Black Pine Valley. This land was once entirely under water and housed Bonneville Lake, the largest land locked lake in North America many millions of years ago. The lake which at its peak measured 20,000 acres eventually drained into the Snake River. The great Salt Lake of Utah remains as a small, previous portion of this great body of water.

The Black Pine Valley is also home to the Ferruginous Hawk, North America's largest hawk. These birds, which are the size of eagles nest in the many Juniper bushes found throughout this valley and feed primarily on Jack Rabbits and rodents.

After listening to Amanda's tirade about religious cults and their oppression of women for a bit longer I got to speak with my children. They were all excited about the U.F.O. goo I was bringing them from Roswell and Emily in particular was looking forward to her alien meat.

I stopped briefly at a rest stop along the road to stretch my legs and shave. As I was shaving in the far right of three sinks in the restroom I couldn't help but notice how uncomfortable people felt when they came near me to wash their hands. I guess they had not seen a homeless guy shave at a rest stop before.

What was even more entertaining was the fact that the paper towel dispenser on their end of the sink was empty but the one on my end was full. I watched with humor as man after man would reach for a paper towel from the empty dispenser, then after realizing it was empty, look down at the full dispenser beside the eccentric homeless guy shaving at the rest stop, then hesitate, not reach for a paper towel and then walk out of the rest room drying their hands on their pants or shorts.

After getting back on the road I passed through Boise, Idaho right in time to catch the five o'clock rush hour traffic jam. I would actually drive the entire length of Idaho today and not stop until I got to Oregon. I would visit Idaho again in its northern panhandle on the way back east and I would have loved to stop and visit its southern portion today but I was in the middle of a heat wave. The temperature was over 110 degrees and there was still smoke everywhere from all the forest fires. I was burning up in the cab of my truck with the air conditioning on full blast and I didn't even want to spend any amount of time outside.

Just before crossing into Oregon I saw cowboys herding cattle in fields riding on the backs of motocross style dirt bikes as opposed to horses. This site took me back to so many fond memories I had riding dirt bikes with my buddies growing up back in West Virginia.

I remember that in junior high most of my friends had gotten dirt bikes or four wheelers. A couple of them even had those dreaded three wheelers that are now outlawed from production. After tipping one back and breaking my left wrist one time I understand why they are illegal to produce. Every law of physics goes against them from a safety stand point.

Anyhow, all of my friends had dirt bikes except me. I had tried to collect aluminum cans or find odd jobs to save the money to get one but at 15 years old in a small town that didn't provide any work opportunities for teenagers as their were not even enough for all the adults my efforts were in vain.

I remember coming home from school one day and my mother told me there was a bunch of trash on the back deck that I needed to put into the shed out back so that the local dogs would not get into it.

"OK," I lamented at the idea of having to do a chore.

I grabbed the bags of trash and moped to the shed. When I opened the door I had the biggest surprise I had ever had up to that point of my life as in the shed sat a brand new Suzuki DR100 dirt bike!!! I jumped on it immediately, not even shutting the door or saying anything to my mother and road up the dirt road behind our house that ran along the south fork of the Cherry River and did not come back until dark.

It seemed that my friends and I spent every day light hour that we were not in school on those old dirt roads with our dirt bikes. I took really good care of that bike the entire time I had it until I sold it a few years later to pay for a week long cross country camp at Grove City College in northern Pennsylvania. I hated to part with it but distance running had become my new love and I knew the investment in the camp would pay off as it did. Before going to the camp my best mile time was five minutes even but the next track season it would drop all the way down to my 4:33 best. I learned so much about proper training techniques at that camp.

My thoughts soon shifted to my own son Christian. I was really feeling bad that he had gone through a divorce and was now living 3,000 miles away from the home he knew. I had had such a perfect, enjoyable childhood and I was fearful of the experiences he and his sisters were going to go through.

I was brought back to the present when I noticed the sign welcoming me to Oregon. I stopped at the welcome center, took my shirt off and went and stood under the sprinkling system that was watering the grass. Though it would be dark in another hour it was still over 100 degrees and I was willing to do anything to cool down.

After getting completely wet I used the facilities then came out and talked to two really nice women, one about seventy years old and her fifty year old daughter. Our conversation drifted all over the place, from my trip across the country to my upcoming duties with the National Guard, but it eventually made its way to eBay. They had noticed my eBay power seller sticker that I proudly donned on the back of my truck. It turned out that these two ladies ran an antique business in Oregon and most of their sales were transacted these days over the internet.

They referred to eBay as "feebay" due to the site's always rising fees and told me to check out www.ubizz.com and www.bidzig.com, two sites that offered online auctions but according to them, for much lower expenses. They had actually constructed their own site, www.tias.com/stores/lml where they were now selling most of their wares.

I inquired as to the whereabouts of the closest Wal Mart and they informed me I would need to go to La Grange, Oregon which was still about an hour north. After finishing our conversation I got in the truck and hit the road en route to La Grange.

I pulled into the town of La Grange just after dark and quickly located the Wal Mart. I went inside to use the restroom and buy a snack and couldn't help noticing that this was the cleanest Wal Mart I had ever been in. I guess I was quickly becoming somewhat of a Wal Mart cone coir.

On the way out of the store I noticed a row of recycling bends where people were cramming plastic bottles and tin cans into these large green receptacles. I had always heard that Oregon was a pretty "green" state and I guess that trickled down to the local Wal Marts. Just as Wal Mart had adapted to Roswell with their U.F.O. mural on the front of the store they were adapting to the lifestyle of this local community as well.

I left the store and went back to my truck, which I had already parked within the nomad camp at the far end of the parking lot. I inflated my air mattress and unrolled my sleeping bag, which I was now very comfortable in doing and climbed in the back and slept for the night.

22

I woke up the next morning in La Grange feeling hungrier than I had in a long time. I had not stopped to eat much the day before, not wanting to get out in the heat and the smoke so I passed up on settling for a bowl of cereal this morning and went to the local Denny's. Here I ate 3 eggs, sausage links, bacon, toast and three large pancakes. I got it all for the fair price of $5.49.

Before leaving Denny's I asked my waitress Aimee, a girl about my age who was probably hot ten years and twenty pounds ago where the local library was. I wanted to get on the internet and email my friends and family of my where-abouts. She told me how to get there so I left the restaurant, deciding to stop for gas at the gas station just next door before heading on to the library.

After pulling up to the pump at the gas station I got out to pump my gas. The attendant working this morning was filling up an R.V. on the other side of the gas island and told me he would be right with me.

"That's OK," I said pleasantly. "I can do it."

As I took the gas handle off of its holder and began to stick it in my truck I heard the attendant yell, "NO!!!"

I turned around and saw that he was running straight at me! He was coming with such ferocity that I actually felt physically threatened. As he stepped up on the gas island to come to my side I actually got in a fighter's stance fearing I was going to be attacked.

This young man of maybe twenty years tripped as he came off of the gas island and landed into the side of my truck, taking the pump out once he got his footing.

"I can't," he panted, "I can't let you pump your own gas!"

"Why not?" I asked incredulously.

"Your not (pant pant pant) from around here are you?" he asked.

"No," I said, wondering what that had to do with anything.

"It is against state law in Oregon for customers to pump their own gas," he informed me. "I didn't mean to startle you but I didn't want you to get in trouble if a cop drove by."

"Oh," I said relieved.

I then looked over at the middle aged couple in the R.V. who were looking in our direction smiling, as if they had been entertained by this incident.

It seems the state of Oregon outlawed customers from pumping their own gas in the 1970's due to many law suits that were arising from spilt gas. After seeing the law was not really needed, but realizing how many extra jobs in created for the state, the state's leaders decided to leave the law in effect.

"Well man," I said to the attendant, "I can understand that but you might want to be a little less dramatic next time. I was getting ready to knock you out!" I said this as I was catching my breath from the excitement myself.

"I'm sorry," he said. "I just don't want any of my customers to get in trouble."

After fueling up at what had to be my most exciting visit to a gas station ever I got back on the road and headed for the library. It was only eight o'clock local time and I was hoping that they didn't open as late as most public libraries.

As I drove through Main Street in La Grange I noticed that the town was immaculately well kept. There was no litter to be seen. The streets looked as if they were swept daily and all the store fronts were well maintained.

I made my way to the library but was disheartened when I walked to the door to see that it would be another 2 hours before they opened. As I was walking back to my truck I passed who I assumed to be the librarian who was coming toward the building. She was an attractive woman in her early fifties, very trim and fit, but she walked like she had a broom stick up her a—.

"Do ya'll really not open 'till ten?" I asked in my best southern drawl, hoping that maybe if she found me charming enough she might let me in early.

"Why do you talk like that?" she asked very pretentiously.

"Talk like what?" I said, confused.

"Like that," she said, enunciating and drawing out "t-h—a-t."

"Where are you from?" she quickly followed up.

"Virginia!" I said with pride.

"Oh," she said, very dismissively. "Yes," she then continued. "We really don't open until ten."

With that she let herself in the library and then gave the door an extra tug once inside to make sure it had locked safely behind her.

"Well," I said out loud. "At least back in Virginia they would have let me in to use the internet."

Not wanting to waste two hours of precious traveling time I decided to leave La Grange and continue on toward Washington State. I was glad that I had set my "no driving after dark" rule because Oregon was absolutely beautiful and I would not have wanted to miss its scenery by driving through it after dark.

After going for several miles on the interstate I was hearing the "call of the wild" so to say telling me to get off of the interstate and take a back road through this beautiful land. I answered this calling and soon pulled off and found a road on my atlas that would take me 47 miles through the Umatilla National Forest. I quickly made my way onto this back road and never regretted it.

I wound my way up county route 244 and never took my eyes off of the scenery. Along the road ran a beautiful mountain stream like the ones that lined the roads back in West Virginia. The hills were green and covered with beautiful ever greens. I saw the first mule deer I had ever seen in the wild along this road. At several points I passed several of them grazing. They looked up as if only half interested in me as I passed by.

At one point I stopped to walk along the banks of the stream that I had been following. I peered into its clear water hoping to see trout though I saw none. I did however, happen across a recently shed skin of some sort of snake that was about four feet long. I knew it was fresh because it was still moist and had not yet grown dry and flakey. It had probably been shed just this morning.

I got back in the truck and made my way to the small community of Ukia. I certainly would have missed this town had I blinked. The local public school housed grades kindergarten through twelfth all in the same building.

After making my way to the interstate I stopped at Pendleton where I ate lunch out of the back of my truck and then fell asleep laying sideways, just inside the tail gate. I usually didn't sleep in the middle of the day, but as I was ahead of schedule for making it to the west coast due to the previous day's long drive I didn't fret about the nap.

I woke up and got back on the road and almost immediately crossed Lake Wallula and into Washington. After making my way to the town of Prosser only a short while later, I sought a place to access the Yakima river as I had not bathed in a couple of days.

I quickly found public access to this river and pulled in to park. I decided I would try to call Maia before getting my kayak off of the truck so I opened my cell phone and dialed her number.

It was so nice hearing her voice when she answered the phone. Every time I heard her speak I could see her beautiful face in my mind's eye. I was still amazed that I had met this beautiful creature and that she had given me her love.

"So where are you boyfriend?" she asked as I walked over to look over the bank and into the river.

"I am in Prosser, Washington at the Yaki!!!!!!"

Before I could get my entire location out I fell on some extremely dry grass along the bank and slid on my butt all the way down to the river's edge, a distance of about twenty yards. Feeling like an idiot and hoping no one had seen, which unfortunately a family swimming in the river had, I walked back up to the top of the bank and called Maia back.

"Are you ok?" she asked immediately when she answered the phone."

"Yeah, I'm OK," I said in an embarrassed voice.

"What happened?" she asked.

"Oh, nothing," I said. "I just fell on my butt and slid down the river bank."

"Are you sure you're OK?" she inquired again.

"Yeah," I assured her. "I think I bruised my pride because some swimmers saw me but I am fine."

"You'd better be careful boyfriend," she laughed. "I want you coming back to me in one piece."

"Trust me," I told her. "Knowing you are back there for me to come back to gives me even more motivation to make it back in one piece."

Maia and I talked for about half an hour. I told her of all that had happened on my trip since I had talked to her last and she told me about how her days had been going. She kept a pretty regular schedule of working out at the gym, always buffing that gorgeous body of hers, and working at the restaurant in the evenings.

She told me of some movies she had recently seen and all I could do was think about how much I would have enjoyed going to see them with her. Or, should I say how much I would have enjoyed going to the movies to see her. Whenever we were together the world around us may as well have stood still because she was all I ever noticed.

I hate to say it but at many times I was not the best listener when we talked in person because I would get lost in her eyes and barely hear her words. She would point out to me times when she knew she was repeating herself with me and I told her about how I was probably lost in her eyes the first time she told me whatever it was she was retelling me. I don't think she ever believed me but it was the God's honest truth. As much as we were together, every time we would get together again it was as if I was re-meeting the most beautiful woman I had ever seen in my life. She seemed to grow even more beautiful with each passing day and I couldn't help but take notice.

I got off of the phone with Maia, which I always hated to do and then took my kayak down from the truck. I was already wearing a pair of running shorts in an attempt to stay as cool as possible so all I had to do was ditch my shirt, grab my shaving bag and then head down to the river.

There was a family of Mexicans swimming in the Yakima River. There was a mother and father, not much older than me and their six kids. The parents were sitting on the bank talking while keeping and eye on their children which ranged in ages from 2 years to 16 years old.

I put my kayak in and talked to some of the kids while I began floating down stream.

"Is this water pretty clean?" I asked the oldest of the group, a girl.

"They find dead cows in it every now and then," she said.

"Well, as long as they don't find dead people in it I guess," I said.

"Oh, they found a dead person in it not long ago," she informed me. "But it's rained pretty hard a few times since then so I'm sure it is safe."

"OK," I said, reluctantly continuing down stream.

Once I made it through some small rapids and around the bend I pulled over to the side and participated in my strange, yet necessary ritual of shaving and bathing in the river. I would actually be making it to Seattle by dark and would be seeing my kids. Olivia had always been a stickler about me shaving. She hated it when I had any stubble. I don't know if it was because it irritated her face when we snuggled or if she just didn't like how it looked.

After bathing, wondering if I had actually gotten dirtier bathing in this "river of death" as the Mexican girl had described it I began making my way back upstream. I had no problem paddling through the currents I had recently descended. Though my kayak was only a recreational kayak, meant to be used on ponds, lakes and very slow moving rivers I had actually taken it through class five rapids in West Virginia. This however, was not done intentionally.

Several years ago I went to Richwood, West Virginia for a trout fishing expedition I had fantasized about since childhood. One of the 7 major rivers that flowed its way through the mountains surrounding my home town was the Cranberry River, named after the small, wild berries that grew in the forests surrounding its head waters.

The state stocked the Cranberry for a length of about twenty miles with trout that they raised in one of their many hatcheries. Though the river was easily accessible along the stocking route, there was a part of it which stretched for about five miles before it dumped into the Gauley River that was not easily accessible. There was no road along the river at this portion and it was nearly impossible to get to by foot due to the rough terrain and numerous rattle snake dens throughout the area. I had always imagined that if I could reach this section of the river, say by boat, that I would find huge trout in overwhelming abundance.

In March of 2004 I took my kayak and tried to do just that. I was happy to find that my hunch was right. In a period of only three hours I caught over fifty trout! I don't remember catching any under twenty inches in length either, except for a few native brook trout which at ten inches in length were very large for their species. I caught mostly rainbow trout that day along with a few brown trout, one at nearly thirty inches!

The rapids on this river were more treacherous than any I had ever kayaked but the fishing was so exceptional that I found it to be worth it. I just had to make sure to have my pole secured to the side of the boat in plenty of time before I hit each section of rapids so I could maneuver my way through the water.

At one point along this journey I reached an exceptionally long hole of calm water. I was catching fish on nearly every cast. I would actually cast the rooster tail spinner I was using as bait in an area I wouldn't imagine there would be a trout just to see if I would catch anything and sure enough I would. I had hit the mother load!

However, I did not realize how dangerously close I had gotten to the white water at the end of this large hole. When I did, I secured my rod to the side of the boat, using the tight bungee cord attached to the boat's side to hold it down. I had been in the middle of the river so I could cast to both sides and I realized that I was not going to be able to paddle to the safety of either bank. I would have to ride the rapids and hope I had the skills to make it.

Another thing I had not noticed until it was too late was that this section of the river was not simply one of rushing currents. I had made my way to a set of falls, consisting of three main drops of about five feet high each.

As I went over the first fall I leaned back as far as I could in an attempt to adjust all of the weight to the back and thereby hold the nose of the kayak up. This worked, but the force with which I hit the water at the bottom of the drop forced the kayak to completely submerge about a foot down and take in a lot of water.

The next drop curved at an angle to the left. Here the waters were crashing violently into a large boulder at the side of the stream. I thrust my hips out to my right in an attempt to make this turn but due to all of the water in the boat I continued rolling to my left and was turned upside down. This had never happened to me before but I had my life vest on and I was able to kick out of the kayak underwater, almost instinctively.

When I popped up out of the freezing water (there was still ice hanging from the ledges of the cliffs along the river) I was facing upstream, from where I had just come. As I realized I had survived this spill I let out an adrenaline fueled laugh, but quickly stopped laughing as the water whipped me around to face the other direction and I realized where I was heading.

Just ten yards down stream there was a huge rock slab that had slid into the river who knows how long ago. The waters were rushing under this slab, trapping everything they had taken under it with them. I saw a log jam made up of trees much larger and stronger than me that had spent who knows how much time pinned beneath this rock.

Again, almost instinctively I reached my left arm out and grabbed onto a boulder that was sticking up out of the water in the middle of the stream. I hung on with every amount of strength I possessed as I knew that if I did not this would certainly be my last day on earth.

The force from the water whipped me around to the back side of this rock and I was able to climb to the safety it provided on top. Though it was cold and I was soaking wet I could not yet notice this as a mix of adrenaline and fear rushed through my veins like I had never experienced.

I sat on top of the rock for about five minutes, catching my breath, calming down, and assessing my situation. I was trapped by rushing water on both sides. The bank was ten yards away on my left as I faced downstream and about eight feet away to my right. As much as I didn't want to do it, I knew I would have to dive into the river on my right and swim like hell to make it to the bank before the waters pulled me down into the doom that awaited under the rock slab.

After working up the courage to do so, I dove with everything I had, reaching out to the bank on my right, and began digging with my arms to get to its safety. I was able to reach the bank and climb out of the river. I then walked through the woods to the bottom of the calm hole of water below the falls. When I looked up at the third fall I saw just how lucky I had been to have fallen out at the second.

This third fall was the steepest of the three and sitting out about four feet from the drop was a long pine log that stretched across the entire width of the river. My kayak had nosed dived coming over the fall and was stuck straight up and down between the rushing water and this pine log. Had I been able to maneuver past the rock slab in the second fall I certainly would have broken my neck, been pinned and drowned in this third drop. This had to be the closest to death I had ever come.

Very carefully I made my way across this pine log, crawling like a baby, and muscled my kayak loose. Once it got to the other side of the log I swam along beside it and guided it to the bank at the bottom of the calm hole below.

I felt as if I had accomplished something when I made it to the bank below the calm hole. This is when the adrenaline wore off though and I realized first how cold I was and then secondly, that I had lost all of my gear including my paddle. I was now literally up a creek without a paddle.

Knowing I faced the threat of hypothermia I stripped off all of my wet cloths, climbed to the top of a boulder that was one of the few places in this deep ravine that was receiving sun light, laid my clothes out to dry, then laid down on the rock itself to absorb the heat it provided. As I laid there I thanked God for getting me through this ordeal and began praying that if nothing else he would allow me to find my paddle.

I laid there for twenty minutes or so and managed to heat back up enough to where the threat of hypothermia was gone. I then stood up and put on my shorts. I decided to go shirtless as I figured I would stay warmer bare backed than by putting on my wet shirt.

As I walked down to the bottom of this hole, climbed on top of another boulder and peered downstream, I was flabbergasted to see yet another answer to my prayers. Downstream, which was made up of much calmer waters, the river was about thirty yards wide and only a couple of feet deep. There was but a lone rock sticking up in the middle of the river, maybe six inches above the surface, and my paddle was evenly balanced across the top of this rock. Again, I do not believe in coincidences and didn't view my paddle resting here as one. Besides, if you were to do the math, figuring the width of the stream, where my paddle had entered the water, etc there was no possible explanation for why my paddle had ended up where it had. This had truly been the answer to prayer.

Thinking back on this experience in West Virginia made these currents of the Yakima river seem even more mild.

"I can't believe you paddled upstream," one of the little Mexican boys said to me as I reached the swimming hole.

"I've paddled through much worse," I said with a grin, remembering the deadly waters of the Cranberry River.

I got out of the river, pulled my kayak back up the bank and secured it to the top of my truck. I ate a sandwich and some plumbs and then got back on the road and continued toward Seattle. I was as excited as I had been yet on this trip because I knew that by night fall I would be seeing my darling children.

23

It was only a three hour drive from where I had bathed in the Yakima River to the city of Seattle, Washington. Though the scenery was as beautiful as I passed through the Cascade Mountain Range and the Mount Baker Snoqualmie National Forest as I had seen on any part of this trip, I'll admit that I didn't pay extensive attention to it because my mind was focused on only one thing; my kids!

It had been nearly two months since I had seen them and I missed them dearly. I had talked to them at least every other day on the telephone but that was nothing in comparison to actually being with them.

I was not expected to arrive in Seattle for another day or two so with excitement I called the kids as I was descending the western side of the Cascades and drawing ever closer to the city.

"Hi Daddy," Emily said when she answered the phone.

"Hi crazy "Em," I responded, using the nick name she had rightfully earned through her dare devil ways.

"Hi crazy Kevin," she laughed back as she always did every time I called her crazy Em.

"When are you going to get here Daddy?" she asked, as she always did when I had called her from the road.

"Well crazy Em," I began. "I am going to be there in about an hour!"

"Woo Hoo!!!!" she let out in a big, excited scream.

"Daddy's gonna be here in an hour!" I heard her tell her brother and sister. I could hear them celebrating in the back ground.

"Hello!" the now unpleasant voice of Amanda came across the phone.

"Hi!" I said, still excited that I was going to be seeing my children soon.

"Are you really going to be here in an hour?" she asked.

"Yes! Isn't it great!" I answered.

"No Kevin! It's not great!" she said, but still unable to dampen my spirits.

"I was not expecting you for a couple of more days!" she said.

"Well I'll still stay as long as I was going to so this gives you a couple more days to yourself," I told her, trying to guide her to the positive side of the situation.

"Uh!" she sighed. "I guess! But the apartment is a mess and I need to go to the grocery store and I don't want to hear you complain about it!"

"Amanda," I began. "I just want to see my kids. I'm sure I won't even notice your mess."

Amanda then gave the phone back to Emily who I talked to for a while before also spending some time talking to Olivia and Christian. I got off of the phone with them just as I began to be able to see the city of Seattle. I generally did not like cities, having grown up in the mountains and now being a country boy, but this city was a pleasant site for my eyes because I knew what waiting for me within its limits; my kids!

I had printed off the directions to Amanda's apartment from map quest before beginning my great journey and finding her neighborhood, street and even her apartment building was not hard. What was hard however, was finding a place to park.

Amanda lived on Bellevue Avenue which was in the middle of a part of town known as "The Hill." I soon began thinking that "The Hill" was where all of societies misfits and other young folks still trying to "find themselves" or figure out who they are lived. I saw everything from men walking around in kilts and skirts to guys walking what I was assuming were their girl friends around on leashes. I saw just about every hair color except for those that appear naturally.

I finally found a space barely big enough to fit my extended cab truck into and parked. It was so far away from Amanda's apartment that I had to walk a few city blocks to get to her building, passing freaks and geeks of all sorts in doing so. I couldn't help but stare at all of their piercings, tattoos and strange attire as I made my journey down the side walk.

When I got to Amanda's building the front door was locked so I called Amanda to ask her to come down and let me in. In less than ten seconds after hanging up the phone my kids were busting through the front door of the building and jumping into my arms, all three at the same time, almost knocking me over.

"Daddy! Daddy! Daddy!" Is all that I heard.

"I missed you guys so much!" I said as I gave out a big group hug and then went around passing out individual hugs.

Christian was in dire need of a hair cut but other than that he looked the same. Emily had lost another front tooth but besides that she still looked the same as well. Olivia had not lost any teeth nor had she seemed to grow any but what had been my big brown eyed girl with long brunette hair was now sporting hair that had been dyed pink!

"What did you do to your hair Livy?" I asked her as we pulled away from our hug.

"Mommy wanted me to look like I fit in in Seattle so she had my hair dyed pink," she said, not seeming to like it too much herself.

"Yeah, mom tricked her," Emily added. "She dyed my hair purple but the dye came out in a week. Olivia's hair has been pink ever since we got here."

"Well I love it Olivia!" I said to make her feel better. Then I gave her a big hug and said, "Now you're my big brown eyed pink haired girl and I always wanted one of those too!"

The kids and I made our way upstairs to their mothers apartment and I saw that Amanda was right, the place was a mess. Even more noticeable than the mess though was how small this apartment was. It could not have been any bigger than 450 square feet! There was a small living room, an even smaller kitchen, a bathroom that was smaller yet, and only one bedroom.

"Where do you guys sleep?" I asked the kids.

"We sleep on the couches!" Emily said with excitement as she dove onto one of three couches that was crowding the living room.

"This is my couch Daddy!" Olivia said as she dove onto a couch on the opposite side of the room from her sister's. "The one in the middle is Christians!"

Kids being as they are it didn't seem to bother my children that they were living in such cramped quarters. However, it was breaking my heart. Where had I sent them to?

Emily rushed me into the kitchen where she had art work she had painted for me drying on the small table that only sat three if that.

"I made these for you after we got off of the phone!" she told me.

She had painted me three pictures. One was a picture of me standing beside a U.F.O., one was of me in my kayak in the middle of a river, and the third was a picture of me standing, holding hands with all of my kids in front of our old house in Virginia.

"Where's our surprises?" Olivia spoke up from behind me.

"They're in the truck!" I told her. "I should probably move my truck closer any way so do you guys want to go with me to move it and get your stuff?"

"Yeah!" they screamed.

Amanda just glared at me as she told me where I could park my truck. There was a small lot behind her apartment building where I could park in the visitor's spot for up to two hours. She informed me that if I was there a minute longer that the Apartment manager who watched the lot like a hawk would have me towed.

"Nice to know you have such accommodating and friendly neighbors," I said.

"Don't bad mouth my neighbors," she barked. "I like them better than those dumb rednecks in Virginia!"

The kids and I walked down the street to get my truck. I carried Olivia on my shoulders as I had done so much back home and Emily held my right hand with her left tightly and stared up at me the whole time. Christian walked on my left side and went on and on about what was going on on his favorite T.V. show and how many Yugio cards he now had.

When we had made it to the truck and shut the doors, almost in unison all three kids said, "Quick Daddy! Take us back to Virginia!"

"What?" I asked, floored by their request.

"We hate it here Daddy!" Emily, who had appointed herself my children's spokesperson years ago informed me. "We just tell Mommy we like it here so we don't hurt her feelings!"

It killed me to hear this as I drove the truck to the back of Amanda's apartment building and parked in the visitor's spot which had obviously been built for one of the so many compact cars I was seeing in the city. I had been thinking that the kids were making the most of this and enjoying their time in Seattle but I guess that had just been wishful thinking. I began finding that my experience of being reunited with my kids was one that was bitter sweet. I was ecstatic about seeing them but I was not happy about their living arraignments or how they honestly felt about them.

After parking the truck we went back upstairs. We went back to the kitchen so I could get a drink of water and awe at Emily's art work some more.

"I'm walking over to Starbucks to get a coffee!" Amanda scorned at me. "Don't you dare snoop through any of my stuff!"

"Amanda," I said in a defusing tone. "I am only hear to see my kids."

After Amanda left the apartment I did snoop in her refrigerator. I wanted to make sure that my kids were at least eating. I opened the door and found that this was not the case as there was only a half empty gallon of milk and a small block of cheddar cheese. This site broke my heart even more.

"So what do you kids want to do this evening?" I asked.

"Let's go over to the park!" Olivia said without having to think.

"Yeah Daddy!" Emily agreed. "Me and Livy can show you the game we play on the jungle gym!"

"Do you want to go to the park Christian?" I asked my son.

"I guess," he said, not seeming to care what we did as long as we were all together.

After Amanda came back with her coffee the five of us went to the park which was only a few blocks away. Amanda made sure to walk about ten yards ahead of the kids and me I'm sure to give the impression to anyone passing that she was not a part of our family. I guess she wanted to let her single status be known.

We made it to the park in just a few minutes and I was treated for an even larger freak and geek show here. I saw more men in skirts, multi colored hair and tattoos and piercings of various assortments. What I now saw also were same sexed couples walking through the park holding hands and at times kissing.

It had always been my attitude that whatever goes on between two mutually consenting adults was their business. However, I also had always believed that out of decency for the general public, it should be kept in the bedroom. I would have been no more happy about my kids witnessing hetero-sexual couples making out right in front of them at a local park.

I ignored the freak show as much as I could and focused on my children. It had been too long since I watched my girls play on the monkey bars. I loved pushing them on the swings and I got to do this again today. Christian, who had out grown the playground scene some time ago stayed at my side as we watched his sisters and he and I talked as if we were the best of friends, not father and son.

We stayed at the playground until dark. We then made our way back to the small apartment on Bellevue avenue. I was again carrying Olivia on my shoulders and holding Emily's hand the whole way back.

"So where are you staying tonight?" Amanda asked scornfully when we got into her apartment.

"Oh, sleep with me on my couch!" Olivia said. Emily then echoed the same request.

"No!" Amanda shouted.

"You are not staying here tonight!" she then said as she glared at me through piercing eyes.

The girls started begging her to let me stay, even coming to tears while doing so but Amanda would not budge from her position. She never changed her mind and it looked like I would be staying at the local Wal Mart. I wondered what sort of mural this one might have painted on the front. The scene of a local punk band with multi-colored hair perhaps?

I asked Amanda if she would at least have the decency of pointing me in the direction of the local Wal Mart. She quickly went about the task of writing me out directions.

"Here!" she said curtly as she thrust the small piece of paper she had written them on in my face.

I said my goodbyes to my kids as they cried and I did all I could do not to.

"Don't worry," I said with a hard fought up smile. "I'll be back first thing in the morning. When I get here why don't we load up your stuff and go camping for a week!"

I had been thinking of this idea the whole time we had been at the park. I wanted to get my kids out of this city that they didn't seem to be to happy in and get them back to a more familiar place. We had camped so much back in Virginia, and even in West Virginia and I was sure they would love the idea, which they did.

I left the apartment building, got in my truck as I was being glared at through a window buy a middle aged lady with hair shorter than my own military hair cut, who I assumed to be the manager, and drove off in search of the Wal Mart.

I followed Amanda's directions to a "T" but I found no Wal Mart. Amanda had sent me into the heart of the bad side of Seattle. All I could see by looking in any direction were bars and liquor stores.

I had adjusted well to the time changes as I had moved across the country but even at that it was now almost eleven o'clock west coast time and I was very tired after all of the energy I had used with my kids. I decided I would just pull into the side lot of a closed liquor store and spend the night there. That was until I turned the engine off and less than a minute later heard a distant gun shot!

I immediately started the truck back up and headed in the direction from which I had come. I didn't remember seeing any Wal Marts as I entered Seattle but I imagined anywhere on the outside of town would be better than here!

I had to drive for nearly an hour to get back to the outskirts of Seattle. It was now past mid night and I was not being too choosy about the lot I picked. I noticed a very large church off of the interstate to the right and took the next exit and made my way to this house of God.

I was actually able to pull around to the back of the building and park in the lot right up against the woods. I wasted no time in moving my gear to the cab of the truck and inflating my air mattress. I quickly unrolled my sleeping bag and climbed in for the night. I was quickly asleep.

In the middle of the night I was awakened by a loud crashing sound coming from the woods to my left. I opened my eyes but did not move. Then I heard it again. This time however, it was closer. Whatever it was it was coming my way.

This is when I realized I was in Big Foot country!

Everyone knew that the Pacihc North West was home to the largest and most reclusive man like land mammal in North America. The state of Washington actually recognizes Sasquatch, his Indian name, as one of the state's animals due to a hair sample that was found in the state years ago that did not match up to any other known animal through DNA testing.

I had seen way too many documentaries on this large, supposedly friendly creature in the past to know that he was real. Not only was he real but he was coming out of these Pacific North Western woods to pay me a visit as I lay there in the bed of my truck.

I thought about trying to climb out of the back of the truck and seek safety in the cab but the crashing sound had gotten too close. I could now hear it at the wood's edge. Big Foot was ready to make his way into the parking lot.

As I lay there, my heart racing, I was wishing I had hugged my kids one last time. I was wishing I had been a little more pleasant to Amanda. I was wishing I had called and talked to Maia one last time and I was feeling guilty for not having called my parents enough. I prayed to God that if he spared me from my impending doom I would be a better father, son, lover and friend!

As I was finishing my prayer I broke out in a sweet as I sensed this creature rush past my truck! I could hear the heavy panting outside that was coming from something that was not human! Winston Churchill often talked of Britain's "Finest Hour" during World War II. This, I knew, would be my "Final Hour."

After realizing that the beast had passed and was continuing its way across the parking lot toward the church, I sat up just enough to peer out of the window to my right.

I looked on with relief as I saw that my "Big Foot" was nothing more than a coyote chasing a cotton tail rabbit in the hopes of capturing a mid-night snack.

"Ah!" I sighed with relief as I laid back down.

I began chuckling to myself, much like Ichabod Crane in the Legend of Sleepy Hollow when he realized that what he had mistaken for the galloping hooves of the devil horse carrying the Headless Horseman was merely pussy willow buds thumping on the log beside his head. However, just as he had stopped laughing when he heard the cackling of the Horseman mocking him, I too stopped laughing when I heard a deep, monotone growl coming from the woods! It may have been another coyote. It may have been something else. Perhaps it was Big Foot. I made no attempt to find out and was fortunate enough to fall back to sleep with no more interruptions throughout the night.

24

I woke up early the next morning as the sun shone through the back glass of my truck's topper. I knew the kids would still be sleeping so I took my time in preparing a cup of Regina's tea and a few fried eggs on my Coleman stove. I sat on the tail gate and ate my breakfast, staring up into the woods behind me both wondering what it was I had heard the night before and still chuckling to myself over thinking the coyote I had seen was actually Big Foot coming to get me.

After eating I packed all of my gear and headed back into town. After weaving through the freaks and geeks of "The Hill" I again secured the guest parking spot behind Amanda's apartment building. I looked up and waved with a smile to the apartment manager who was gawking down at me. I guess she was not too used to my friendly southern ways because she never returned the gesture.

I called up to the apartment and just like the day before all three kids charged down the stairs to greet me. They told me they had been up for hours waiting on me. I guess I was bringing them as much excitement as any Christmas morning ever could.

We wasted no time in carrying their belongings down from the small apartment and putting them in the back of the truck. The girls made sure to pack one bag full of clothes and another full of stuffed animals each. Christian had his bag of clothes and a duffle bag full of Yugio cards and assorted video games for his game boy. I had always limited his time allowed on video games back home but this week I would just overlook this. This was to be a time of joy for us all, not a time for me to be playing knit picking father.

I was too happy to be making my way out of the city and my kids seemed very relieved as well. As we began climbing up the Cascade Mountains the kids informed me that their mother had never taken them this far out of the city.

"We never go anywhere!" Emily said.

Once about twenty miles out of the city, we stopped at a shopping center in a small community to buy groceries for our trip. After having come through this way the day before I knew it would be our last chance to do so.

We went into the store and when the kids asked me what they could get I told them they could get whatever they wanted. They were overjoyed with this concept.

"I'm getting some Doritos!" Olivia said. Doritos had always been her favorite snack and she informed me that she had not had Doritos since leaving Virginia.

"I'm getting strawberries!" Emily said. She loved strawberries more than anyone I knew.

"What are you getting?" I asked Christian.

"I don't know," he said. "I'll find something." I knew he would come back with a bag of snack sized candy bars of some sort.

Christian and Emily took off together to pick out their goodies and Olivia stayed with me and rode in the cart. She was starting to get too big for this but it reminded both of us of all of our shopping sprees back home so neither of us thought she should get out and walk.

After grabbing two bags of Doritos for Olivia, one Ranch flavored and the other Cheddar Cheese, we then began focusing on the necessities like bread, milk, lunch meat, canned soups etc. Half way through the store we met up with Christian and Emily. Emily was carrying three quarts of strawberries and a big bag of plumbs.

"I got these for you Daddy!" she said as she held up the purple fruits.

Sure enough, Christian had a bag of bite sized Milky Way candy bars. I too had always kept an eye on the amount of junk food my kids ate back in Virginia but I was willing to let this slide now.

After getting a few more necessities we made our way to the front of the store and paid for our purchases. We spent almost $200 on groceries. We may have bought too much but remembering the site of Amanda's refrigerator it didn't bother me. I would make sure that my kids ate like royalty over the next week.

We made our way back to the truck, loaded our groceries in the back and then continued climbing the Cascade Mountains in search of a place to camp. After taking several wrong turns that led nowhere we eventually made it to Lake Easton State Park on top of the mountain. We were about seventy miles east of Seattle.

I went into the small park office and paid for a tent site that we would occupy for a week. After getting back in the truck the kids and I drove around the park to check it out before going to our site. We were happy to find that there was a small beach with a swimming area at the lake as well as a playground. We decided that we would return to these facilities after we set up camp.

We rolled around to our camp site and quickly began setting up the larger of my two tents. We had used this tent to camp in as a family before and it provided plenty of space for all of us.

While we were setting up the tent I couldn't help but remember the giant grass hoppers in New Orleans as well as all the tree frogs and lizards. I told the kids about them and Emily especially seemed really excited.

"Did you take any pictures?" she asked.

"Of coarse I did crazy Em," I told her. I then went to the truck and took out my digital camera so I could show her the evidence.

"Whoa!" she said when she saw the sight of one of the grass hoppers I had taken a picture of while holding a dollar bill up behind it in the background.

"That thing is huge!" she exclaimed. "I wish you would have brought me one for a pet!"

"I knew you would have wanted one Emily," I said. "I was thinking while I was there about how lucky those critters were that you weren't there with me because you would have captured them all."

"Heck yeah I would have!" she said. "I would have put them all in your truck!"

"I bet you would have," I chuckled, knowing she would have.

After getting the tent set up the kids dove into our stock pile of groceries. It was time for lunch but instead of enforcing a healthy meal of some sort I sat back and watched with joy as Olivia dug into her bag of Cheddar Cheese flavored Doritos, Emily sucked down succulent strawberry after succulent strawberry, and Christian devoured one miniature candy bar after another.

"Mom never lets us eat like this!" Olivia said as she chomped on her Doritos.

"You never used to either," Christian said in my direction. "What is up with you Dad?"

"Don't get too used to it," I told them. "I haven't seen you for a while so I'm a little soft. I'm sure I'll harden up after a day or two."

After finishing their food the kids all wanted to go swimming.

"Did you bring your bathing suites?" I asked.

"I did!" Christian said as he began digging in one of his duffle bags to find his trunks.

"I knew I forgot something!" Emily said, smacking the palm of her right hand against her forehead. "Livy!" she shouted toward her little sister. "You were supposed to remind me!"

"Hey, don't yell at me!" Olivia said just as temperamentally. "Your not the boss of me!" she then said. This seemed to be a popular saying these days among second graders.

"It's ok girls," I interjected. "We're roughing it. You can just wear some shorts and a t-shirt. We're not trying to impress anyone."

"Yippee!" Emily yelled. She had always been so excitable. Again, I have all of the emergency room bills to prove it.

We waited for Christian to change into his swimming trunks and then we headed to the lake's beach. There were about two dozen other campers swimming and sun bathing here and the kids wasted no time in getting into the water.

"Ahhhhh!" they all said in unison as they pulled up their shoulders and opened their mouths wide.

"This water is freezing!" Emily stated.

"Do you want to just get out and play on the playground?" I asked them.

"No way man!" Emily said. "We're swimming!"

I sat on the beach and watched my children as they played in the water. I had walked into it up to my knees and found that they were right. The water was very cold. I had to wonder if this lake was glacier fed like many of the lakes and streams in this part of the country were.

After sitting in the sun on the beach's soft sand for a while, made up mostly of fragmented limestone, I again walked into the water up to my knees.

"Look over here Daddy," Emily said in a somewhat mischievous tone.

When I turned to my right to look her way I knew that something was in store for me as she offered me her crooked little grin.

"Get 'em!" I heard Christian yell from behind me just before he jumped on my shoulders and Olivia took me out at the knees. My kids had booby trapped me and I was now laying down completely in this chilling water.

"What the!" I yelled while making only half an effort to get away. I wanted to make them think I was trying to free myself from their grips while giving them the joy of thinking I could not.

Emily made her way over to get in on the action too. She began splashing the lake's ice cold water in my face and then dove on my head when I shut my eyes, forcing my head to go under water.

Since they had gotten me completely wet, I stayed in the water and played with the kids for a long time. I was freezing but I didn't let that stop me. Besides, it was warm enough on the beach that all we had to do was get out and lay in the sand for just a minute or two before warming back up.

After an hour's worth of swimming we made our way over to the playground. I took turns pushing Emily and Olivia on the tire swing as Christian would chase what ever girl I was not pushing at the time around on the jungle gym. We were having as much fun as he had ever had back in Virginia. For now, we may as well have been back in Virginia. Neither the kids nor I were thinking about our situation of being separated and of them living in what I would consider to be unde-sirable living standards in Seattle.

After exhausting ourselves on the playground we got back in the truck and made our way back to the tent site. We all grabbed some dry clothes and walked over to the shower building that was only about thirty yards away from our site. We changed into dry clothes and then headed back to our camp.

As evening drew on we ate again. This time though I made sure to be a little more strict and made the kids eat some real food before devouring their goodies. We all ate either canned spaghetti and meat balls, sandwiches, or both. Afterward the kids had their snacks of choice and I ate some of the plumbs Emily had been thoughtful enough to get for me.

With about an hour of daylight left we decided to go for a walk on one of the many trails in the camp ground. We chose a trail that ran along the bank of the river that was flowing swiftly below the dam that blocked this river to form the lake.

We walked up the trail about a mile, then turned around and walked back. When we got back to the bank Christian decided to go back to the tent, which was in sight of the trail but the girls wanted to throw rocks into and play in the river. I stayed with the girls.

As we were standing there on the bank of the river a baby cotton tail rabbit made its way to us.

"Look girls," I said in a hushed tone as I motioned toward the bunny.

"Don't move and be very quiet," I told them.

The girls didn't move, which was very surprising of Emily. I was afraid she would try to capture this small, delicate creature but she did not. The rabbit made it's way to the girl's feet, sniffed them, then came over to me and did the same. As unconcerned as this rabbit had been in approaching us it left us just the same.

While the girls were throwing rocks into the river my cell phone rang. It was Maia.

I asked my girls if they minded if I took the call and they told me it was ok. As much as I loved Maia, I did not want to take time away from my kids to talk to her if it was going to be an issue with them. They were so into throwing rocks however, that it wasn't.

"Hello beautiful Maia," I said when I answered the phone.

"Hi boyfriend!" she said. "How are you?"

"I am wonderful!" I told her. "I have been with my kids the whole day and I am happier than I have been since I saw you last!"

"That is wonderful Kevin," she said. "I know how much you've missed them and I am glad you guys are finally getting to spend some time together."

Maia and I talked for only a few minutes as it was now growing dark and I needed to get the girls back up to the tent.

Before getting off of the phone with Maia I had told her about all the freaks and geeks I had seen in Seattle.

"Yeah!" I said. "They all have purple and blue and green and pink hair! I have never seen a bigger collection of miscreants in my life!"

After hanging up the phone I turned around and saw that Olivia was crying.

"What's wrong baby?" I asked as I made my way to her and kneeled down to give her a hug.

"I don't like my hair being pink!" she cried. "I didn't want it to be pink but Mommy tricked me and told me it would wash out in a week and now it is always gong to be pink!"

I realized that Olivia had heard what I had said to Maia. I felt terrible.

"Oh Honey!" I consoled her. "You hair is beautiful. It's ok for little girls to have pink hair. That's why you can buy pink haired baby dolls in the stores."

"Really?" she said, beginning to regain her composure.

"Yes Honey," I continued. "It's just weird when grown ups have pink hair. Honey, you are the most beautiful little girl in the world regardless of what color your hair is and Daddy loves you just as much as when your hair was brown."

With that I picked her up into my arms, took Emily by the hand and we all made our way back to the tent. I never had to worry about Emily getting jealous whenever I told Olivia she was the most beautiful girl in the world. Emily was a Tomboy and Olivia was a girly girl. Whenever I did complement Olivia due to some feminine attribute Emily usually just rolled her eyes. She often referred to her little sister as "high maintenance."

When we got back to the tent we found that Christian was already asleep inside. Emily quickly laid down on one side of a futon cushion we had brought from one of their couches and I laid Olivia down on the other side. She was already asleep. She had fallen asleep while I carried her up the hill. Emily was asleep in five minutes.

I went outside and laid down in my portable hammock that I had sat up at this camp site just as I had back in New Orleans. I gazed up through the branches of the tall pine trees growing in the park and into the night's sky. The stars were out in full on this clear summer night. Without any artificial light coming from the city that lay seventy miles to our west I could see the stars as clearly as I could from the country back in Virginia. I laid there and thanked God for seeing me safely across the country and reuniting me with my children. After my prayers I went into the tent and laid in the middle of my girls.

I did not go immediately to sleep as tired as I was. I lied there and looked at my children as they slept. This was something I always loved to do back in Virginia. I was always humored by how Emily would always curl up into a little ball and not move through the whole night. Olivia did just the opposite. She would sprawl out spread eagle and kick like crazy. Most nights when she crawled into my bed after a bad dream or when she was sick I would end up on the couch or the floor, but definitely somewhere else, much like the time when she spent six months with me in the living room when Amanda and I were splitting up.

I never really watched Christian sleep. With him I listened. He always breathed really loud. So loud at times, that it woke me up in the middle of the night. He talked a lot in his sleep too. I always tried to make out what he was saying so I could tell him about it the next morning but it was always incoherent gibberish. In spite of Christian's loud breathing and Olivia's kicking I was soon fast asleep myself.

25

The kids and I spent the next day much like we had the day before. We went to the lake to swim in the icy waters and then played on the playground once we were finished swimming. We would come back to the camp site to eat every other hour or so, and I did firm up and enforce the rules when it came to eating real food over junk food. Then we would head back to the lake for more swimming. By the end of this second day the kids and I looked like walking prunes with wrinkled up fingers and toes from spending so much time in the water.

We went for another walk on a different trail this evening. We didn't see any bunny rabbits but we enjoyed our time just the same.

After our walk we all grabbed a change of clothes, a couple bars of soap and a couple of towels and made our way over to the shower house. The girls went into their's and Christian and I went into the men's room. All of us were done pretty quickly except for Olivia. She loved to take her time in the shower, modeling after her mother no doubt.

Christian decided to walk back over to the tent and Emily and I stayed behind to wait on Olivia. As I sat outside of the shower house listening to Olivia sing the latest Carrie Underwood hit while she showered, Emily began turning over rocks and fallen tree limbs to see what sort of vermin she could harass.

"Emily, what would you do if you turned one of those rocks over and there was a rattle snake under it?" I asked her.

"I'd catch him!" she said with the voice of excitement.

"That is what I'm worried about," I told her. "How about not turning over any more rocks but if you find a critter on the ground you can catch it as long as it's not a rattle snake, ok?"

"Ah Dad!" she said, disappointed.

Emily did manage to catch two moths that were hanging out on the side of the shower house. For some reason when she stuck them on her shirt sleeve they just sat there and didn't even try to get away. When Olivia finally made her way out of the shower house, now humming a Natasha Bedingfield tune, Emily took one of the moths from her sleeve and put it on Olivia's.

"Thanks Emily," Olivia said appreciatively.

Olivia usually couldn't stand bugs. I guess she had come a long way in the past couple of months.

The girls and I then joined their brother at the tent site. He had gone in the tent and begun playing one of his video games on his Game boy. Again, as much as I believe video games, like cable, turn a child's brain to cheese I wasn't about to say anything to him for doing it.

"So do you guys want to hear a ghost story before going to bed tonight?" I asked the kids.

"Yeah!" Emily and Christian shouted in unison.

"No Daddy," Olivia said, tilting her head down and looking up at me with her big puppy dog eyes as she offered me that pouting lower lip of hers.

"Ah come on drama queen," Emily scoffed at her. "You know you want to hear one you just want attention."

"Hey!" Olivia whined.

"It's ok Liv," I said. "I won't tell one if your scared." I was playing along with her drama. I knew that as harsh as Emily's assessment of her little sister's actions had been, it was a correct assessment.

"Ok Daddy," Olivia finally gave in. "But only if I get to sit on your lap while you tell it."

"OK sweetie," I said.

"God Livy!" Emily chided.

"This is a story called, 'The Ghosts of Turkey Ridge,'" I began with my best Vincent Price imitation.

"We've already heard this one Dad," Christian said while rolling his eyes.

"Shut up Christian! I like it! Tell it again Dad!" Emily said all in one quick breath.

"More than ten years ago," I continued, "While I was in college, I had decided to go back to Richwood to go Turkey hunting. I went in on a Friday evening having hoped to get in sooner but I had been held up taking an exam."

"When I got to my parent's house I decided that though there was not much daylight left I would hit the woods anyway. If nothing else I might get onto some turkey tracks that I could return to the next morning."

"Is this really a true story Dad?" Olivia asked.

"Of coarse it's true Livy!" Emily answered for me. "You know Dad turkey hunts all the time so shut up and listen to the story!"

"Emily," I said. "You really need to stop telling people to shut up."

"Just shut up and tell the story Dad!" Emily said. She immediately started laughing and said, "Dad, you know I'm just kidding! Ha Ha Ha!"

"Ok," I said, continuing with the story. "I drove to the mouth of Saxmon Hollow on the edge of town. This was one of my favorite places to hunt. The top of the mountain was actually named 'Turkey Ridge' because of all the turkeys that lived there. They seemed to spend the fall and winter on one end of the long ridge of the mountain top and go to the other end in the spring when they laid their eggs."

"After parking my car I got my old twenty gauge single shot shotgun out and hit the woods. I soon made it to the game trail that was on top of the mountain, stretching its way across Turkey Ridge."

"I soon found where a flock of turkeys had been feeding, which was obvious by all of the turned up leaves, and I began to track them across the ridge. I knew I was running out of daylight but the scratching and tracks were fresh so I decided to push on anyway, hoping I could actually jump the flock before dark."

"Just before it was too dark to see I heard the roar of a shot gun come from no more than fifty yards ahead of me! Someone had beaten me to the flock!"

"As I walked on to investigate I was met by an old man with a hen turkey strung over his shoulder."

"'Did you bust the flock up pretty good?'" I asked him.

"'Naw,'" he grumbled. "'You should be able to come back up here in the morning and call 'em back in.'"

"'I think I might go out there and call a bit tonight and see if I can find where they roost.'" I informed this older gentleman.

"Daddy?" Olivia asked.

"Yes Honey?" I said.

"Was the guy as old as you are now?"

"No honey," I chuckled. "He was even older."

"Wow," my little girl said with awe. She had a way of making 33 feel older than it was.

"Anyway," I continued as Emily just glared at Olivia for having interrupted me again. "The old man told me that I had better get out of these woods before dark. When I told him I wasn't worried because I knew the place like the back of my hand and that I had a flash light, he said, 'Boy! They's things up here you don't know nothin' 'bout and aint no flashlight gonna keep ya safe from 'em.'"

"With that the old man was on his way."

"Whatever! I thought to myself. That sure was one crazy old coot!"

"I walked about another hundred yards and tried to call the turkeys with my diaphragm turkey call, the kind you put in the top of your mouth. I called several times but got no answer so I decided I would leave the woods. It was now dark so I got my flashlight out only to find that the batteries were dead!"

"What did you do Daddy?" Olivia asked.

"He walked by the light of the full moon Olivia! You know this story!" Emily said firmly.

"That's right Livy," I went on. "I walked by the light of the full moon."

"The moon was full on this dark October night, just before Halloween and there was not a cloud in the sky. This made it easy for me to get through the woods without a light."

"When I had gotten about half way to the car I noticed the light coming from several fires down the hill below me. Even though I could see by the light of the moon I decided to go down and ask these apparent campers if they had a flashlight I could borrow and then return to them in the morning when I came back again to go turkey hunting."

"As I drew close to the fires I stopped when I sensed something was not right. When I took a closer look I saw that there were about a dozen men in some sort of uniforms. I drew closer and it looked to me that the men were wearing the same uniforms the southern army wore during the civil war."

"Mommy says the people in the south think we're still fighting the civil war," Olivia offered. "Is that true Daddy?"

"No honey, that's not true," I told her.

"Anyway," I said again. "As I got even closer to the fires and the men surrounding them I could actually hear them talking."

"'We can make it to the river by the end of the day tomorrow if we start early enough,'" a gentleman who appeared to be the leader said."

"I couldn't figure out what river they were talking about. The closest big river was the Gauley but it was only 15 miles away. You could make it there in twenty minutes if you drove the speed limit."

"'We can meet up with reinforcements there and we'll be out of this pickle,'" the apparent leader spoke again."

"Something was going on here I thought. I didn't know what it was but I didn't want to find out. There were no civil war reenactments in this area. I didn't even know of any battles that had been fought in this area."

"As I started to make my way back up the hill I stepped on a dry branch. As it snapped the men at the camp took noticed and peered through the darkness in my direction. The leader of the group gave some sort of hand signal and all of the men scrambled to grab what looked like flint lock muskets and quickly spread out across their perimeter."

"I stood as motionless as I ever had for more than twenty minutes, not making a sound. After about this long the men dispersed and went back to sitting by their fires. I continued making my way up the hill but this time was sure not to carelessly step on another branch."

"After making my way to the top of the hill I continued following the path to my car. I got in it and drove home as quickly as possible."

"When I made it back to the house my dad asked me if I had seen anything. I told him I had trailed a flock of turkeys to roost but I did not tell him about the strange men I had seen gathered around the camp fires. He decided that he would go with me the next morning."

"When my dad and I made it to the woods the next day I told a little white lie. I told him I had seen the turkeys down over the hill where I had actually seen the men. I wanted to go down the hill and investigate the scene with the light of day on my side."

"When my dad and I made it to the spot of the camp fires of the night before I couldn't believe what I saw. Or should I say I couldn't believe what I didn't see?"

"There was no evidence that anyone had been there the night before! There were no abandoned fire pits and the ground was not pressed down anywhere from where tents had been."

"Did your dad think you were lying about the turkeys?" Olivia asked.

"Livy!" Emily shouted. "Would you please just shut," looking at me and thinking of what she was about to say, she then corrected herself and said, "Would you please just be quite and stop interrupting?"

"No Liv, he never thought I was lying about the turkeys," I told Olivia.

"Anyway," I said for the umpteenth time, "My dad said, "'Huh, look at these.'"

"I went over to see what he was talking about and found that there were several rock piles about six feet long and three feet wide. They had been there for a long time as moss and weeds were growing in them and a tree was actually growing out of the center of one of them."

"'What is this?'" I asked my dad.

"'Well,'" he began. "'It could be one of two things,'" he said.

"He informed me that there could have been an old home site at this place years ago. He told me that when homesteaders would set up their properties they would often clear all the rocks away from their garden sites and pile them in piles like this to later come back and use for fencing."

"'Look around and see if you can find any sort of foundation from an old house,'" he said.

"We looked and looked for about ten minutes but found nothing."

"'You said it could be one of two things,'" I pointed out to my father when our efforts to find the foundation of a house failed." "'What was the other thing?'"

"'Well,'" he began." "'Back during the civil war when soldiers got killed, any survivors would often burry their fallen comrades in shallow graves then mark them with rock piles so they could later return and recover the bodies.'"

"'Really?'" I said."

"'Yeah,'" he continued." "'You know, it's been rumored since the days of the civil war that a small group of confederate soldiers where heading toward the Gauley river to meet a larger group of soldiers but got lost somewhere in these mountains and where never seen again.'"

"'Really?'" I said again."

"'Yeah,'" he went on." "'The story goes that a group of Union soldiers over-took them in the woods and decimated them.'"

"So basically, what I had seen the night before, the ghosts of Turkey Ridge, where the ghosts of the confederate soldiers who had gotten lost and slain in these woods 150 years before."

"As much as I loved hunting turkeys on this mountain I never returned to do so again."

"That is creepy," Christian said as I ended the story.

"Not as creepy as the first time you told it," Emily said as she made her way into the tent and her little pink Barbie Doll sleeping bag that she never really liked.

"Daddy, I'm scared," Olivia said as she snuggled up tightly against me.

"I'll keep you safe honey," I said hugging her, letting her think that I was buying into her dramatics.

Christian, Olivia and myself then joined Emily in the tent and we all slept soundly through the night, in spite of the tall tell I had just told.

26

The next few days with my children at Lake Easton State Park were the happiest I had known since my children had left me for Seattle. We spent our days at the lake swimming in the ice cold water and making sand castles and volcanoes on the beach. We spent hours at the playground. I twirled Olivia around over and over in the tire swing, watching her pink hair flap out with the beauty of butterfly wings. I watched as Emily caught nearly every insect in the state of Washington and I listened to Christian tell me all about the upcoming West Virginia Mountaineer football season. Though he had moved away from West Virginia when he was only three years old, he remained loyal to the Mountaineers.

At the camp site I loved hearing the beautiful music of, "Daddy! Daddy! Daddy!" This was the chorus. The versus were "Make me some Ramon Noodles. Open me a can of soup. Walk me to the bathroom. Let's go swimming again."

I did not realize how much I had missed being a father. I know that these constant demands from children drive a lot of parents crazy, as they did me at times, but for the most part I thrived on it.

When the day finally rolled around that I was to take the kids back to their mother's small apartment in Seattle I was not too happy about it. I prolonged it as much as I could. We didn't leave the park until late in the afternoon and we stopped to eat twice during the 70 mile trip back to the city. I knew that the kids and I were not even hungry when we stopped the second time but I did not want to part ways with them. I was able to lure them into a Burger King on this second stop with the prospects of the cheap toy that came in the kid's meal.

After making it back to "The Hill," I parked in the small visitor parking spot behind the apartment building and we waited nearly half an hour before Amanda came down to the back door of the building to let us in. All of our actions were closely surveyed by the apartment manager the whole time. I waved a couple of times, but just like the time before I got no response.

Amanda finally came down to let us in. She claimed she did not hear the phone ringing because it was in the other of her two main rooms. I didn't buy it and didn't really care what the real reason for her delay was because it had given me more time with the kids.

We carried all of the children's belongings up to the apartment and then Amanda pulled me outside to talk to me. She was attempting to get me to put in writing that I disagreed with the judge's decision back in Virginia and that I was surrendering to her full custody of our children.

"Heck no!," was my response to her when she asked me to do this.

"Kevin," she stated. "You can't take care of the kids! You are homeless, your getting ready to be gone for six months playing soldier and you'll probably go to Iraq when you are finished with that!"

"No one knows if I'll be in Iraq or not Amanda," I argued.

"Oh bull s—t Kevin!" she continued with her tirade. "Your buddy Bush is sending everyone dumb enough to enlist over there as quick as he can get them there! You probably won't come back if you go over there anyway!"

"I'm glad you have so much confidence in my capabilities," I told her.

"Kevin!" she said. "My mother and I went out and bought a life insurance policy on your dumb a—the day you told me you were enlisting in the Guard! She's paying the premiums and if you get killed where splitting the death benefit!"

"That is sick Amanda!" I said disgusted.

"Hey," she began dismissively. "I have to look out for myself!"

"I know you do," I agreed. "But it sounds like it is something you are betting on.... Like you hope I get killed."

"You are of no use to me alive Kevin!" she said coldly.

"Did you ever think I might be of some use to the kids?" I asked. "Why do you want them to grow up without a father so badly? I mean, you moved all the way across the country, and your trying to get them out here permanently. Don't you see any benefits of them growing up with both parents actively involved in their lives?"

"Kevin!" she stated. "It is the father's job to make money and send it to the kids. It is the mother's job to raise them!"

"So my only value to them is financially?" I asked, already knowing the answer.

"Of coarse it is!" she said.

This was coming from a semi-feminist. Amanda was great at playing the role of feminist yet was also able to switch back to the "damsel in distress" mode when it behooved her to do so.

I saw that I was getting nowhere with Amanda and I decided not to waste any more time arguing with her. I was worn out from arguing over the past couple of years and it did no one any good.

"I'm going up to see the kids," I told her in an attempt to end the conversation.

I walked back in the apartment building and up to Amanda's apartment. I sat on one of the three couches in the small living room and positioned myself between Christian and Emily. Olivia came over and sat on my lap. They were watching the latest episode of Hannah Montana on television.

Shortly after I had sat down and gotten comfortable with my children Amanda barged in the door and said, "Kevin, I think it is time for you to leave!"

"Not yet Mommy," Olivia said.

"Kevin," Amanda began, looking at me, not Olivia. "Leave! You are not welcome in my home!"

Not wanting the kids to have to witness a scene I got up to leave. The kids and I all exchanged hugs and kisses. The girls cried as I was leaving and again, I painted on that hard fought up smile that was as fake as Amanda's feminist views when she attempted to use them.

As I was exiting the apartment Amanda decided to get in one more cheap shot in front of the kids.

"You're a thief!" she said. "You still owe me the money from your retirement plan!"

She was correct in her accusation. She was entitled to half of my IRA and I had used the money in an attempt to save our house and to feed the kids while she was gone for six months and was sending nothing back to help out. I intended to start making her installment payments once I shipped off to basic training and began drawing an income form the military.

"I'll start sending you money as soon as I get to Fort Benning," I said in a non-confrontational tone.

I took one look back at my kids, which inspired them to come hug and kiss me again. I then said my last goodbye and headed down stairs to my truck.

"Your truck is going to be towed if you are not out of here in ten minutes!" the apartment manager yelled down to me from her window. It turned out she could communicate.

"I'm leaving now Mam," I said with a pleasant southern accent.

"Don't call me Mam!" she said just before slamming her window shut.

I made my way off of "The Hill" and eventually out of Seattle. I was traveling east now on interstate 90, the same road that had gotten me to Seattle. After a little more than an hour I passed Lake Easton State Park. I thought of the great time the kids and I had had during our week there. I wish the week had not ended so soon.

When I got to the intersection of I90 and I82 I remained on I90 heading east. I had come up from Oregon on I82 so I was now venturing into unraveled territory for me on the trip.

I am sure the scenery between this major intersection and Spokane Washington which was some 150 miles away was as beautiful as it had been through the rest of the state but I paid no attention to it. All I could think about where my children. My heart was breaking thinking about being away from them again and also thinking about their living situation in that small apartment back in Seattle.

As I drove through the Cascade Mountains of the Pacific Northwest I tried to think back to where everything had gone wrong. Amanda and I really struggled financially in the early years of our marriage, but by the time we split up we were doing really well. I had managed to become successful as a stock broker and she never had to work. She only did work occasionally because she wanted to. It seemed that we were taking vacations regularly, almost quarterly, whether we spent a week in a cabin in the mountains of West Virginia or a week in a condo at the Outer Banks of North Carolina.

I had never been an abusive husband physically or mentally and Amanda had always been a good wife and a loving mother. I know that our views and core values were changing as we aged and I knew too that they were heading in opposite directions. I was wishing I had been just a little more tolerant of her views and perhaps less sharp in mine. However, I had to accept the fact that if I were to change who I was for someone else that I truly would not be living. I just hated this so much for the kids.

I had to remember too that I had found Maia. If Amanda and I had never split up I would not have Maia today as the love of my life. If only there could be some sort of middle of the road where I could be happy with Maia but not have to watch my kids go through what they were going through. Rarely though does real life ever seem to offer this middle road.

I drove on for hours actually crossing into the northern pan handle of Idaho before I was tired of hurting. A question I had begun asking myself years before when I was in a state of emotional pain was simply, "Have you had enough yet?"

I had had enough of this pain for now so I decided to do the best thing I knew to do about it. Pray! As Abraham Lincoln was known to say on several occasions, "At many times I have found myself driven to my knees in prayer, simply because I had nowhere else to go."

I certainly could not take to my knees as I drove into Idaho but I certainly did decide to pray. I asked God to please get me and my children through the rest of these tough times. I thanked him for getting us through them so far and asked that he guide us through the rest of the way.

As I ended my prayer I began ascending a steep hill. After saying "Amen" I looked up and was astonished at what I saw!

I was driving through fields of wheat and scattered throughout the fields were large irrigation systems. They basically consisted of long rows of PVC pipes that sat about six feet off the ground on giant tractor wheels, making it easy for the farmers to move the systems.

As I looked up the sun was beginning to set just behind the top of the hill. All of the irrigation systems were running and the sun light refracting through the water created rainbows, dozens of them, all over the fields ahead of me. I had never seen this many rainbows in my life.

Again, I do not believe in coincidences. I took this as an answer to prayer. In the bible the rainbow is symbolic as a promise to Noah after the great flood that God would never destroy the world again. He would not put man through the torment of the forty days and forty nights of non-stop rains.

I took these rainbows in the wheat fields of Northern Idaho as a sign from God that I had made it through the roughest of my turmoil. I felt as if he were telling me that things again would never be this bad.

I felt put to ease as I pulled into the Wal Mart parking lot in Coeur d' Alene Idaho, only fifteen miles across the state line from Washington. In spite of my woes of the day I was able to climb into the back of the truck and get to sleep with relative ease. I think too that I had been emotionally exhausted from the day's events.

27

When I woke up in Coeur d' Alene the next day it was a Saturday morning. I was still tired both physically and emotionally from being with my kids for a week and then having to leave them so I decided I would spend this Saturday morning as leisurely as I had so many back at my house in Virginia, when I had a house.

The bed of my truck was now my living room. My bathroom was an empty gallon jug for liquids that I was always sure to dump and rinse each morning and Wal Mart restrooms and road side rest stops served for solids. My kitchen was my tail gate and my refrigerator a large, red cooler. I had a personal office too; the passenger seat of my truck. However, just as I had at home in Virginia I did most of my paper work in the living room, or truck bed.

On this lazy Saturday morning, the first thing I did was fill out an application for employment with A G Edwards out of their office back in Virginia. I had talked at length about going into recruiting for the National Guard after completing basic training with Master Sergeant Spicer, the gentleman in charge of recruiting for our part of Virginia before I left for my trip but I was torn between which avenue to take after completing my training. I felt as if filling out the A G Edwards application at least would make me feel better about my children's situation. It made me feel as if I was being as pro-active as I could for the time being.

After filling out the application and dropping it off in the mail box in front of the Wal Mart I returned to the truck and ate a bowl of cereal. I then propped my pillows up on the back of the cab and began writing of the previous weeks activities in my journal. I had propped the topper up and left the tail gate down to allow the cool breeze to flow into the truck and keep me comfortable. Though it was the middle of the summer, the breeze and lack of humidity made it feel like Virginia in the fall.

As I wrote in my journal, and then switched over to reading more of McCullough's "1776," I would glance up and wave at passersby when I could feel them staring. It felt no different than when I would often waive at my old neighbors when they drove by when I was reading on my front porch in Virginia. I had really gotten used to my state of homelessness.

After spending literally hours reading and writing in the back of my truck I decided I would find a Laundromat. I had not done laundry yet on my journey and I had run out of clean clothes.

I drove into Coeur d' Alene and stopped first at a dry cleaners that I thought might also house some washing machines and dryers. I was greeted at the counter by a lovely middle aged woman and a beautiful girl in her late teens if not early twenties that I was assuming was her daughter. They looked a lot alike.

As I was asking them for directions to the closest Laundromat I could hear yelling coming from an office located just behind them.

"You cost me five hundred God d—n dollars!" I heard a man yell in an angry tone.

"Go back out to the main road and take a right," the older woman said, acting as if she did not hear any shouting at all.

"Five hundred God d—n dollars!!!" the angry voice came again.

"Sounds like someone lost five hundred dollars and aren't very happy about it," I said, smiling in the direction of the girl. She looked at me as if she hadn't heard a word I said, or didn't care if she had. It made me wonder if this was common practice around here.

The angry man then walked to the door of the office, gave me an angry look, then slammed the door and continued his tirade on what I was assuming was a non-productive employee.

"Go three blocks then take a left," the older woman continued.

Then I heard a loud bang as if the angry man had either punched the wall or slammed whoever the victim of his tirade was into it.

"Take a right at the first light and it will be on the left," the woman said, finishing her directions.

"Thanks," I said. "See ya later."

I looked over at the younger girl and smiled. She actually smiled back, revealing her beautifully perfect teethe. Her actions were met with a snarl and an unapproving look by the other woman who had basically just confirmed she was the mother. I certainly did not want to get this girl into trouble with the angry man in the office so I quickly left and headed for the Laundromat.

I found the Laundromat with no problem and was happy to notice a "help wanted" sign on the door. I went in and began loading my laundry into one of the washing machines and was greeted by a really friendly and somewhat attractive woman about my age. She talked me through the process of exchanging my money in for a store card that was required to be used with the machines.

When I asked her about the "help wanted" sign and let her know I was interested in short term employment her attitude changed. She was still friendly toward me but no longer as conversational as she had been. I didn't know if she thought I was hitting on her or if she didn't want to reveal too much about herself to me in the event we would become co-workers, but there was a definite change.

"The owner is out of town and won't be back until next week," she told me.

"Oh," I said. "This won't work then. I should be crossing the Mississippi River heading back east again by next week."

"Where are you heading?" she asked.

I then told her about my trip. I told her where I had been so far and what I had seen.

"That sounds so exciting," she said, beginning to warm up again.

"I'm just a homeless guy trying to make the most of my circumstances," I told her.

"Homeless?" she asked.

"Yeah," I continued. "I lost my house as the result of a pretty nasty divorce and I'm now living out of my truck. I decided I may as well drive all over the country and see this place."

With that she informed me she had some paper work she was behind on and quickly made her way to the small office in the back of the Laundromat.

"Note to self," I said out loud. "Don't tell pretty girls about all of your disfunctionalisms in the first conversation."

I then chuckled as I continued loading my laundry and inserted the store card. I had seen a Kinko's right across the street so I decided that while my laundry was in the wash I would walk across the street and check my emails.

I made my way across the street and was greeted at the Kinko's by a friendly lady in her late forties or early fifties named Barbie. She informed me that I would need to buy minutes for the internet on a Kinko's card. What was it about this town and store cards?

When I told her I would just pass because I didn't want to deal with filling out all of the personal information required to get a store card she looked around to make sure no one was looking then handed me her employee card.

"Here," she said. "You seem like a nice guy. Take as much time as you need."

I thanked her kindly and then went to the computer and checked my email. After emailing my friends and family of my whereabouts I went through and read the few emails that were of any importance and then deleted nearly one hundred spam's. I used spam guard but it seemed as if the spammers were always figuring out ways around it.

After finishing on the computer I went back to the counter and talked to Barbie for about twenty minutes. Barbie informed me, after finding out I was in the National Guard that her practically adopted son, a good friend of her real son, had been to Iraq twice already and wanted badly to go back. He felt his work there was important and Barbie felt the same.

I told her of my trip up to this point and she told me that her husband had actually gone to New Orleans with their church and helped rebuild houses too. I happened to have my digital camera in my pocket so I showed her some pictures I had taken when I was in New Orleans. She seemed especially interested in the ones of the giant grass hoppers.

Our conversation eventually made its way back to the war on terror. Barbie seemed to understand the threat posed by our enemies and was in full support of the war. However, her manager had made her way to within ear shot of our conversation and at this point told Barbie that she needed to get to work. I was assuming that perhaps this young lady was not quite as supportive.

I left the Kinko's so as not to get Barbie in trouble and headed back across the street to check my clothes. When I got there, I was happy to find that my clothes were finished washing. I put them into a dryer, inserted my store card to get the machine started and then headed out to my truck. One thing I had not done while in my "living room" this morning was balance my check book. I wanted to see how low on funds I was running.

When I had completed this task the numbers proved grim. It was not a question of "if" I would run out of gas money but "when" I would run out of gas money.

I decided that I would need to make a few cut backs wherever I could. I was no longer staying at state parks so I couldn't make cuts there. I had already gotten Maia a tee shirt on my trip, one from Roswell with aliens on it, and I had already loaded my kids up with toys, so I figured I could just pass up buying any more goodies for my loved ones. I could not do anything about the ever rising gas prices but I could make sure to never go over the speed limit, unless if I had to out run more forest fires. And, I decided, I really didn't need to be buying all of those plumbs at three dollars a pound.

As I often did in times of need I bowed my head and prayed. When I had finished, just like the time I had seen the rainbows, I found it very hard to believe what I took notice of when I raised my head.

I had parked at the edge of the parking lot of the Laundromat that sat beside a small field. All of the trees around me had purple leaves but these were not the purple Maples I was used to seeing on the east coast. These were something else indeed.

I looked at the ground and noticed that there were purple, golf ball sized round objects all over the ground. I got out of the truck to investigate.

Once in the grass of the field I bent over, taking one of these objects in my hand and laughed out loud when I realized what it was. I had parked right beside a wild plum orchard and there were more ripe plumbs on the ground than there were in any bend in any grocery store I had ever been in.

I went to the back of my truck and opened the lid on my cooler. I then went into the field and began picking up as many plumbs without defects that I could get my hands on. I loaded them into all the pockets of the cargo shorts I was wearing. I would take a load over to my cooler, put them in it, then return for more plumbs. I made sure to get more than I thought I would eat on the remainder of my trip.

After rejoicing like I had hit the mother load I went back into the Laundromat and began folding my dry laundry. I struck up a conversation with a pleasant woman in her mid fifties who was folding her laundry beside me.

The woman I met was named Janice Magnesun. Janice was originally from California. She had retired from a phone company and had moved onto a ten acre tract of land on the outskirts of Coeur d' Alene. She had a daughter in her twenties and she was also caring for her aging mother who lived with her.

I told Janice about my trip when she inquired as to why I was in the area. I told her about how I was trying to walk in the foot steps of men and women who might not think I was so crazy for making material sacrifices in my own life for a cause that was bigger than me, which at this point in time I felt was our war on terror.

Janice informed me that though she didn't care much for George W. Bush she was a supporter of the war on terror and she was glad that we had a Commander in Chief who was not afraid to take the war to the enemy. Everything she said reminded me of what Thoral Wardel in Utah had told me, except she did not have a son in Afghanistan.

I finished my conversation with Janice just as we both were finishing folding our laundry. We both said our goodbyes as we left the Laundromat together. She was heading for home and I was heading east, getting ready to begin crossing the Rocky Mountains heading into Montana.

Before I made it too far out of the town of Coeur d' Alene though I crossed over the river that went by the same name of the town. Noting its crystal clear, glacier fed waters I decided to find public access to it and participate in my homeless bathing ritual.

I took the next exit and found access to the river with ease. It was such a nice day that I decided to run a few miles before getting my kayak off of the truck and hitting the stream. I was now on an old dirt road and I thought it would be the perfect place to run being how there was practically no traffic. I had to keep in mind that I couldn't afford to get completely out of shape on this trip because when I got back I would be heading off to basic training at Fort Benning.

As I ran down this dirt road I marveled at the scenery. I was surrounded by deciduous forest with the stream running along beside the road. With no humidity the air was clear and I could see as far as the mountain tops would allow me to see.

At my turn around point I noticed a huge Osprey nest built on top of a pole of an old telegraph line. The line had long been abandoned and it provided the perfect home for this large, eagle like bird.

As I turned around and started heading back to my truck I saw the inhabitant of this nest circling above me with a small cut throat trout in one of its talons. This was a sight like I had rarely seen. Once, while boating on Lake Moomaw back in Virginia I was fortunate enough to witness a bald eagle dive bomb the top of the lake and come away with a trout in its talons. Seeing this Osprey with it's catch of the day reminded me of that time.

I had worked up a nice healthy sweet by the time I got back to the truck. The temperature was probably hovering close to a hundred, but again, with no humidity my run had been as comfortable as any run at six o'clock in the morning back in Virginia.

After walking for a few minutes to catch my breath I took the kayak off of the truck. I dug through my duffle bag in the back and located my shaving kit. I then took it and the kayak down to the river's edge and got in the water.

The Coeur d' Alene river was absolutely gorgeous! Though I passed over holes that where fifteen feet deep the water was so clear that I could see even the smallest pebble on the river's bottom. I saw cut throat trout numerous times darting away from me as I passed them by.

I floated past a local swimming spot. Here there were ladies sun bathing, children swimming, men fishing and practically everyone but the children drinking beer. I waved as I passed and just about everyone waved back.

After making my way around the next turn in the river, making sure I was out of site of the swimming hole above me, I got the kayak out on the side of the bank and entered the water to take a bath with my "soap that floats."

The water in this river was just as cold as the water at Lake Easton had been. I found it to be both reviving to me and comforting on my leg muscles that I had just taxed while on my run. I enjoyed the crisp clean feeling the water was giving me so after I had bathed completely I stuck around and swam for a while before heading back.

I finally got back in my kayak and began paddling upstream. I passed the swimming hole and all of its inhabitants again as I continued toward my truck. Most of them watched in awe as I paddled upstream through some slightly swift currents. I felt almost guilty when people took notice of this like I was some kind of super human athlete. With the aerodynamics of the kayak and the back current always provided close to the bank, paddling upstream really was not as hard as it looked.

Once I made it to where I had parked, I got the kayak out of the river and safely secured to the top of my truck. I put away my shaving kit and got out my two empty water jugs to take down to the river and refill before heading on my way. I always made sure not to get these jugs confused with the one that I used as my "bathroom" in the middle of the night.

I went down to the stream and filled my jugs. I stood up and took in the beauty of the area one last time and then headed back for the truck. I put my jugs of water back into my cooler which was now overflowing with wild plumbs, got into the driver's seat, then headed back for the interstate. It was time to begin crossing the Rockies and head back east.

28

As I drove on Interstate 90 heading east I was now crossing the northern portion of the Bitterroot Mountain Range. I was almost at the exact spot the Lewis and Clark expedition had been when they first crossed over these mountains just over 200 years ago. Fortunately for me though I was crossing them in the comfort of a modern vehicle in the middle of the summer. The Lewis and Clark party had crossed these mountains on foot during mid September.

Though September means the weather is just starting to cool off back in Virginia, through much of the south, and many other parts of the United States, September can be a treacherous time of heavy snow and dangerously low temperatures in these Bitterroot Mountains as the Lewis & Clark Expedition was to find.

When the Lewis and Clark expedition encountered the Bitterroots, a mountain range they would have to cross to be able to make it to their destination of the Pacific coast, they were none too happy to finally reach them. For some time up until reaching this point, all of the men in the group had been looking to their west, toward these mountains, dreading the day they would eventually make it to them. Even while they had been in the warmer, lower lying valleys heading this direction they could see the snow covered mountain tops that looked nearly impossible to cross.

From September 16'th through the 27'th of 1805, the men would find that their worst fears would come to fruition as they crossed through this part of their journey. What they found when they began passing through this portion of the land was mountains nearly impossible to climb, forest and brush nearly too thick to get through, and snow and cold like they had never known. On the first day alone the snow had poured all day and the men, who where hard pressed to follow any semblance of a trail were constantly having the snow that had accumulated on tree branches above them fall on them throughout the day.

To make matters worse through this pass there was little to no wild life that the party's hunters could kill for food. On one evening, the hunters returned to the camp with only 3 grouse, nowhere near enough food for all of the men in the party.

The men of the Lewis and Clark expedition had to resort to eating some of their horses while journeying through these snowy mountains. At times they even resorted to eating their candles. The candles had been made out of wax that contained bear fat and the men figured they would provide some sustenance.

Another problem the men had during this part of their journey was that their horses were running away at night. Not only were the men starving but their pack beasts were too and they would leave the camp at night in search of grass on which to feed. The men lost valuable hours worth of traveling time during daylight hours because they had to spend up until mid afternoon at times locating their horses.

The expedition finally made it over these mountains with the help of their Indian guide Toby, and by the thoughtful hand outs from and ration exchanges they made with a small group of Nez Perce Indians they had encountered while in the mountains. Though the threat of Indians, mainly the Blackfeet and Oglala Sioux were one of the most dangerous threats to the expedition once they were west of the Mississippi, the occasional run in with friendly Indian tribes could certainly be attributed to the success of their journey.

Thinking back on how miserable of an experience those brave men over two hundred years ago had gone through I shuddered. I thought of how so many of us don't realize how good we have it today. Whereas many folks would point out to me the desperation of my own situation, I took heart knowing the Lewis & Clark men would have traded me places for anything in the world at any time.

Shortly after crossing into Montana I noticed a yurt, one of the mongoloid round houses I so desired to live in, sitting on the side of the mountain off to my left. It was green in color and had a wonderful deck around it. The yard was landscaped to where it looked like the whole property had sprouted naturally out of the mountain.

I had started fantasizing about living in a Yurt while I was struggling with trying to keep my house. Yurts are very sturdy and, according to people who live in them very comfortable as well. One of the biggest drawing points to me though is the fact that they are very cheap. You can purchase a brand new thirty feet in diameter yurt for about twelve thousand dollars. Get some cheap land in West Virginia for a song and a dance and you could have your entire home and the land it is on paid for for under twenty five thousand dollars and never have to worry about rent or a dreaded mortgage payment again.

It was becoming evening and due to all of my activities back in Coeur d" Alene I had not eaten much throughout the day. I took advantage of a rest stop about seventy miles west of Missoula. I got out and ate a can of spaghetti and meatballs and about half a dozen of my newly acquired wild plumbs.

After I finished eating I walked over to use the restroom and plug my phone in for a quick charge. As I walked on the sidewalk leading to the restroom I noticed some prairie dogs hanging out along the wood line behind the building, just as I had seen at a rest stop while making my way to the west coast.

After plugging my phone in to charge and using the restroom I went back to the truck to retrieve some trail mix I had bought while I was camping with the kids in Washington. I made my way behind the restrooms, got down on my knees and began trying to lure these small critters in with the trail mix.

When I first knelt, the dogs were about thirty yards away from me. I first tried to fake them out and draw them closer by acting as if I was throwing something their way. The kids and I loved to implore this trick on unsuspecting sea gulls while at the Outer banks of North Carolina. When we did this there we would draw birds in from hundreds of yards away and man were they pissed when they saw we were joking. At times they would dive bomb us and we would have to seek shelter in our rented town house.

These prairie dogs bought the trick as well and slowly started making their way toward me. There was a brave leader who led the pack, stopping every few seconds to look back to make sure his troops were following.

Once the prairie dogs got to within fifteen yards I actually started throwing real trail mix. I knew I could heave the mixture of small nuts, raisins and dried bananas that far and I wasn't willing to find out just how these small animals attacked after thinking back on some of the actions of the sea gulls.

As the prairie dogs ate I intentionally began throwing the trail mix less far, drawing the animals even closer to me. I wanted to see how far they were willing to come for a free meal. After some time of getting used to me I was actually able to draw them to within arm's length. I would simply hold the trail mix out in my hand and drop it. The little critters would grab it, then sit back on their haunches and eat it while keeping an eye on me the whole time.

After I ran out of trail mix I got up to go get my cell phone and get back on the road. When I stood up, the little prairie dogs scattered, screaming in all directions. Once they made it back to the safety of the wood's edge they stopped and looked back at this giving, yet intimidating man. Intimidating to them at least.

After getting my phone I got back in the truck and continued heading east on I90. I was heading toward Missoula and the Clark Fork River, named after the point where Lewis and Clark had split up to investigate different parts of the surrounding land on their journey back east, had drawn up beside the road and I took note of its splendor. At times I had to make sure not to run off of the road and into this river because I was looking at it so much.

While looking at this beautiful stream it occurred to me that I had not yet done any fishing on this trip. This river reminded me so much of the wonderful trout streams back in West Virginia more than any other I had seen so far so I made a vow that tomorrow I would fish. There wasn't much time left in the day since I had spent so much time in Coeur d' Alene so for now I planned on getting as far east as I could before stopping for the night.

By the time I did decide to stop I had made it to Butte, Montana. I pulled off of the interstate and gassed up for $51 at a gas station that also housed a gambling casino and several restaurants. I went inside to get a foot long Italian sub from Subway after getting my gas and to inquire as to the whereabouts of the closest Wal Mart.

I was greeted at Subway by a fairly attractive middle eastern lady in her mid thirties. She was telling me how she had pulled two shifts the day before and was doing the same today because her help had not shown up.

I was glad that I had stopped to ask for directions for the Wal Mart because I would have never found it on my own. It turned out that it was in the town of Butte and about three miles off of the interstate.

I paid for my sub which I took to go and then got in my truck and headed to Wal Mart, eating my sandwich as I drove. I easily found the Wal Mart according to the directions I had received and wasted no time in making my way over to the nomadic caravan at the far end of the lot.

There were more campers and R.V.s here tonight than I had seen yet in a Wal Mart parking lot. I made my mind up that the next morning I was going to talk to some of my fellow travelers and find out a little bit about them. I bet there had to be someone with a story as interesting or more so than mine.

After moving my gear to the cab, filling up my air mattress and unrolling my sleeping bag I climbed into the back of the truck. Though I was tired I did not go to sleep just yet. I had been thinking of my beautiful Maia back in Virginia as I so often did and decided to call her before going to bed. It was late enough back east to where she should have been finished with work for the night.

I was disheartened to get only her voicemail and not her. Maybe she wasn't finished with work yet, or maybe she was already in bed herself.

I left her a brief message letting her know where I was and that I was ok. I also let her know that I loved her.

I always felt as if there was something lacking when I told Maia that I loved her. I knew that these three little words were the standard in our society when it came to letting someone know that they were of the most importance to us, but what I felt toward Maia was stronger than any emotion I had ever known before. I felt as if I should invent a word to replace the word "love", a word that meant love to the tenth power! I don't know, I guess I just hoped that when I told her I loved her that she never took it the same way as she had from doubtless numerous other men who had told her the same thing throughout her life. What I felt for her was real, rare and radiant. I was certainly wrapped around her finger, her heart, and every other part that she possessed.

I laid down on the comfort of my air mattress and thought of Maia. Oh how I longed to have her with me tonight. It wasn't just for the thoughts of the physical pleasure we would no doubt enjoy if we were together but I longed for that spiritual feeling I always got when she was with me.

Often times, after we made love I would lay my head on her chest so I could hear her breath and listen to her heart beat. I would soon find my breathing pattern matching hers and somehow my heart would beat in time with hers as well. It would feel as if, though our bodies were no longer physically entwined in the heat of passionate love making our souls would unite as one as the dust from the previous storm of passion would settle. God I missed Maia. Perhaps I would dream of her tonight.

29

I awoke the next morning greatly rested. To my disappointment, I had not dreamed of Maia. I had not dreamed at all. I had slept so deeply that it felt as if I had just closed my eyes before opening them gain but it was now 8:00 a.m. the next day.

I got out of the back of the truck and looked around to see who among my fellow nomads I might strike up a conversation with. To my amazement, they were already all gone. I was the only one who remained. These people came and went like thieves in the night.

After eating a quick bowl of cereal and enjoying a cup of Regina's tea I went into Wal Mart to buy a very inexpensive fishing rod. I knew I would be tapping into my dwindling gas money supply but the Clark's Fork River had called to me the entire day yesterday and I couldn't pass up answering it.

Just before leaving on my trip I had been kayaking and cat fishing on the Rivanna Reservoir back in Charlottesville, at the exact spot Maia and I had gone kayaking on that lovely Sunday afternoon when she had officially become my girl friend. I had stayed on the river until after dark and when I was taking my kayak out of the water both of my poles that I had secured to the side of the kayak got caught on a small sapling at the bank's edge. Since it was dark, I could not tell that this had been the case and I broke both of them in half as I tugged the kayak up over the bank and out of the water. Fortunately though, my reels were still in perfect working condition and I was able to find a pole here at the Wal Mart in Butte, Montana for only $6.99. Sure, it was not the top of the line but it would do the trick for me.

As I was paying for my pole along with some Montana post cards I would mail to the kids, my parents and Maia after leaving the store, I spilled change from my fanny pack all over the floor. I had been gathering the change through the coarse of this trip and since the bag it was in now weighed about five pounds I decided to start spending it on incidentals to lighten the load and to conserve my bank funds for gas. Nearly all five pounds of the change went on the floor as I unzipped the bag, not paying any attention to the fact that it was upside down.

The two lovely middle aged women in line behind me courteously got down on their hands and knees and helped me pick up the change. I was embarrassed, which they could tell by my red face and one of them mentioned that this happened to her all the time. I doubted the truthfulness of her statement but I could appreciate her attempt to make me feel better.

After gathering my change, paying for my purchases and thanking the ladies who had helped me clean up my mishap, I left the store. I went to the truck, leisurely filled out and addressed my post cards, dropped them in the mail box in front of the store and then got on my way, continuing on Interstate 90 east. I was trying to hug the same route Lewis and Clark had taken two hundred years before.

When I had gotten only thirty miles east of Butte I spotted yet another forest fire in the distance. This one did not appear to be nearly as big as many of the fires I had seen through Utah and Idaho and I was hoping that due to this fact it could be easily contained.

Unfortunately I was no longer following Clark's Fork along the road. I had lost the river somewhere around Butte and was now desperately looking for one of its neighbors in which I could kayak, bathe and fish. It would be about another half an hour after seeing the small forest fire before I found another river promising me the opportunities I was desiring.

At Livingston, Montana I entered the valley between the Gallatin and Absaroka Mountain ranges. It was at this point where I also began traveling along side the Yellowstone River. Though a bit wider and more fierce than Clark's Fork it was beautiful none the less and I decided it would do for my activities.

I took state route 89 north at Livingston and was able to find public stream access within site of the interstate. Before taking my kayak off of the truck I walked down to the river bank to view the scene.

There were several people swimming in the deep hole of water below the bridge that crossed the river here and there were several others who were taking out a large pontoon type boat they had floated down the river in from some point upstream. As I spent time on the river here today I would see many such folks doing the same thing.

I made my way back to the truck and took down my kayak. This time, aside from just loading my shaving kit I also took a small cooler I had in the truck and packed it with a can of spaghetti, several plumbs, and a twenty ounce bottle of water. I generally ate my lunch on the tail gate but I wanted to get to the river badly and I thought it would be very relaxing if I ate on the bank.

I also put my old reel on my new pole and secured it to the bungee cord at the side of the kayak. After taking a few lures out of my large tackle box and putting them in a smaller one that I then put in my pocket, I grabbed my paddle and life vest and headed down to the river. I was in the water and the middle of the Yellowstone River in no time.

As much as I wanted to fish and as badly as I could use a bath, my first priority was lunch. I paddled upstream, passing underneath a bridge, and made my way to the other side of the river were a large sand bank was provided. I got the kayak out of the water and sat on the back of it and ate my can of spaghetti and then followed it down with my plumbs. I was sitting there trying to remember the last time I had had a hot meal, but I couldn't.

After putting my empty spaghetti can and used plastic fork back into my cooler, as I had practiced the act of always taking anything I took into the wilderness with me back out my entire life, I got back into the kayak and began making my way downstream.

This Yellowstone river was astonishingly beautiful. It was forty yards in width here and though deep at times, say fifteen feet or more, its winding body would also give way to shallow rapids where my kayak would actually drag on the bottom.

I could look up in any direction and stare straight into the Rocky Mountains. Though it was the middle of July I could still see snow caps on the highest ranges. I could only imagine passing through here in the winter!

As I floated swiftly downstream I cut through western cow fields and past old log jams and immensely eroded river banks. Though the water was quite swift at times I never felt as if I were facing any danger. I was concerned however, about my trip back upstream that I would eventually have to take.

With this thought in mind I decided to finally pull my kayak over to the bank about a mile downstream from my truck. I had made the turn around a bend in the river and the swimmers upstream would not be able to see me participating in my strange, homeless ritual of bathing, though I was so far away from them now I doubt they would have been able to tell what I was doing anyway.

Before bathing I decided to fish for a bit. I figured I might actually have a better chance of catching something before I lathered the water up with the soap that floats than I might if I waited until afterward.

I pulled out a ¼ ounce rattle trap lure from the small tackle box I had put in my pocket. This lure is a small silver fish shaped lure made out of hard plastic that has a couple of bee bees in the center to give it that "rattling" sound as it is pulled through the water. These lures retail for about $5.00 each but I was able to buy just over 400 of them at a Dick's Sporting Goods sidewalk sale the spring before for $1 each. I sold the overwhelming majority of them on eBay at $4 each, allowing me to undercut the retail price but still quadruple my money, and saved about twenty or so for my personal use. I rarely lost a lure, maybe only once every two years, so I doubted I would ever need to buy another rattle trap again in my lifetime.

As much as I cast toward the bank, in the center of the river, both above and below the swift water, and both upstream and down I didn't catch a thing. I didn't even get any bites. This was a far cry from the success I had had just a few years before on the Cranberry River back in West Virginia. I was not disappointed to any great degree though as I was simply enjoying being on this beautiful stream in these beautiful mountains more than anything. Besides, I wasn't really paying much attention to the fishing I was doing. While I was reeling my line in I was gawking at the snow covered mountains.

After casting several more times unsuccessfully and after another large pontoon boat had passed me by I decided it was time to bath. I reeled in my lure and secured my rod to the side of the kayak. I then took my razor, shaving cream and soap out of my shaving kit and began my ritual.

The water of the Yellowstone was cool but nothing like the waters of the Coeur d' Alene River in Idaho or Lake Easton in Washington. I had been making my way into lower elevations since leaving Idaho and I would suppose this is why the water was getting warmer.

After shaving and bathing, I put my toiletries back into their kit and then began the long, arduous ordeal of paddling upstream. It hadn't occurred to me that perhaps I should start paddling upstream and bathe there when I got in these rivers for that purpose so that once I bathed I wouldn't have to break a sweat and ruin my perfect state of cleanliness because there would be no effort involved with simply floating back downstream.

The first part of the journey back to the truck was relatively easy, but the closer I got back the more swiftly the water flowed. At one point, in spite of the gawking onlookers at the put in site, I did get out and walk along the bank, dragging the kayak up through the water at my side.

Once I got back to the truck I chatted with a couple of college aged girls sunbathing on boulders by the river's edge, as their boyfriends glared at me from a distance as they swam in the river. It was nice to know that these young, muscular, good looking men considered me a threat, but it was obvious that there was no need for them to as their lady friends never even looked my direction as we talked. They were too concerned with making sure they didn't get any tan lines across their back, where they had undone what little strap their skimpy bikini tops did provide.

After gawking a bit more at these girls, I mean talking a bit more with these girls, I loaded my gear in the truck, secured the kayak to the top and then hit the road. I had been at the river for a couple of hours and I was now continuing my journey taking interstate 90 east again.

Remembering the advice Thoral Wardle had given me in Utah about helping farmers in Montana I kept my eyes open for an opportunity. What appeared to be an opportunity to me came only ten miles down the road when I saw a sizable farm just off of the interstate. In the fields there were hundreds of the small, fifty pound hay bails that few farmers cut these days. Most hay is now prepared in those big, one thousand pound circular bails that are later picked up with a sharp spear attached to the front of a large farm tractor and either loaded onto a hay truck or taken back to the barn one at a time by simply using the tractor.

With the smaller, fifty pound square bails there was still quite a bit of manual labor involved with putting the hay away. Generally, and as we did when I helped neighbors put up hay when I was a kid back in West Virginia, a couple of people would walk through the fields and move all of the loose bails into centralized piles throughout the field. A flat bed truck would then make its way to the piles and one or two people would throw the bails onto the truck to another person who was in charge of stacking the bails neatly in such a way that as many as possible could be hauled in one trip. The truck would then make its way to the barn, where all of the bails were unloaded and stored, and then would return to the field for more loads.

Hoping that this was still how things were done, as it had been nearly twenty years since I had helped out with this type of work, I took the next exit and headed for this farm. After turning onto the local road running parallel to the interstate I traveled only a quarter of a mile back in the direction from which I had just come. I then turned left and headed up the long dusty driveway to the old farm house that sat a couple of hundred yards away at the end of the drive.

As I pulled behind the house where I saw both a Ford F150 and a Buick Century parked, both at least twenty years old, I was greeted by the wagging tail of some sort of mongrel who had to be just as old as the vehicles he seemed to be guarding. He barked at me, not in a threatening tone though, as I got out of my truck. I think he was trying to give the impression that he was doing his job as a guard dog but I also got the impression that he received visitors very rarely and he was happy to see me stop by.

After shutting my truck door I bent over, allowed him to sniff my hand so he would feel comfortable with me, and then petted him on the head and rubbed him behind the ears once I felt comfortable with him. As a runner I had been bitten by more than one dog in my life and I was always a little leery.

After making my way up three broken wooden steps that led to the porch at the back door of this house, I knocked softly at first, and then a bit more forcefully as it seemed no one had heard me the first time.

The back storm door of the house was open, allowing the breeze to blow into the kitchen. I could see that all of the windows within site of me were open to allow the same as well. After having gone door to door as a stock broker for several years I had learned to "psychoanalyze" a house and its inhabitants quite well.

I could tell from this house that it was occupied by an old man, probably a widower, who was in his late seventies or early eighties. More than likely he would need help with his hay, but due to his generation's mind set he probably would not accept help. The issues of false pride and economics would play into his decision. Though he probably had hundreds of thousands of dollars in fixed annuities and bank CD's scattered all over the county, he probably felt as if he were broke as a joke and only a month's worth of bills away from living on the street. This was common of the old WWII generation who went through the great depression as children.

I found that part of my hunches were correct as a man of about six feet tall and 78 years in age came limping down the hallway, through the kitchen and to the back door. He was not limping due to any type of apparent injury or illness, but simply due to many years of working the land surrounding his home.

"What can I do ya for?" he asked as he looked at me suspiciously yet curiously.

"I am driving through the area," I began to inform him, "And I would like to help out with some farm work if I could because I fear I may run out of gas money before I get back to my destination of Virginia. I see that you have quite a bit of hay bails out in the fields," I continued. "I have put up hay many of times in my youth and I wouldn't mind helping you put up yours if you didn't mind the help."

He looked at me, still suspiciously and curiously for a brief moment before finally speaking. "What are you doing all the way out here from Virginia?"

I had dealt with many farmers as clients back in Virginia when I was a stock broker and I had learned that though they might not always understand all of the technical mumbo jumbo of Wall Street, as few people, including those of us in the business did, one thing they did understand was honesty. They also appreciated sincerity. It seemed that for some reason farmers were better judges of character than just about anyone else in any other profession. I knew there were times that I had been awarded business by these folks, not because I had the best investment idea or hottest new product, but because they could tell that I believed in what I was talking about and they felt I was being honest with them.

With all of this in mind I began to explain myself.

"Well," I started. "I have recently enlisted in the Virginia National Guard. I have also just sold my house and technically until I go to basic training at Fort Benning Georgia next month I have nowhere to live. I decided that I would use this time to drive around the entire country and take a look at this great land that I have enlisted to fight for."

As I finished my explanation I waited as he continued to glare at me, choosing his words carefully before he spoke.

"I'm seventy eight years old and I aint seen most of this country," he did say when he spoke. "That sounds like one heck of a trip?"

"It has been!" I informed him, feeling as if I was starting to build a report that may lead to some gas money. Besides, I was getting good vibes from this older gentleman and believe I would have built that same report even if there were nothing in it for me to do so.

"So why'd ya sell your house?" he then asked.

"I went through a nasty divorce and some things came up there at the end that I could have never predicted, and as a result I had to sell," I said. I was trying to give a straight answer without going into too gory of details.

At this point the gentleman shifted his stance, raised an eyebrow and said, "My wife and I were married for sixty years before she passed!"

I had blown it! The WWII generation rarely participated in the practice of divorce that their offspring baby boomers had made such common place. They believed in working through their difficulties at all costs and staying together. Unfortunately, I had found that even some of my best clients while I was a broker would not transfer their accounts to me when I left Edward Jones and went independent because I had done so as a result of my divorce.

This was one of the most hurtful things about my divorce that I never saw coming. I found that, even without knowing my circumstances, there were many people who were quick to judge me because of my failed marriage.

This didn't happen just among older folks either. I had friends who were married and in my own age group who my ex wife and I had known for years who all of a sudden would not speak to either of us after we split up. I would see some of these people at school functions or in the stores or restaurants surrounding our area and when I attempted to waive or speak, they would turn and quickly go the other way. It was as if they thought I had some sort of divorce virus that they might catch it they got too close to me.

"I aint got no need for any help with my hay," the old man finally spoke again.

"Ya know," I said, trying to not take no for an answer, "I am really gonna be in trouble once I cross the Mississippi and I am willing to work for practically nothing. I'll work all day for $50 a day. I figure two days of that and we can have all your hay put away and I will be ensured to have enough gas money to make it back to Virginia."

With this, he went into deep thought, more like he was remembering something though than thinking about my offer.

"Ya know," he began. "There's a bunch of Mexicans that come through here every now and then makin' the same offer. I guess a lot of people hire 'em or they wouldn't come around."

"Well if some of your neighbors are reaching out to the Hispanic community, couldn't you try to help an American soldier?" I asked. At this point I was desperate for a "yes" and I had resorted to the pity factor.

"Naw," he said, not taking the bait. "I aint got no need for help but I appreciate you coming by."

The old man and I continued to talk for another twenty minutes before I left. He told me that he had grown up on this land and lived in the house his entire life. This was the case with many of the farmers in our country from his generation. That is a big reason for all of those hundreds of thousands of dollars worth of bank CD's too. True, their generation had practiced thrift, but they never had to pay a mortgage either. If you figure the average mortgage today of roughly $1,000 never having to be paid, over a thirty year period we would all save $360,000.00 just from the principle! We would save two and a half times that once you figure your not paying the interest.

Though I was a bit frustrated by not being helped by this gentleman, I kept my cool and remained mature and listened to him intently as he continued to talk. He told me of his wife and how she had died just a couple of years earlier form cancer. They had raised six children in this little house. All of his children were still living and were quite successful, according to him.

After our conversation ended I got back in the truck, petting this man's mongrel one last time as I did, and got on my way. Though I was not able to take care of my quickly approaching gas money problem I was not out anything either. Though he was unwilling to help me, I did enjoy talking to this farmer and was leaving with no less than I had come with. Nothing ventured nothing gained.

About two hours after leaving the farmer's house I crossed into Wyoming. As I did I was passed by a car with Florida license plates. This was the first vehicle I could remember seeing since Texas that was further away from home than I was.

For some reason the road along this part of Interstate 90 was reddish in color. It reminded me far to well of all those tar tan tracks I had run way too many laps on in the past. Many people considered the four lap mile and the eight lap two mile, distances that I ran in high school to be "long distance." These races were nothing compared to the twelve and a half lap 5k and even longer twenty six lap 10k that I ran in college. I couldn't help but think of all those laps as I rolled down this long, now gently rolling road. I had entered the great plains and what were the turns through the Rocky Mountains had now given way to the undulating hills of the great grass lands.

It was growing dark just as I entered Wyoming so I did what I had gotten used to doing so much during this time of day while on this trip and sought out the closest Wal Mart. It was not off of the first exit at Sheridan, Wyoming, nor was it off of the second. It was however, just off of the third exit, its tall blue sign shining to me like a beacon.

I pulled off the exit and into the parking lot and made my arraignments to sleep for the night. Where I could not get in touch with Maia the night before, and didn't even have the luxury of dreaming of her, tonight I was able to reach her and we talked for nearly an hour before I went to sleep. God was it good to hear her voice!

30

The next morning I awoke at 8:00 a.m. and again was the only member of the nomadic caravan that was left in the parking lot. When I had pulled in the night before there had been half a dozen others. By the time I had finished my conversation with Maia that number had doubled. However, I was now the lone ranger.

I went into Wal Mart which housed a small McDonald's restaurant and ordered a sausage, egg and cheese biscuit and an orange juice. I hated fast food, especially McDonald's fast food, but I was longing to have something hot in my stomach. Though I had gotten comfortable with the idea of spending the nights in the parking lots at Wal Mart I still was a little antsy about cooking a full blown meal there.

After finishing my breakfast I got back on the interstate heading east. I quickly passed the city of Buffalo, Wyoming and couldn't help to think of the large beasts that the city no doubt drew its name from.

The mighty buffalo once roamed these great plains that cover parts of ten different states and make up 1.25 million square miles of our nation's land. The combined area of the plains is larger than the territory of Western Europe, to include the British Isles. The plains are said to have been formed millions of years ago from flowing waters coming down from the Rockies. This part of the country is believed to have once been a great inland ocean and the plains were the gently rolling and downward sloping bottom of this great ocean's floor.

The bison is said to have made its weigh across the Bering Straight that connects the continent of Europe to Alaska millions of years ago, just as humans did. For an uncountable number of years herds of these large beasts roamed the plain's area as it was the perfect territory for an animal that is required to eat no less than thirty pounds of grass a day to maintain its existence.

Since these beasts were so large and ran in huge herds few threats were posed to them by any naturally appearing predators. There were herds of these beasts so large that it is said that if you were to sit in one place and watch from the time the first buffalo passed by until the last in the herd passed by, that you would have to sit for three months!

It is known that in areas where there were falls on river ways, such as Niagara Falls on the border between Canada and New York, when these large herds of buffalo would make it to the stream for water, many of the unfortunate animals in the front of the pack would actually be pushed over the falls by the crowding of the animals in the back of the herd.

The Lewis and Clark expedition wrote of their first encounter with a grizzly bear that was feeding on a buffalo at the bottom of some falls on the Missouri river that had suffered this very fate. They also wrote of how incredibly hard it was for the men to kill this large bear. It made them curious about what other great beasts they may encounter as they continued their journey west.

It is sad to think that as numerous as the buffalo were, existing literally in the millions even through the early 1800's, that they were nearly wiped out of existence in only fifteen short years. Between the years of 1870 and 1885 white settlers and frontiersmen took a heavy toll on this great animal of the plains. Buffalo Bill Cody became famous throughout the country for killing 4,000 buffalo in only two years. Like the passenger pigeon that once flew in flocks so large that they would block out the sun when they flew by overhead, people did not understand what they were doing when they were on their way to wiping these large mammals out and nearly into extinction.

Fortunately, there would soon be hope for the dwindling buffalo population of our nation. By the late 1880's buffalo had disappeared from practically everywhere in the United States except for in Yellowstone National Park. Though hunting the buffalo in the park was an illegal act, it happened at the hands of poachers anyway and what was once a herd of over two hundred buffalo in the park was quickly reduced to less than thirty.

Around this time, Henry Bergh founded the American Society for the Prevention of Cruelty to Animals, or ASPCA for short. He was able to get legislation passed that would further protect the dwindling buffalo population.

At the turn of the next century the buffalo found another friend in President Theodore Roosevelt, one of my favorite presidents. "Teddy," as he was popularly known as among so many Americans was a huge conservationist. During his presidency all of the land that he set aside to be used as federal park land, if combined, would be larger than the entire country of France!

Though Roosevelt was a big game hunter himself, actually passing up the opportunity to run for a third term for president in the 1908 presidential election to run off to Africa and hunt big game there, he believed in being a respectful sportsman when it came to hunting. He did not believe in hunting pregnant female animals and he believed that one should always track and kill any wounded creature so as to eliminate its suffering.

Roosevelt found himself drawn to the plight of the buffalo, perhaps from having witnessed their condition first hand when he had spent some time in the Badlands of North Dakota as a rancher twenty years before his presidency. With his help, the American Bison Society was formed on December 1, 1905. The creation of this body saw that congress provided land for the buffalo in Oklahoma and Montana. It also saw that domestic buffalo were released in these areas and that the population would be further protected from hunters and poachers so they could reproduce and replenish the plains.

For the first time many Indian children who had only heard the stories of these great beasts from their parents or grandparents were now gathering on their reservations to see them in real life. Often, when the beasts were hauled in to be relocated by train, the trains were met by Indian families who had brought their children to see these creatures.

I thought of the great fall and magnificent comeback of the buffalo as I continued driving over "Crazy Woman Creek," and wondered too if the lady this stream was named after had been any relation to the woman in Texas for whom "Woman Hollering Creek" was named after. Had they gone through a similarly horrendous ordeal?

As I continued rolling over the plains with the cruise control set on 60 m.p.h. I thought of how it felt much like riding an air mattress in the ocean at the beach just behind the point where the waves broke. Steadily up; steadily down, steadily up; steadily down. Fortunately I had never been prone to car sickness. Christian always had been and as much as I would have enjoyed having him and his sisters along for this trip I am sure I would be seeing his breakfast again if he were riding with me here.

As I continued through the plains I passed a group of no less that thirty cyclists. I don't know if it were a club, a tour, or just a group of friends but their caravan stretched for nearly two miles. I passed the middle aged ladies with big butts first, then made my way up to the front where the trim, fit, lean and mean looking men and women in their late twenties were leading the way.

I finally came to and passed through the town of Gillette, Wyoming. I couldn't help but be reminded of my native West Virginia as I made my way through Gillette.

Wyoming is the largest producer of coal in the United States, with West Virginia coming in a close second. Though Wyoming produces more coal than West Virginia, the mountain state back in the Appalachians boasts the largest amount of highly efficient and cleaner burning bituminous coal. This area of Wyoming that I was now passing through held so much of the state's energy reserves that the city of Gillette boasted itself to be "The Nation's Largest Supplier of Energy." Weather this was actually true or not I did not know, but I'm sure it drew tourists.

31

As late morning turned to early afternoon I crossed into South Dakota. I pulled off at Sturgis, home of the largest annual biker festival in America to check my map to see exactly how I had to go to get to the next site on my trip, Mount Rushmore. I also wanted to inquire about possible employment at a small lumber mill that sat just off of the side of the interstate.

I first pulled into the parking lot at the mill's office, deciding that if I was going to get another rejection I would get it out of the way quickly then enjoy my afternoon at Mount Rushmore. Sure enough, rejection is what I got.

The owner was not in when I walked into the empty offices. When I came back out I saw that I was practically being bum rushed by a shirtless, long haired fork lift driver in his late forties who was missing his two front teeth. I got the feeling he hadn't been out of the pen for too long.

"What do you need?!" he both asked and yelled at the same time.

"I was stopping by to see if you guys could use an extra man on the green chain," I said.

"We have a full table!" he informed me, yelling again. "Get on outta here!" he then screamed as if I were a stray dog raiding his trash cans.

With that I headed toward my truck, not really too upset. Though I needed the gas money, working on a green chain in a lumber mill was hard work. Basically, after the saw cuts the logs into boards, the men on the green chain stack the boards according to their lengths and grades, or quality so to say of the boards. The better boards are considered "FAS" and are used for walls and floors in houses and the lower grade boards are considered either "1, 2, or 3 common" and are often used on the inside of furniture, providing for a strong frame but remaining out of site due to their visual defects.

When I had worked for Georgia Pacific in Buena Vista, Virginia after Amanda and I were just married, I stacked boards on the green chain for ten hours a day five to six days a week. When I started this job I weighed 165 pounds but after two months on the green chain I was down to 135 pounds and both Amanda and my mother forced me to go to the doctor for a complete physical because they were afraid I had either tape worms or cancer. After the doctor completed his physical, which included the always uncomfortable two fingered prostate exam, he simply informed me that I worked on a green chain; something I already knew.

After getting back in my truck and plotting my coarse on the atlas, with the long haired, toothless fork lift driver keeping an eye on me the whole time I got back on my way. I continued on interstate 90 to Rapid City and then cut down state route 16 to the small town of Keystone, which was home to Mount Rushmore.

This part of South Dakota, both along I90 and Rt. 16 was home to more bill boards than I had ever seen in one place. These hideous eye sores were practically one on top of another! I wondered why the local government didn't do something about this.

When I got into Keystone, I saw hundreds of people walking the side walks of this town that was no more than 100 yards long. Within that small space however, there were knickknack, trinket, and gift shops of every kind imaginable. There were the old photo shops were one could dress up in western garb and be photographed as if they were part of the old west. None of this stuff drew too much excitement from me and I was more than glad to pass all of these tourist trapping businesses up and go straight to Mount Rushmore which sat on top of the mountain just south of the town.

When I first saw the faces of Presidents Washington, Jefferson, Teddy Roosevelt and Lincoln staring down at me from high atop their peak as I made my way up the winding mountain side my heart skipped a beat. I had seen this place in so many pictures and documentaries but had never seen it in person. This was one of the places I had greatly looked forward to seeing while on my trip across America.

I paid my $8 admission and pulled my truck into the parking lot. I got out and began making my way to the entrance of this great American monument, passing through crowds of people from all over the world. I must have overheard conversations in a dozen different languages as I made my way through the marbled courtyard that housed the flags of all fifty states below the mountain.

Looking up at this magnificent work of human accomplishment I couldn't help but think of the Buddhist monuments in Afghanistan that had stood for thousands of years before the Taliban blew them to smithereens. If the Taliban were to have their way here in this country do any of us think for a minute that the same fate would not befall Mount Rushmore? That sounds far fetched, but on September 10'th, 2001 if anyone would have said that terrorists would hijack four of our airliners and fly them into the world trade center towers and the pentagon they would have been institutionalized.

I also thought of what these four great men would do if they were alive in our times. I could just see it now!

Abraham Lincoln would put himself in charge of keeping all free nations in tact, preserving our democratic way of life. Thomas Jefferson would use his great diplomatic skills and would be successful in getting even the French to rally to our side. Washington would take charge of the armies, as he had during the revolution and see that our soldiers were triumphant. T.R. would resign from public office, come back out west and rally his "rough riders," and then participate in the war effort just as he had in the Spanish American war. He would lead a great charge in the mountains of Tora Bora that would end the war! If only we could be fortunate enough to have all of these great men living at the same time.

As I made my way up the wooden board walk that would take me right under the President's noses I marveled at this wonder. I first was impressed with the size of the sculpture. The dimensions of Washington's head alone were so that the Sphinx of Egypt could lie between the end of his nose and the beginning of his eyebrow. T.R.'s mustache measured a whopping twenty feet across. Even Lincoln's character adding mole was sixteen inches wide. By the time it was complete Mount Rushmore would become the largest carved monument not only in the nation, but the world.

The entire work, which was led by engineer Gutzon Borglum would take sixteen years to complete, beginning in 1925 and not seeing completion until 1941. When the work started we were celebrating the roaring twenties and when it was completed we were just about to enter WWII.

Borglum was an enigmatic individual, as it would take one to have the vision he possessed for Mount Rushmore, an idea that often times infuriated the people of South Dakota who felt that his "pie in the sky" idea was just that, as well of a waste of money that could have been better spent in other areas. He was the son of a polygamist Mormon father from Idaho who had two wives at one time and a total of eight children. His father would eventually abandon his Mormon beliefs and actually leave one of his wives, Borglum's birth mother, and keep only one wife, who was actually the sister of the other.

From childhood Borglum thought that one person could make a huge difference in the lives of all and he considered himself to be just one of those people who could stand out and make a difference. He had been considered weird and eccentric all of his life so it was nothing new to him when the folks of South Dakota found him and his ideas strange as well. He paid no mind to the locals, at one point referring to them as mere "horseflies."

The entire story of Borglum's life is just as interesting as Mount Rushmore itself. He was an entirely self made man, teaching himself to read and making himself worldly by traveling to Europe, where he spent much of his twenties fine tuning his art skills. He had hoped to be wealthy and well known by thirty, but by the time he entered his third decade he found himself financially broke, unknown, and facing a divorce from his first wife.

In spite of his difficulties, Borglum pushed forward with his dreams, returning to America and helping out with artistic works throughout the country. He would eventually get his break, or at least what appeared to be his break, when he was contacted by the Daughter's of the Confederacy to carve a large likeness of Robert E Lee onto a mountainside known as Stone Mountain in Georgia.

Unfortunately, his work in Georgia did not go to plan. After a ten year struggle with the endeavor he was only one tenth of the way finished with the work. The powers in charge of the operation, the Stone Mountain Association, fired Borglum and in a fit of rage he destroyed all the models he had created of the work. Viewing the models as part of their property, the Stone Mountain Association swore out a warrant for his arrest. By the time Borglum made his way to South Dakota to begin his work on Mount Rushmore he was a fugitive running from the law.

Though Borglum was known to possess the ability to charm anyone into doing whatever he wanted, he was also known for his temper that he would unleash on anyone who would not do his bidding. He was an egomaniacal genius who's mood often changed like the direction of the winds on Mount Rushmore.

Money was often tight for his project in the Black Hills of South Dakota as it was in his personal life. There is a story of Borglum pulling into a filling station for gas one time and the station's attendant let him know that he would require payment before he could fill his car. When Borglum asked the attendant if he knew who he was, the attendant answered, "I know exactly who you are. That is why I am required to get payment first!"

In spite of this, Borglum was often able to use his strong willed personality and his reputation as the creator of Mount Rushmore to gain free gas or free admission into movie theaters on a number of occasions.

Mount Rushmore, which appeared to have been created with the ginger finesse of a clay sculptor, was bored into the mountain with the use of hammers, anvils and dynamite. Borglum could have perhaps created a much smaller, more articulate work to celebrate the times in America but he was a man who believed that size did matter. At one time he said, "There is something in sheer volume that awes and terrifies, lifts us out of ourselves."

I found myself being lifted out of myself as I stood there, staring up at the rock hard faces of these great former leaders of our nation. This is exactly why I had come on this trip in the first place. I wanted to get out of myself. I wanted to stop focusing on my own recent hardships and focus on something much bigger than myself. Standing here today at Mount Rushmore provided me that opportunity.

It is interesting to note that Borglum, who actually died suddenly from an unforeseen illness at age 73, just a couple of years before Mount Rushmore was completed, intentionally left three inches worth of rock on the face of the structure. Before the carving would be as complete as Borglum wanted it to be, these three inches would have to be removed. Borglum knew that the rate of wind and rain erosion was one inch per 100,000 years hence, it will be another 300,000 years before Mount Rushmore is actually "completed." Borglum did this so that his work would stand the test of time.

Thinking of this, I thought of how some things are worth fighting for. If Borglum was willing to sacrifice so much during is personal life to create this magnificent monument it was the least those of us in following generations could do to preserve it.

32

I spent several hours at Mount Rushmore, taking the guided walk led by a park ranger and taking several pictures. As I left I continually looked back at those huge stone faces while I drove back off of the mountain as if we were all saying goodbye to each other. I passed back through Keystone and all the cheesy little businesses and then continued on past all of those ugly billboards until I made my way back to Rapid City.

Though it would be dark in just over an hour by the time I had made it back to Rapid City it was still 105 degrees. I located the Wal Mart, got a bite to eat at the local Golden Coral restaurant and then went to the theatre and watched "Transformers." I knew I was splurging by eating out and going to a movie but I had to figure out some way to get into air conditioning and out of the heat.

After seeing the movie, which was a real let down after seeing the awe of Mount Rushmore I made my way back to the Wal Mart parking lot. I pulled into the nomadic caravan beside a tow behind camper and started moving my gear from the back of the truck to the cab so I could sleep for the night. It was now 10:00 p.m. and it had cooled enough to where I would be able to sleep comfortably.

Before I was done getting set up the man who was staying in the tow behind camper beside me came over to strike up a conversation. Though I was tired from the long day I viewed this as an opportunity to finally talk to another nomad.

"Hey neighbor!" this friendly man in his late sixties said as he walked up to the back of my truck as I was climbing back out, having just unrolled my sleeping bag on top of my air mattress. "I guess we're neighbors tonight huh?"

"I guess we are," I said to him, just as friendly as he had greeted me.

"I've been here for a week!" he informed me. "The engine in my truck died and I've been having a hard time figuring out how to get it fixed. I finally got in touch with a guy who is gonna come tow it to his shop tomorrow."

"So where are you heading?" I asked.

"Alaska!" he said.

"Alaska?"

"Yeah," he continued. "I have a couple of daughters up there. I'm gonna go by and see them and then spend a few months panning for gold on some land I've leased up there."

"That sounds like a good time," I added.

"Oh it is," he agreed. "I have already been up there once this year. I usually make the trip twice a year."

"Really?" I asked, astonished. "That is a lot of driving."

"Well, its what I do these days," he said.

"So you pretty much are a full time nomad?" I asked.

"Yeah," he chuckled, throwing his head back. "I guess you could call me that; a nomad."

"So how long have you been living this way?" I asked.

"Since 1993," he stated.

"Really?" I said.

"Yes," he continued. "My wife died of cancer back then and she and I had traveled around a lot in the sixties before our kids were born and I just decided that I was going to do it again. I'm a retired school teacher from up in Delaware so I get a pension from that and I get a disability check from a trucking accident I was in. That makes it all possible financially."

"A trucking accident?" I asked, wanting further explanation.

"Yeah," he went on. "I used to drive a truck and I was in a wreck and it messed up my rotator cuff," he said as he grabbed his right shoulder with his left hand and began moving his shoulder in a twisting motion.

"I couldn't move my arm for a couple of years," he said. "I was dealing with some doctors where I was living in Ohio at the time who kept trying to fix me and couldn't. I moved to Maryland and the doctors there fixed me right away. I went back to my old doctors and told those quacks they must have gotten their degrees from W.V.U. (West Virginia University). I told them I was form West Virginia and I knew how those people there were and I bet they had gone to W.V.U. And sure enough I was right! They had!"

He kept going on about his injury, his surgery and the "quacks" from W.V.U. who he claimed wanted only to keep him drugged up on OxyContin when it occurred to me what exactly he had said.

"Wait a minute," I interrupted as he was explaining every detail of his operation. "Did you say you were from West Virginia?"

"Yeah," he said, discounting my question. "A little town called Montgomery. You wouldn't know of it even if you were from around there."

As he started his medical mumbo jumbo again I cut him off once more.

"I know exactly where Montgomery is. I am from Richwood, just over an hour away from there."

"No kidding," he said, his eyes lighting up. He had forgotten all about his medical jive at this point.

"Yeah," I said. "I used to go to Montgomery and run a 10k road race they held there every year. West Virginia Tech is located in that town."

"Yeah," he said. "I know Richwood well. I used to go camping in the Cranberry wilderness up there every summer when I was in high school."

"I almost got killed kayaking on the Cranberry river a few years ago," I told him.

"You kayaked the Cranberry?" he said astonished. "Don't you know there are class five rapids on that river?"

"I do now," I laughed.

This was the beginning of a conversation that would go on for three hours. Though it was late and I was tired I had met a fellow hillbilly in the middle of a Wal Mart parking lot in South Dakota and I was not going to pass up an opportunity like this. We sat on the back of my tail gate and went on and on.

I found out that this man's name was Robert "Buck" Rogers. He had grown up in Montgomery, West Virginia and was a graduate of Glenville State College, the same college I had attended for years before transferring to and graduating from Fairmont State.

There was a very popular tourist road that ran through the Cranberry Wilderness outside of Richwood known as the "Scenic Highway" and it turned out that Buck had done the surveying for this road one summer when he was in college. My father and I used to run, bike and hunt along that road when I was growing up.

He also used to spend quite a bit of time during the summer in those days hanging out at Watoga State Park in nearby Pocahontas county, a place I had actually taken the kids camping before.

We talked of many things that night. Buck told me that the first time he and his wife took a cross country trip that they had done so with the first two of what would later become their four children. They had a car at the time and their two year old daughter would sleep in the front seat and their infant daughter would sleep in the back while Buck and his wife slept outside on the ground.

"Yeah, that first trip was to Colorado and back," he said. "And that was before they had interstates!"

Buck was doing a lot of reminiscing about his wife Rhonda, who was part Cherokee Indian and part white. I told him I could appreciate the unique beauty that came with a combination like that because I was dating a girl who was part Sioux Indian and part black. He pulled out a picture of his wife taken when they had first met when she was only 19 years old and sure enough she was a looker.

"Yeah, I hated her when we first me," he told me. "I was a patient in the hospital there in Montgomery. My appendix had ruptured and she was my nurse. She came in every night and woke me up and gave me four shots. Every night! I could not stand her!"

He told me that when he had gotten out of the hospital that Rhonda had arraigned for several of her friends and herself to go hiking with Buck. Ironically her friends bailed out on their plans at the last minute and it was just her and Buck.

Buck told me that he was a perfect gentleman throughout the hike. On the way back to the car though, Rhonda slipped on some rocks and fell to the ground. When he bent over to help her up, she laid a lip lock on him and he too eagerly returned the gesture.

"She admitted to me when she was on her death bed that she fell on purpose that day," he said with a smile. "She said she knew the car was only 80 yards away and that if she didn't get me there she might not ever."

Buck also told me of some of his trips to Alaska. One in particular was quite interesting. It seems that Buck liked to go to Alaska and pan for gold, often staying in old abandoned mining cabins well off the beaten path and inaccessible by vehicles. One time he was trapped in such a dwelling for several days as a storm came through and brought with it 60 m.p.h. winds.

"I had to hold on to the side of the cabin with one hand when I went outside to pee so I wouldn't get blown away," he said.

He told me of some small, gopher type rodents called parkas that stayed in the cabin with him during the storm. He said they would come in through a hole in the floor and would chew on the bottom log of the wall of the cabin and eat what little food he could afford to share with them. He said that whenever he would stand up though they would scurry in fear but could never seem to find the hole that they had come in through to escape.

"You sure the parkas weren't from West Virginia too?" I joked.

While Buck and I were talking we were joined by another nomad, 64 year old Reinhard Ohlhoff, a man of German decent. Reinhard was staying on the opposite side of my truck as Buck. I was parked right in the middle of them.

Whereas Buck was nomadic full time and did not even own a home, Reinhard was only nomadic part of the year and he spent his winters at his home in Florida. In the summers Reinhard liked to go to Canada and leave the humidity of the southern United States behind.

Reinhard grew up in a village located in the northwestern corner of Germany. He said that during WWII the British would fly over his village on their way back home and would dump whatever munitions they still had in their planes on the homes in his town. He could remember as a small child hiding behind a three feet thick concrete wall in his basement. He wasn't exactly sure why he was doing it at the time, he just remembered doing it.

Reinhard started his nomadic ways years ago with a truck and a topper, just as I had. He later moved up to vans, one of which he was now driving. He claimed he hated tow behinds mostly because of the excessive gas involved with having to pull them.

As I sat in that Wal Mar parking lot with these two gentlemen I viewed it as an opportunity to pick their brains on this nomadic way of living. They were more than happy to teach me the tricks of their trade.

First of all, they explained to me that within the counter culture of nomads there were actually two sub-cultures. You had the R.V.'ers and then the true nomads. The R.V.'ers were basically yuppies who had mortgaged their homes to buy over priced R.V.'s and they stayed in the Wal Mart parking lots because they couldn't afford the lot fees at the state parks. They would go to the parks once a week or so to take advantage of the dump stations for their septic systems. R.V.'ers usually were paranoid of the true nomads and considered them lesser-thans.

The nomads, however were genuine people and did what they did as a way of life. These folks generally lived in trucks, like myself, vans or tow behind campers. They were not out on an annual vacation but rather lived like this through out the year. They were generally people who possessed free spirits and wondering souls and who could not stand to be tied down to the same place for any extended period of time.

Buck and Reinhard told me that a nomad should always pack more gear than he thinks he will need because it is better to have something and not need it than to need something and not have it. They told me that Flying J truck stops were good places to shower because you could do so for $7 and they even provided you with a towel, soap and a wash cloth. I told them about how I bathed in rivers and lakes and I was proud to see that these two pros were quite impressed.

They also told me to stay off of the interstate as much as possible. They said that most of the beautiful parts of the country are the places well off the beaten path. I told them that I had found this to be the case when I decided to get off of the interstate in Texas and cut through the "gut" of America.

They told me that it was a good idea to take a break in the middle of the day. This is when it was hottest and it would be hardest on the engine of your vehicle. They said they generally liked to find a body of water of some sort and nap under a shade tree while they let their vehicles rest.

Lastly, they told me to use the pay phones at the Wal Marts to make any 800 calls, such as those to pay credit card bills etc. This would allow me to save the minutes on my cell phone. I had never thought of that one.

Somewhere in the middle of the night our conversation started to trail off as the three of us grew very tired. I wanted to stay up and talk to these guys until the sun came up but I just couldn't. Nor could they. We said our good nights and then we all three climbed into our different yet similar dwellings and went to sleep for the night.

33

After staying up so late having such a wonderful conversation with Buck and Reinhard I did not wake up until 9:00 a.m. local time the next morning. The caravan was gone, all except myself, Buck and Reinhard. Though I was just getting up I could see that Reinhard was already up and about, walking around looking at the outside of his van with a cup of coffee in his hand, and I could overhear Buck in his camper next door talking to one of his daughters on his cell phone, giving her the update of his break down predicament.

I went into Wal Mart and had another greasy McDonalds breakfast biscuit and orange juice, used the facilities and then went back out to my truck. I was greeted by Reinhard who asked me if I would like to view the inside of his van. I let him know that I would be happy to.

When I got inside what appeared from the outside to simply be an ordinary van I was amazed by what I saw. He had a full sized bed, a television, a shower, a toilet, a refrigerator and even a kitchen sink! This thing was set up to be lived out of year round as far as I was concerned.

"Would you believe I got all of this for only $13,000?" he said with a proud, German accent.

"This is unbelievable!" I told him. "You should just sell your house in Florida and live in this thing all year."

"I've thought about it," he laughed.

As Reinhard and I were talking we were joined by Buck who walked into the van as if it where his, cup of coffee in hand.

"Would you like some coffee?" he asked.

"No thanks," I said. "I really do appreciate the offer but I don't drink caffeine."

The three of us picked up our conversation from the night before as if it had never ended. I really felt a bond with these fellow nomads and I wished I could have spent more time with them. I even told them that at this point.

"Why don't you come to Alaska with me?" Buck offered.

"I would love to," I honestly told him, "But I have to ship off to basic training in just a couple of weeks."

"That's right!" Buck said disappointedly as he remembered we had talked about that the night before. During our conversation that night I had told both of them about the reasoning behind my trip across America. They were supportive of both the reasoning behind my trip and my decision to join the Army National Guard.

"Well when your done with all that," Buck said, "You and I need to get together and spend a summer in Alaska."

"Two hillbillies hanging out together for the summer in Alaska," I said. "What would the Eskimos do with us?"

We all three laughed at that one.

Buck and Reinhard helped me plan my day's journey on the atlas. They both kept trying to convince me to back track some so I could shoot down into Colorado. As much as I would have loved to I knew I couldn't because of both my time frame and my gas money situation.

Finally accepting this, they warned me of a supposedly wretched odor, caused by field fertilizer that I would smell as I continued on I90 through the eastern most portion of South Dakota, Nebraska and even into Iowa.

"I would certainly take a different route if I were you," warned Reinhard. "I never go through there this time of year it is so bad."

"He's not kiddin'" Buck agreed. "I don't go anywhere near there myself and if you do you'll wish you hadn't."

"I'm sure you guys are right because I've never been there but I have to stay on schedule so I don't turn up A.W.O.L." I told them.

"Okay," Buck said. "Just remember that we warned you."

After spending a little more time with my newly made friends I took care of all the business of rearranging my truck back to order and then hit the road. Reinhard and Buck waved me farewell as I left the Wal Mart parking lot and continued heading east on I90, the route they had warned me of taking.

I was only able to drive for a couple of hours before it was mid day due to my late start because of staying up so late the night before. I decided to take Buck's and Reinhard's nomadic advice and I began seeking out a body of water to kill a couple of hours. I didn't have to look for too long as I soon came to Oacoma, South Dakota, a place in the state where I90 crossed over the Missouri River. I pulled off of the interstate and quickly made my way down a dirt road that took me right to the water.

I was ready for lunch but before I ate and bathed in the waters of the Missouri I wanted to get a quick run in. I had not ran as much on this trip as I had hoped to. It was easy to do in the first part of the trip because I had the convenience of the showers at the state parks. However, when I started staying in the parking lots I no longer had this luxury. Though I could have showered every day for the week I was at the park in Washington, I only ran a couple of days while there because it was so hard to get away form the kids long enough to do it. This was no fault of theirs though, as they would have let me go just as easily as they did the couple of days I did run, but I did not want to leave their sides.

After backing my truck up to where I could let the tail gate down to face the waters of the Missouri, I quickly changed into a pair of running shorts and laced up my running shoes. It was about 100 degrees so I chose to run with no shirt.

I made my way back to the hard top and began running along side the Missouri. I soon veered left onto a road that went about a mile out to a public park. This was perfect because it was a half a mile or so from my truck to this road so out and back would give me three miles.

The first part of the run went smoothly but I began to feel uncomfortable on the way back. I think that since I had been running along a gradually declining grade I had gone out too fast and I was now paying the price.

By the time I got back to the main road and only had a half mile to go I was really hurting. I had stomach cramps, calf cramps and an oncoming headache. I thought of stopping, something I had done less than a hand full of times in my nearly twenty year running career, but then I thought of something better; my weakness prayer.

Leaning into the hill and grasping at my now hurting side, I mouthed the words, "God, please give me your strength in my time of weakness." I know that in times of trouble or during challenging situations a lot of people "dig deep" or "look inside themselves" for that "inner strength" to get through it. I've always believed that any strength, talent or skill that I possess is not of my own accord but is a gift from God so years ago I quit trying to look to myself to come up with solutions for problems and just started going straight to the top!

Once again this prayer was the answer and God saw me through the rest of the run. I made it back to the truck winded and hurting but I made it back to the truck.

After walking around for a few minutes to catch my breath I grabbed my shaving bag, kicked off my shoes and socks, and walked into the Missouri river to shave and bath. The water was soothing, especially after my difficult run, but I was inconveniently joined in it by a nasty horse fly. Just as I began shaving this son of a gun bit me on my back right shoulder blade and I nearly cut my throat when I jerked my razor down in pain. I ducked under the water as I felt him land on my back again for another bite.

For the rest of the time I shaved I did so neck deep in the water. I could still see and hear him flying around my head but my hair worked as little sensors so that when he did land on my head I would know it before he bit me and I could smack him. Just as I finished shaving I managed to land a shot that killed him dead.

With the fly gone and my face shaved I was able to enjoy my bath. I was already completely wet from the way I had to shave and avoid the fly so I simply walked onto the bank and lathered up with soap. I then walked back into the water and swam around to rinse off.

I made my way back to the bed of my truck and prepared lunch. I ate two ham and cheese sandwiches and a handful of Idaho plums. I didn't want the crust from my bread so I pealed it off the sandwiches and threw it on the ground beside my truck for whatever vermin might come by and get it later. I then inflated my air mattress and unrolled my light sleeping bag so that I could nap in comfort. Again, I rarely napped during the day but knowing I was simply following the advice of a couple of pros, Buck and Reinhard, I viewed it as a guilt free treat today.

I had fallen asleep, though I don't know for how long when I was awakened by the loud squawking of a couple of obnoxious sea gulls. It seems that these two birds had eaten the crust from my sandwiches and were demanding more. This was pay back I guess from all those times I teased the sea gulls at North Carolina's Outer Banks.

I had no more food that I was willing to share with these ingrates so I waved them off and tried to go back to sleep. That is when I was visited by the ghost of horse fly past. It began nipping at my toes and then was joined by a friend who was doing the same. In other words, my peaceful mid day rest was over. I got back in the truck and headed east.

Shortly after getting back on the interstate something I had feared might happen throughout the entire trip finally did. The engine light came on! Oh no!

I quickly took the next exit and parked in the side lot of a gas station. I popped open the hood and got out to investigate. I stood there looking at the running engine as if there was actually something in there that I might recognize, but the fact is that there was not. Though I am a firm believer in regular maintenance of a vehicle I know absolutely nothing about how that maintenance is performed or what any of the parts under the hood are. It's just a man thing I guess to at least look at the engine like you know what you are doing.

After looking at the engine for a couple of minutes I closed the hood and got back in the truck. I turned the motor off, counted to ten, prayed and then restarted it. The check engine light did not come back on when I restarted the truck. I rolled back onto the interstate and continued on my way and I am happy to say that the light never came back on throughout the rest of the day.

As afternoon became evening I decided it was time to start locating a Wal Mart here on the eastern side of South Dakota. That was until I began smelling what had to be the foulest odor I had ever smelled in my life!

At first I feared my truck might be burning oil, but when I rolled down the window I could tell that the odor was definitely coming from outside as it hit me in the face like a bully in gym class! This was the odor that Buck and Reinhard had warned me about and I wished like crazy now that I had heeded their warning. It was the foulest smell that I had ever smelled! The fertilizer causing this stench was obviously spread thickly over every field in this part of the country.

The closer I got to the Nebraska state line the worse the odor got. At times I stopped for gas or a snack and I had to hold my breath any time I got out of the truck.

I had done so well at abiding by my "no driving after dark" rule while on this trip, but this was the point in the trip to break that rule! There was no way I was going to spend a night in the back of my truck with this odor!

Most of the days on the trip so far I had driven anywhere form 280 to 350 miles per day. However, in my attempt to escape the wretched odor coming from the fertilizer in all the fields surrounding the interstate I drove for more than 500 miles this day. I drove until 2:00 a.m. I did not stop driving until I reached Council Bluffs, Iowa in the far south western corner of the state. I had veered onto I29 south some time ago and would not travel on I90 anymore. It seemed that the farther south I went after veering onto I29 the less and less I could smell the stench. By Council Bluffs the odor was entirely gone.

As late as it was I was not so tired that I was worried of any risk of falling asleep while driving. I am assuming this was due to sleeping in, being used to staying up later than this from the night before, and because I did manage to get somewhat of a nap in today before being awakened by the sea gulls. I managed to find the Wal Mart, which did have signs up against overnight parking and had no caravan in the lot. In spite of these facts, it was 2:30 in the morning and I was not going to drive anymore. I would risk a ticket. I not only slept in the lot but I got in the back of the truck and slept on the comfort of my air mattress. I had become quite brazen since that first night in a Wal Mart parking lot back in Roswell, New Mexico.

At four o'clock in the morning I was awakened, terrified actually by what sounded like something trying to claw its way into the back of my truck. When I sat up I saw that I had backed the truck up so far at the edge of the lot that the end of the bed was actually parked over a sprinkling system at the edge of the grass. As loud as it was I was so tired that I didn't even get up to move the truck. The way I saw it, I would get a good night's sleep in spite of the sprinkler system and I would have one shiny clean spare tire in the morning. I went back out like a light!

34

Though I was up late the past two nights now I still woke up at 8:00 a.m. local time. I was happy that no one had attempted to enforce the "no over night parking" signs in the parking lot.

I went into Wal Mart and bought some ice and bread before returning to my truck and starting the day's drive. I didn't feel good at all, now starting to show the signs of sleep deprivation. Fortunately, it would be a short day as far as driving was concerned because my next stop, Independence, Missouri was only about three hours away. I wanted to stop in Independence and spend some time at the Harry S. Truman Presidential Library and Museum. Truman was one of my favorite President's.

Though I could ordinarily make the drive in one straight shot without stopping, I stopped half way between Council Bluffs and Independence to take a long nap at a rest stop. I had the time to spare and I much needed the sleep.

After stopping at this rest stop I went into the bathroom and plugged my cell phone up for a free charge as I had gotten so accustomed to doing. I then went out to a picnic table and ate a couple of bologna and cheese sandwiches and half a can of sweet yams.

I then got my felt sleeping bag out of the truck and spread it out on the ground under a large sycamore tree. I was far enough east now to where I was beginning to notice familiar trees and plant life. After laying on the sleeping bag I decided to go all out as far as comfort was concerned so I returned to the truck and got my pillows as well. I had long ago gotten over the stares of fellow travelers as I just made myself at home at any rest stop or Wal Mart parking lot.

As I lay on the ground, not really asleep but not really awake, I found my thoughts drifting back to the days of the previous spring when I had spent six months alone with the kids. Times were really tough for us there at the end and I was making the decision to buy groceries and not pay bills on several occasions. One of our most common dinners had become frozen fish sticks, store brand macaroni and cheese and canned corn. As poor as we were I still tried to have a meat, a starch and a vegetable at every dinner.

I was in such a state of semi-consonances as I laid on the green grass on this warm day that it felt like my body had transcended to a fourth dimension and I felt as if I were sitting there at the table with my kids eating dinner. Emily was sitting to my right and Olivia was to my left, the way we always were so that both girls could sit beside me. Christian was straight across the table from me and the little neighbor girl KiKi was squeezed in between Christian and Emily.

I often referred to KiKi as my adopted daughter because she spent so much time at our house. She always had the luxury of eating two dinners as she ate with us every day and then again with her family, who always ate a couple of hours after us.

As I came back to complete conciseness when a tractor trailer running down the interstate began shifting into lower gears I found that I was crying. Instead of fighting back my tears I let them flow. I know I am a man, and soon to be an infantryman at that, but I believe that allowing ourselves to feel pain is a part of the human condition that sets us apart from animals. It is not just our thumbs that make us different than apes.

I really had mixed emotions. Though it was sad to look back on the hardships we had been through, I could honestly say that sitting around that table every evening eating our fish sticks that came five pounds to the bag for only a couple of dollars were truly the best days of our lives. They were the best days of my life anyway. Though I didn't have two nickels to rub together, I had my children, including my adopted daughter KiKi.

I don't know how long I had been out but it must have been for some time as when I retrieved my cell phone it was fully charged. It generally took at least an hour to get a full charge.

After packing my gear back into the truck I got back on the road. I got to Kansas City, Missouri shortly thereafter, where I took a wrong turn and had to circle around the city for nearly an hour before finding the right way again. This was the only time on the trip this happened and I attributed it to my lack of sleep.

After finding my way again I soon came to Independence. I located the Truman Library pretty easily but I got there only twenty minutes before it closed. At least I would know where it was in the morning when I came back.

On my way to locate the closest Wal Mart, which I wouldn't need for several hours as it was nowhere near dark, I noticed a sign for a lake and a park. Since I had the time to kill I decided I would go to the lake and get in a run and a bath.

I made my way through a small suburb of Independence, which I'm sure had really grown since the days that Truman had lived here, and found the lake with ease. As I was driving down to the parking lot I had to stop in the middle of the road for a while as I saw something I had never seen before. A doe had been crossing the road and her fawn decided that it was time to eat, right there in the middle of the road. The young deer fed on his mother's teat for about two minutes before she shook him off and continued crossing the road, allowing me access to the lake.

Whereas my run yesterday had been very uncomfortable my run today felt great. There was no humidity and it was now evening, a much better time to run than in the middle of the day. I started at the lake but ran up into a mature subdivision, the type where not all the houses looked the same and the houses were actually spread quite some distance apart.

I had planned on only running for twenty minutes but the run felt so good that I went for thirty. I made my way back to the lake, walked around for about ten minutes to cool down, then grabbed my shaving bag and went to the water for my homeless guy bathing ritual.

When I got to the water, there were several families picnicking and swimming and a few guys fishing. It was tricky positioning myself in between all the people so as not to disturb any of them but I managed. I tilted my head to wish them all hello as they watched me as I entered the water, wearing only my skimpy running shorts and the pair of sandals I had switched into. I'm sure they stared in wonder as I began lathering my body up with Ivory soap, but again, I had stopped noticing such things by now.

I finished my bath, swam around a little bit in the warm water and then returned to my truck. I drove back to Independence and continued to seek out the Wal Mart.

I got to the Wal Mart right at dark. I did not see the caravan and when I pulled up at the far side of the lot I knew why. There were more "no over night parking" signs posted. Again, like the night before I decided to ignore them. That was until I saw the little white golf cart with the flashing yellow light on top coming my way.

Fortunately I saw the cart before I had rearranged all of my gear so I simply started the truck back up and got back on the interstate to find another Wal Mart. I was able to find one only ten minutes further down the road. I pulled in, this time finding the caravan, pulled up beside it and organized my sleeping gear in the back. Before going to sleep I called my kids and had a wonderful conversation with all three. The only down side of our talk was when the question that always came up arose; "Daddy, when do we get to see you again."

It was tough answering this question now. Just a couple of weeks ago the answer was only a couple of days, but now, it was at least six months. I never came right out and said it in those terms because six months to children as young as mine may as well have been ten years. I simply said, "I'll be back as soon as I finish my training. It will go by fast."

I attempted to call Maia, knowing she would still be working. I simply left her a message letting her know where I was, that I was safe, and that I loved her and couldn't wait to see her again. The one silver lining at the edge of the cloud was that I would be seeing Maia again soon, if only for a couple of days before not being able to see her again for months as well.

I was asleep by ten o'clock this night and it was a much welcomed early night to bed. The past couple of nights had worn me out and I wanted to be completely rested the next day when I visited the Truman Library. I wanted to take in every exhibit of our 33'rd president that the library had to offer.

The next morning I awakened fresh, lively and ready to hit the Truman library. It would be another hour before it opened which gave me plenty of time to eat a bowl of cereal in the back of the truck and make my way back to the heart of Independence where the library was located.

When I did finally get to the library I waited for about ten minutes for the doors to open along with a dozen other people. We all chatted briefly about the weather and about Truman and then the doors finally opened.

After paying my admission I was drawn first to the oval office that sits right across from the admissions desk. The office was set up exactly as Truman's had been when he served in the white house. The big globe, which was a gift from General Dwight D. Eisenhower sat in front of the fire place. One of the most famous pictures of Eisenhower and Truman together is one where they both had their hands rested on opposite sides of this globe. On the presidential desk sat the famous sign that read, "The Buck Stops Here."

I looked at every crook and cranny of the office before heading down stairs to start the exhibit. On my way down stairs I thought back on how simple of a man Harry S. Truman was and about how, in spite of this simplness, there could have been no better man to step in and fill the shoes of F.D.R. when he died less than three months into his fourth term.

Harry Truman, like so many of our past presidents came from very humble beginnings. He did not go to college, he spent much of his life before getting into politics as a farmer, and he was the first president to be born in a hospital. His ancestors had migrated west like so many people in the early 1800's in the hopes of laying claims to much more fertile farming land than what was to be had back east.

Harry Truman was born in 1884 in Lamar, Missouri. His family would later move to their farm on the outskirts of Independence. As a child and young man,

Truman put in long hours helping with the family farm, a fact that would instill in him a work ethic that he carried through life. Interestingly, his middle initial "S" stood for nothing. His parents simply gave him this initial instead of a middle name.

As a youth, Truman had longed for a military career but was unable to get into West Point due to his eye sight. However, with the outbreak of WWI and America's eventual involvement in the conflict, Truman found himself being drafted and he went to France and served in an artillery unit. He saw action in which he displayed great leadership qualities, was admired by his men for doing so, and thus was promoted to the rank of Captain by the time he completed his duties in 1919 and returned to Missouri.

After the war, Truman married a childhood friend, Bess Wallace, and set up a haberdashery shop with his war time friend Eddie Jacobson. Though his business which specialized in men's wear flourished for a time it soon floundered and Truman found himself going into politics at the local level.

Truman's first elected spot was that of county judge. Though the title sounds like one of the legal world it is not. County Judges had responsibilities in those days much like that of modern county commissioners. Truman's main area of oversight was infer structure and he specialized in roads.

After years of getting in good with the local democratic party machine Truman eventually ran for a seat in the senate. He was elected but was not the most effective senator. Though he had built a reputation for possessing integrity during his years as judge, many people were leery of him due to his connection with the Pendergast family who ran the democratic machine in Missouri. Old man Pendergast, the family patriarch would actually spend time in prison for tax evasion.

Truman's most effective feat though as a senator was when he took the helm of a military finance committee during WWII. Truman's duty was to visit weapons and equipment plants and make sure that there was no fiscal waste. To his dismay he found that there was quite a bit of it. Proving that his reputation for integrity that he had earned years ago was justifiable, he held nothing back when giving his report of the wasteful spending to the congress. This elevated his reputation in the eyes of his peers and constituents to another level.

In the 1944 presidential election F.D.R. decided to drop vice-president Henry Wallace from the ticket and with much coaxing, Truman took Wallace's vacancy. The democrats knew of Roosevelt's faltering health and knew that they were basically setting the new V.P. up to be the next president and they felt that Truman would be a better person than Wallace for the position. Sure enough, 82 days after the election their hunch became a reality and upon Roosevelt's death Truman was sworn in as president.

There is a story that Truman approached Eleanor Roosevelt after hearing of F.D.R.'s passing and offered to help her in any way he could. She thanked him with a smile but let him know that he would be the one needing the help now.

Mrs. Roosevelt was right as we were still at war with the Japanese, though Germany had already surrendered. Though the great depression was all but over, the American economy had not been too far removed from its darkest days. Though Russia was a friend during the fighting in Europe, they would soon become a foe of more than half a century in the cold war. The atomic bomb had just come into existence and Truman would be the first chief executive to have to decide weather or not to use it. The weight of the world had certainly fallen onto the shoulders of a simple farmer from Independence, Missouri.

Truman took charge of the nation and all the issues it faced with the courage of a lion. He did indeed decide to drop the atomic bomb on both Nagasaki and Hiroshima, stating that "to posses a weapon so great that it could end the war immediately and thereby save millions of American casualties and not use it, would be irresponsible." Until the day he died, December 26, 1972, he never regretted having nuked Japan.

It is my personal opinion that the fact that Truman had seen warfare up close in WWI is why it he chose to use the atomic bomb. No one knew war better than a man who had been there. Eisenhower was known to say that he "hated war as only a man who has seen war can." Truman had seen war too and I'm sure it played into his decision to use the bomb.

When I got to the downstairs portion of the exhibit I listened to the little hand held speaker things they have in these places and could hear Truman's voice as he gave several speeches. Truman's voice was somewhat raspy and high pitched but he was known more so for his hand gestures when he spoke than for his voice. He would constantly hold both hands up and out, about two feet apart, and karate chop the air, both hands moving simultaneously as he made a point of importance.

He had somewhat erroneously earned the name "Give 'em Hell Harry" by the media because of an incident in which he said the word "Hell" one time. In the 1940's I guess that was a big deal, but he rarely cursed and treated everyone in that down home mid-western way that this part of the country is famous for.

I made my way through the exhibit and got to see one of Truman's cars, a 1941 Chrysler Royal Club Coupe which had been donated to the library by someone who had owned the car after Truman. I also saw much of the gear he used during his days as a soldier in WWI. Further down there were original letters he had written to Bess and those that she had written to him. There were also several books that had belonged to Truman when he was a child.

It is interesting to note that when Truman left office he had a very low public approval rating. Like President Johnson from Tennessee though, Truman did not make his executive decisions based upon what was popular at the time, but based upon what he felt was right and in line with the constitution and with the best interests of the American people and the people of the world.

During the Korean war, Truman, after firing General Macarthur, an unpopular act in the eyes of most Americans, realized how dangerous it was to leave the decision to use the nuclear bomb in the hands of the military, thus he dismantled the Department of War and reorganized it under the title of the Department of Defense. One of the stipulations he laid down with the new department was that it must always be headed by a civilian, as opposed to a militant. This decision was made by Truman largely by Macarthur's desire to nuke the largest 20 cities in China to keep them at bay during the Korean war. Many would agree that had this not been done we would have been even closer to using nuclear weapons during the cold war with Russia, thus igniting the process of mutually assured destruction in which both nations would have been destroyed.

Truman is also responsible for starting N.A.T.O., as well as instituting the doctrine with his namesake, the Truman Doctrine, which allowed for the U.S. to provide military assistance to those nations resisting communist take over.

One of the few decisions Truman made as President that he was queasy about was the recognition of Israel as a Jewish state. After he made this decision, which he was highly pressured by congress into making, he said, "I feel that for political purposes I have done something that will come back to haunt America for many years to come." He had such foresight that he could nearly predict our current war on terrorism when he made this decision.

Truman also gets recognition for desegregating the U.S. armed forces. He also ended, at least at face value, discrimination for federal jobs. Truman wanted to go much farther than he did with civil rights at home but his initiatives were repeatedly blocked by the conservative congress at the time.

Though his presidential rating was as low as it was when he left office, history has remembered him as one of the most effective presidents of the last one hundred years. I couldn't help but think of the similarities our current president, George W. Bush, holds to Truman in this regard.

As of this writing, President Bush's public approval rating hovers around 30%. Much of this is directly due to the war in Iraq. However, though I do not think President Bush is perfect I do believe history will treat him much like it has Harry S. Truman.

President Bush has been the first president to directly confront terrorist organizations with military might since the terrorists of the middle east declared war on us when an extremist group in Iran took 52 American diplomats hostage in 1979 and then exasperated the war when another group of extremists bombed the U.S. marine barracks in Beirut, Lebanon in 1982. His initiatives with education, particularly the no child left behind act has reduced illiteracy among American school children drastically. I know of many teachers who have complained of this act since it was passed, but I know that as a sales guy on Wall Street, I always had levels of production to meet. Any other business that produces any other good or service also has production levels they must meet. Why not ask our public school teachers to meet a productivity level as well? President Bush thinks it is not too much to ask as teachers are producing our nation's most important commodity; our future.

Many of the folks who don't particularly care for Bush's supposed "cowboy" tough talk and walk are not fond of his decisions in regard to his use of our military but no one can argue the fact that perhaps seeing what he has been willing to do can be directly related to Libya's decision to disarm as well as the fact that we now have a nuclear free Korean peninsula.

We hear so much about how unpopular the United States is around the world these days but throughout history we have lacked in popularity any time we stood in a solid position of strength. Also, though the war in Iraq is unpopular, never in our history has there ever been a time when more than 50% of our population was in favor of any war we were in, including the Revolution.

Many Americans disapproved of President Reagan's tough stance with the Russians during his presidency, believing that if we gave more concessions to the Russians we could see a less hostile end to the cold war but today the fact is that we no longer have to practice bombing drills and hide under our desks in our schools or offices. Reagan solidly held a position of strength with the Soviets and it paid off. Today we are glad that he was as tough as he was. I believe that a generation from now, when many American Christians can make pilgrimages to Jerusalem without the fear of being blown up at a bus stop by some fundamental, radical extremist group, more of us will be glad that President Bush was the "cowboy" during these times that he has been.

Speaking of other presidents, in the basement of the Truman Library there were many items on display that belonged to Nixon, Kennedy, Ford, Reagan and George H.W. Bush. Being the Reagan fan that I am I took special interest in a pair of his cowboy boots, his Air Force 1 flight jacket and one of his horse saddles that were on display.

To cap off this visit to the Truman library, I finally visited Truman's grave which is just outside the museum in a court yard at the back of the building. His grave is marked with a large concrete cover giving his birth and death dates and a listing of many of his accomplishments. There is also the "eternal flame," a constantly burning torch that was erected in remembrance of this great American.

As I made my way back to my truck and out of Independence I was glad that I had stopped by to see the Truman Library. I had been fond of Truman for some time and I was happy to see first hand many of the artifacts from his life time. As with so many of my experiences on this trip I had to see the blessing in my misfortunes that led me to homelessness. It is almost as if I had to lose it all to gain everything.

35

At some point in the past couple of days I had come to the understanding that I was down to only a couple tanks worth of gas money. I still had not made it to the Mississippi river in St. Louis and it would take me almost a tank of gas in my old Dodge Daguzzler to do so. On my way out of Independence I noticed a pawn shop on the side of the road. Though I would have preferred to have found work along my route I was not able to do so and as much as I hated to walk in the doors of a pawn shop it looked like this was my last option if I wanted to make it back to Virginia.

I pulled into the parking lot and painstakingly grabbed my guitar from the back seat to take inside and pawn. Oh how I wished I could have used this to hustle up gas money on the streets of Roswell as a pan handler but obviously I lacked the talent. They say that it is a poor musician who blames his instrument. I certainly was not blaming my trusty acoustic for my lack of revenue that day back in Roswell but if I wanted to get home I certainly would have to part with it today in Independence.

I walked in and asked some guy in a black golf shirt with tattoo sleeves all the way down both arms if they were in need of an acoustic guitar. I got the standard pawn shop rip you off line of, "No, we don't need any more but we'll take a look at what you've got."

I unzipped my gig bag and held up my Kona acoustic hoping this guy would see the beauty in it that I had. It was not an expensive guitar, only costing me $125 brand new, but it had a lot of sentimental value. I had played it so many nights for my daughters back in Virginia and while camping in Washington and I had serenaded Maia with it on more than one occasion (poor girl).

"That's just a cheap Chinese brand," Mr. Tattoo guy said very sarcastically. "We can give you $25 for it."

"Look man," I said. "I'm in a bind. I have driven from Virginia to the west coast and I'm on my way back and I don't have enough gas money to get there."

Mr. Tattoo guy rolled his eyes as if he had heard these sob stories before, which I am sure he had nearly every day.

"Twenty five dollars won't even get me one tank of gas," I added. "I have to get back because I have to report for basic training in a couple of weeks."

With this, the manager who had been doing paper work at his desk came over to me and Mr. Tattoo.

"Let me see that," he said, reaching out to take my guitar.

"We can give you $75 for this," he said.

"But we can get those new for $75!" Mr. Tattoo said argumentatively to his boss.

"Well this thing looks new to me," the manager said. "You really took care of this thing soldier. What else do you have that you can part with?"

"I don't really know?" I said, amazed that he was willing to give me $75 for my Kona acoustic. "Let me go to the truck and see."

I went to the truck and came back into the store with my Coleman cook stove, an automobile battery charger and my battery operated Coleman lamp.

"How about this stuff?" I said to the manager as I laid my wears on his counter.

He studied over my items with a curious look on his face.

"This stuff all looks new too," he said, leading me to believe he was going to be just as generous as he had been with the guitar.

"I'll give you $30 for the stove, $30 for the battery charger, and $20 for the lamp!"

"You can get that stuff at Wal Mart for those prices," Mr. Tattoo said incredulously. He was right too because I had.

"Go take inventory!" the manager snapped at his employee. "Do these prices sound fair to you?" he then asked me.

"Sure," I said. "They sound more than fair."

With that he opened his register and counted out the $155 he had quoted me on my items. He then looked around and made sure Mr. Tattoo guy or no one else was watching and took out an extra $20 and handed it to me as well.

"Good luck getting home and good luck at basic training," he said to me as he handed me the cash.

"Wow!" I said. "Sir, I am very grateful but I'll admit I'm also a bit confused."

"Hey," he said. "If you're willing to go to war to fight for me, the least I can do is make sure you're not late getting there. Thank you!" he said.

I left the store and I thought of what Eddie Montz had said back in New Orleans.

"People helping people man. It's just people helping people!"

I left Independence with a full tank of gas and a full stomach, having stopped at an all you can eat pizza buffet on the way out of town. I felt as if I could splurge an extra $5 on a warm meal due to the kind treatment I received from the manager at the pawn shop, which had to be a first for anyone who has ever dealt with those kind of places.

The drive across Missouri was pretty uneventful save for a fierce thunderstorm that rolled in just before I made it to St. Louis. I had actually stopped for a quick mid day nap in the cab of my truck when I was awakened by the storm's first thunderous clapping. I tried to sleep through the storm but the repeated thunder kept me from doing so.

I made my way back on the interstate and passed by that huge arch in St. Louis which stood as a monument for the gateway to the west. Today however, it would be my gateway to the east.

I did not stop at the arch due to both the storm and the fact that it would be dark soon but I had been to it several times. Edward Jones' home office was located in St. Louis and when I had worked for them I had to come out here on several occasions for week long training sessions. On all of my trips I made my way out to the arch though it took me several trips before I finally mustered up the nerve to go to the top.

I hate heights. When I got to the top of the arch the day I did ride the little elevator/carnival ride type rig to the top all I could focus on was how the top of the arch swayed in the wind. There are little platforms at the top that you can actually lay on and look out a Plexiglas window to the world below. I remember laying down and looking out the window and seeing the Edward Jones Dome, the home of the St. Louis Rams, when I first felt the arch sway. I didn't jump up immediately because I was afraid that I would puke if I did so. And why was it I was contemplating going to Airborne school at Fort Benning?

As I made my way out of St. Louis I stopped on the east side to eat at the Golden Coral restaurant. I scourged on some lightly sauced barbeque ribs, remembering the time I had seen Maia doing the same when I had seen her at the Golden Coral in Charlottesville, Virginia months before I finally met her. After I had finished eating I was back on the road.

While driving through Illinois I got a call from my father. He called to tell me that on this upcoming Saturday there was a 5k road race back in my home town of Richwood, West Virginia and he thought that it would be nice if I could make it by and run in it. The race was being held in order to raise money to resurface our old high school track.

Resurface was perhaps the wrong term as the thing had never been surfaced in the first place. It was nothing more than a strip of pot holed asphalt that circled our high school's football field. I think it was actually 410 meters around too instead of the standard 400 meters.

A lot of kids always used the patheticness of our track as an excuse to under perform but the way I saw it back then was that if I pushed as hard as I could on every interval I ran on this so called "track" it would make the running all that much easier when we went to meets at other, more prosperous schools who had good tracks. Again, either the glass is half empty or it is half full.

I told my father I would do my best to get back in time, but I wanted to stop off and visit President Lincoln's boyhood home in Indiana and I would not pass that up to make the race. Fortunately it appeared that there would be enough time for me to do both.

I finished my conversation with my father and kept rolling down the road. Honestly, I wanted to make it back and run the race. I had always hoped for a nice track while in high school and though it never came I was ecstatic to know that the future generations would have this luxury. Besides, I did still hold our school's record in the mile so I thought it only appropriate that I be there for the race.

With my desire to run the race in mind, I drove through much of the night to cover as much distance as I could. I hadn't planned on stopping anywhere else before getting to Lincoln City, Indiana, Lincoln's boyhood home, which I would find when I got there was anything but a city. There were more cows than people.

Just before mid-night I made my way off of the interstate and into Booneville, Indiana. This would put me about an hour away from my destination for the next day.

When I pulled into the Wal Mart parking lot I got a very eerie feeling. Maybe it was because there was no caravan. Maybe it was because of the creepy looking middle aged guy with a long beard riding a teenaged girl's bike across the parking lot in the middle of the night. Maybe because it would be the last night I would spend in a Wal Mart parking lot on this trip and I knew my luck had seemed almost too good so far as I had not been busted for vagrancy or ruffed up by any hooligans in the middle of the night.

In spite of this eerie feeling I pulled my truck up to the far side of the lot and prepared my sleeping space as I had so many nights before. Tonight it would just be me and some guy in a van three spaces down from me sleeping here. After preparing my space I crawled into the bed of my truck and fell fast to sleep.

I slept really good all night. I awakened the next day around 8:00 a.m. and just laid there motionless while the sun pierced through the tented windows of my topper. As I lay there, it took me a minute to realize that there was some sort of red and blue flashing reflections coming through the windows of the topper and bouncing back and forth within my sleeping space.

"Oh no!" I whispered out loud.

I slowly lifted my head and peered out of the left side of my topper. I could see that the guy in the van beside me was getting written up by a cop who had his cruiser parked with the lights on in between our two vehicles.

I laid back down and attempted to formulate a plan of action. My feeling last night must have been a premonition that this was coming.

Not to worry. I simply got dressed while I was laying down, making sure that I didn't pop my head up to where the cop could see me through my windows. I then quietly crawled out of the hatch, over the tail gate and down to the ground. As I looked over though to see if I were being watched by the cop, the topper top slid out of my hand and loudly slammed onto the back of the tail gate.

As this happened, both the cop and my neighbor that he was giving a ticket to looked over in my direction. I looked back at my truck as if I didn't notice them and opened the latch and slammed it down a couple of times, making it look as if I had done it the first time on purpose.

"Damn thing sticks sometimes," I said to the two men watching me, as if I had loaded something from Wal Mart into the back of my truck.

This act worked on the cop as he simply continued writing out his ticket. It did not work however, on my fellow nomad as he glared at me as if he were telling me with his evil gaze that he knew exactly what I was doing. I simply shrugged my shoulders in a "what else am I supposed to do?" fashion and quickly got into the cab of my truck to make a quick get away.

I could not see out of the passenger side window because all of my traveling gear that I hauled in the back of my truck during the day was still sitting in the passenger seat. I drove to the other side of the Wal Mart parking lot, parked in the middle of a bunch of cars, and very uncomfortably worked around the cars to put my belongings back into the bed of my truck. I then went in and used the facilities before coming out and continuing on my way, feeling as if I had really gotten away with a close call this time.

I drove for just about an hour before finally getting to Lincoln City, Indiana. Again, this small farming community was anything but a city. There were no sky scrapers or buildings of moderate size to be seen, only corn fields and live stock.

It wasn't hard finding the childhood home of Lincoln as the exhibit seemed to be all that existed in this small community and there were signs pointing to it everywhere. I made my way into the parking lot of the exhibit and got out to take a look around.

The building which housed numerous artifacts from Lincoln's childhood and information on his life and presidency was quite simple. Perhaps the most alluring part of the exhibit though was the grave of Lincoln's mother, Nancy Hanks Lincoln which was located in a wooded lot across the street from the museum.

In the summer of 1818 a disease known as "milk-sick" passed through southwestern Indiana. The disease was believed to be the result of cows eating rayless goldenrod or white snakeroot and then passing the poison from these plants on to their milk, poisoning anyone who drank it. The disease was known to take effect immediately and it usually caused death. Shortly after two of Lincoln's relatives died from this disease his mother became ill with the malady and passed away as well.

Though Lincoln was close to his mother he rarely spoke of her or his feelings about her premature death in his later years. Lincoln was known to take extended bouts of depression and these bouts may have been rooted in the experience of losing his mother at an early age.

Most Americans remember Lincoln for his undoubting leadership during the civil war in which he saw the North to victory and preserved the Union. I have always been amazed by the hardships he faced with his inner demons and how in spite of these demons was able to go on and become one of the most known and respected historical figures the world over.

There was a time in Lincoln's young adulthood when he had been rejected by a young lady with whom he was in love and he actually spent a month in bed in a deep depression. His close friends were so worried about him that they kept a close suicide watch over him until he pulled out of his doldrums.

Lincoln's long time law partner, William H. Herndon records that there were many days when Lincoln would come to work at their law office in relatively good spirits, work for a short time, and then slump into a silent depression. Lincoln would often times during these depressions rest his chin in his hand and stare out the window for up to six hours at a time and never speak a word. During these instances Herndon often left the law office and put the "closed" sign up on the locked door so Lincoln would not be disturbed. Herndon hated to see Lincoln in this state and would leave the office so he would not have to see his friend suffer.

The death of Lincoln's mother was not the only hardship he went through as far as deaths in his immediate family. Lincoln and his wife Mary Todd had four children and only one of them lived to adulthood. Lincoln and Mary Todd buried the other three.

Lincoln had never been close to his father but did become close with his father's second wife after the passing of his birth mother. Lincoln's father, Thomas Lincoln remarried about a year after the death of his first wife. Thomas Lincoln went to Elizabethtown Kentucky with the intent of taking a second wife and did so with Sarah Bush Johnston, an attractive widow who had three children of her own.

Sarah moved her household belongings and her three children into the home of Thomas Lincoln and family and treated Abraham as if he were her natural child. Young Abraham took quickly to his new maternal figure and would speak highly of her and stay in close contact with her throughout his adult life. Though Lincoln was not her biological child, Sarah often hinted to the fact that he was her favorite. She really liked this tall, lanky being and felt as if he held the potential to become a great man, which we all know that he did.

Lincoln's relationship with his father was one that always seemed to be strained. Though there is no record of any sort of dispute that took place between Lincoln and his father to suggest there was a reason for the distance in the relationship it is one that was never warm just the same. Many believe that the reason Lincoln left home as soon as he could upon obtaining the age of majority was to put distance between himself and his father.

Another aspect of Lincoln's life that I find interesting is his numerous failings in both business and politics. Though he was quite successful as a lawyer his first attempt in business was that of a general store owner, an attempt that failed as the direction of growth seemed to be moving away from where he had set up shop in New Salem, Illinois. Lincoln and a partner, William F. Berry ran their store successfully for a while but things went south for Lincoln upon his partner's death and with the population movement heading in a different direction. However, proving that he was a man of character, Lincoln did over a period of time repay all the debts that were incurred in his partner's name on behalf of their business.

Lincoln was successful in winning a bid as a state Legislator. He would serve four terms as a Legislator and one term as a Congressman but he would later lose reelection of this post to Justin Butterfield of Chicago in what appeared to be his end in politics. After his lose, Lincoln returned to life as an attorney and it would be some time before he threw his hat back into the political arena.

When Lincoln did reenter the political arena it was for the newly formed Republican party's nomination for president and was more so for an attempted block of Stephen A. Douglas' nomination than anything else. Douglas, a long time and successful politician held many of the newly formed party's ideals but seemed to be very bluesy about the issue of slavery. Lincoln felt that the time to end slavery had come, that the Republican party was the party to end it, but that Douglas was not the man to lead the party into doing so.

Lincoln and Douglas had many well heated public debates during the campaign and in the end Lincoln was not only successful in getting the nomination but also won the general election as well, drawing favorable support from the heavily populated northeastern portion of the country. Lincoln did not however, win a single state in the south.

Even before Lincoln was sworn in the southern states started to secede from the Union. By the time Lincoln was sworn into office in March of 1862 South Carolina, Mississippi, Florida, Alabama, Georgia and Louisiana had already left the union and had formed the Confederate States of America.

Whereas Andrew Jackson had been successful in keeping ring leader South Carolina from seceding during his presidency by basically surrounding the state with artillery units and in essence saying, "Go ahead, make my day" Lincoln was not yet in office to attempt anything along the same lines or even a different strategy which he no doubt would have taken, being much more of a pacifist than Jackson, and lame duck President James Buchanan had been all but rendered powerless at this time. So when Lincoln finally did make it to Washington he was already up to his neck in troubles facing the nation like it had never seen before. Even during the Revolution and the War of 1812 the nation had been united for the most part, but this time it was state against state and brother against brother.

The results of the ensuing civil war had devastating effects on our nation. With 620,000 deaths we lost more American lives than in all the other wars we have ever fought combined. The effects on the south, mainly at the hands of Union General William Tecumseh Sherman were the most devastating in the country as their livestock and farmlands were decimated. Most of the battles fought during this great war took place on southern soil. It would take the South well into the first part of the twentieth century to fully recover from their losses. The North however, prospered with their victory and nearly untouched infer structure and became the leading industrial region not only of the country but eventually the world.

In Lincoln's successful endeavor to preserve the Union he also was responsible for ending slavery, which freed more than four million people mostly located in the south. Finally, all men "were" created equal, as slave owner Thomas Jefferson had written into the Declaration of Independence when he was only 33 years old. It would be many years however, before blacks truly were treated equal, being given the right to vote etc. and it is still arguable if they are treated equally today in many respects.

We will never know just how much greater of a President Lincoln would have been as his life was tragically ended on April 14, 1865, only five days after Confederate General Robert E. Lee surrendered to Ulysses S. Grant in Appomattox, Virginia. Lincoln and his wife were attending a performance at Ford's Theater in Washington when he was shot in the back of the head by John Wilkes Booth. Lincoln never regained consciousness from the wound and died the next day.

As I stood over the grave of Lincoln's mother in this small Indiana community I thought back on all the hardships Lincoln had gone through in his life. I have heard it said that the turmoil we go through are often to prepare us for greater things in our future. Was it preordained destiny that Lincoln should suffer through the loss of his mother and his children so that he would be emotionally prepared to face the separation of his nation? Had he suffered with extreme depression so that he would be able to handle the heart pangs of a war weary country? Would he have been able to relate to the misery of slavery had he not known misery first hand in his own life? I did not think these questions were far fetched and I do not think Lincoln's troubles in life were of mere coincidence. I believe his misfortunes prepared him to handle the responsibilities he faced as President during our nation's darkest hour in such a way that no happy life filled with joy ever could have.

36

After leaving Lincoln's boyhood home I made only one more stop in Indiana. I stopped at a road side stand where a local farmer and his 12 year old daughter were selling sweet corn. I liked corn on the cob and my father loved it so I decided to buy some ears since I would be seeing him and my mother by the end of the day. The corn was only $2 for twelve ears. I enjoyed talking to the farmer and his daughter as they obviously did me as well because they gave me two extra ears at no cost.

Actually, my father's corn on the cob eating ability was that of legend among our family. He had never entered any corn eating contests but we were all sure that if he had he would have won. He could eat the corn off of the cob in twenty seconds. He did so viciously as he spun the cob around as if it were a spindle on an old type writer, getting nearly as much corn on his face and the table as he did in his mouth.

I remember the first time Amanda ever saw my dad eat corn on the cob. I had told her about it at some point when we were just getting to know each other when we were dating and she obviously remembered the story because when we were at my parents house one time having dinner we happened to be having corn on the cob and when my father started eating an ear Amanda practically spit the food out of her mouth in laughter. I panicked at first, thinking I would have to explain the situation to my upset father but he was in the zone and didn't even notice she was laughing. Amanda laughed non-stop as my father zipped through three ears of corn in less than two minutes, pausing only to put the gobs of butter on them that he put on practically everything he ate.

That story spread among our immediate family so much that our kids used to ask when we could go to Richwood and watch Papa Ernie eat corn on the cob. Soon enough they would get to witness this phenomena themselves. Whereas Amanda had laughed, when our kids saw it they sat back in amazement.

"Wow Papa Ernie," Emily had said. "You really do like to eat corn on the cob!"

Fortunately again my dad was in the zone this time as well and I didn't have to worry about explaining myself.

I blew through Indiana in pretty short order and stopped at a rest area in Kentucky to use the restroom, charge my cell phone and have lunch. As my phone was charging I sat outside at a picnic table and ate a peanut butter and jelly sandwich, several plumbs from Idaho and a raw ear of Indiana sweet corn. Even though it wasn't cooked, the corn was the best I had ever eaten. I was sure my father was going to love this stuff.

After retrieving my phone and talking to the rest stop attendant who was trying to sell me his truck for $2000 I got back in my Dodge Dakota and continued heading east. I passed through Lexington, horse capital of the world and remembered the time I had marched in a pre Kentucky Derby parade with my high school band, the Lumberjack Express. We were a great band for a little school and got invited to many big events which included not only the most famous horse race in the world but also Cincinnati Reds baseball games.

I crossed back into the eastern time zone at some point in Kentucky and was back in West Virginia in no time. Oh how it felt good to be in the place that I truly considered home. Though I had left this state nearly ten years ago now a large part of my heart had stayed behind.

I soon made it to the state capital of Charleston. As I traveled on interstate 64 through Charleston I passed Laidley Field, the place where had I won the state mile championship nearly half my lifetime ago.

I remembered that race as I looked over to the track from the interstate. It was 98 degrees the day of the race and it was the last race of the year. I had finished sixth the night before in the two mile and had my heart set on doing my absolute best in the mile.

Though I thought I was capable of it, winning the mile was not my goal for the day. My goal was the break our school's record which stood at 4:37. I had run a 4:38 at a smaller meet earlier in the season and knew that I could do it, but I also knew that if it was to be done it had to be done on this day.

When the gun went off at the start of the race I tucked myself in at the back of the lead pack which consisted of about six runners. One gutsy runner, Tony Ball from Spencer County High took about a twenty yard lead on the pack in the first two hundred meters of the race and maintained that lead for two and a half laps. It was too hot to chase him down early and I guess we were all hoping he would come back to us. We knew he was a good runner and he had two older brothers who had both been state champions in previous years.

With a lap and a half to go I felt as if the pack were slowing the pace so I passed them on the back stretch heading into the far curve just before going into the last lap. I did not speed up but simply maintained my pace. As I was round-ing out of the turn I saw that I had closed the distance on Ball so I decided to pass him too and did so about half way down the home stretch. When all of this was happening it felt as if my body were on auto pilot. I was in the zone, similar to the one my father enters when he eats corn on the cob.

With a lap to go, the judge fired his .38 caliber starting pistol to signify that it was the last lap and that is when I came to my senses and realized I was leading the state championship mile with only a lap left. At that point all previous plans I had about breaking the school record were off and I set out to maintain my lead.

As I blew down the back stretch and entered the final turn I felt as if my legs, lungs and skin from the heat were all on fire. I had been running all out for two hundred meters and I still had two hundred to go. As I rounded the last turn and went into the home stretch I peered back over my left shoulder, something a runner should never do not only because it costs him six inches per stride but also because the runners behind him view it as a sign of weakness. I saw that Ball was only two strides back and the pack was closing in on us fast.

I tried to dig down and see if I could hit another gear but I could not. As I stated earlier I was already running all out. I knew I would not be able to speed up so my only hope was that I would not slow down.

That had to be the longest one hundred meters of my life. I could see the heat waves rising off of the track and my ears were ringing from the pain I was in. My heart felt as if it were going to pound out of my chest and my lungs felt as if I were inhaling flames.

Only fifty yards away from the finish line I stumbled and almost lost my footing. However, when I heard Ball breathing behind me as he used my mishap to cut my lead to only a stride I regained my footing and ran through the tape to win in 4:33.95 to Ball's 4:34.20. I had become the first individual state champion in track and field in Richwood High School's history by a third of a second. I also ended up shattering our school's record in the event by almost four seconds.

This glorious day happened in my junior year. Unfortunately I would not get the opportunity to defend my title my senior year. Our state's record in the mile at that time was 4:20, held by previous Olympic Trials marathon runner Steve Taylor and I had made it my goal to break the state record my senior year. In attempting to do so, which included running up to sixty miles a week in those freezing temperatures of the West Virginia winter I ended up getting stress fractures in three different places in my left shin and could not compete my senior season.

I sat in the stands that spring as Junior Mike Cox from Athens, West Virginia easily won the state mile championship in 4:24. The next year he would set a new state record with a time of 4:17. Cox would later go on to be coached by Steve Taylor at Virginia Tech were he set a school record and won the P.A.C. 10 championship in the 10,000 meters. Later still he competed in the 2004 U.S. Olympic Marathon trials in Alabama while I watched from home in Virginia while folding laundry and keeping an eye on my three children.

Shortly after passing Laidley Field I drove past the state capital with its huge golden dome. There have been several interesting characters hold the position of Governor in the mountain state throughout the years, be it Republican Arch Moore who served in the 1980's and would go to prison for embezzling state lottery funds or more recently Democrat Bob Wise who had to resign from office just in the past few years for having had a very Clintonesque type love affair with a young lady who was not his wife. Perhaps the most interesting story of any former West Virginia governor however, is that of William Casey Marland.

For years there was a story of a cab driver in Chicago who claimed he had been the governor of West Virginia. The story itself sounded like a far fetched urban legend but the people who were told this story by the cab driver himself actually thought there may be some validity to it because of the sincerity used when he told it. It turns out that the story was very true.

Marland was elected governor of West Virginia in 1952 when he was only 33 years old. He was a graduate of West Virginia University's Law School and the "powers that be" who really ran the state at the time thought he would be the perfect puppet for their bidding. He was young, intelligent, good looking and charismatic.

However, once in office Marland had plans of his own. These were plans that he never informed anyone of until he had the power to attempt to carry them out.

His plans centered around revitalizing the faltering economy in the state by imposing an excise tax on the out of state coal barons who profited like mad from the state's resources. The problem with the West Virginia economy had always been the fact that the interests who owned the land and the resources were located outside of the state, mostly in Pennsylvania and New York. So whereas the state was rich in coal and timber, most of the profits from these resources left the state. All West Virginians could hope to gain through the process of harvesting these resources were whatever labor costs these barons were willing to pay those fortunate enough to get jobs in these industries to have them harvested.

Governor Marland knew that once the coal was gone the jobs that coal mining provided would be gone as well. He wanted to formulate a way to capitalize on the profits the coal generated while it was still to be had, hence his proposal for the tax.

From an accounting stand point, the tax would not have hurt the companies to any great degree as it was very small and also because they would be able to deduct it from their federal tax liability, which was a much higher rate than the state tax, so in essence it would nearly come out in a wash. However, the barons being the capitalists that they were wanted nothing to do with any sort of extra tax.

The owners of the coal companies who at the time employed nearly half a million West Virginian's came to the state and held town hall meetings with the coal miners and their families when the vote was about to come up in regard to the tax. The barons played on the fear of the people telling them that if the tax were passed that they could not afford to continue running operations and would thereby have to shut down and move out of the state. They convinced the miners and their families that they would all be out of a job and that their families would starve.

A scare tactic is all this was. The bituminous coal in West Virginia is five times as valuable as most of the coal that appears practically anywhere else in the world and had the barons taken their ball and gone home, which they would not have done, any number of other coal mining companies would have stepped in to take their place. However, the scare tactic worked and when the vote came up in the state it was defeated.

Governor Marland, who knew that if the tax had passed he would have been able to provide for new schools in almost every county and improve the state's infer structure immensely, became very bitter after the vote failed. The coal barons had turned practically everyone in the state against him and he was not re-elected to a second term.

After his defeat he returned to Illinois, where he was originally from and sank into a deep depression. He developed a drinking problem and in a short time was a full blown, down and out alcoholic.

However, by the time he began driving a cab in Chicago he had gotten sober and was starting to really put his life back together. He even thought about re-entering the world of politics. Unfortunately he developed cancer and died at the young age of 42.

Just outside of Charleston I picked up interstate 79 which carried me to state route 19 which took me south into Nicholas county. Here I took route 55 and shot straight over to Richwood. I had been climbing the Appalachian mountains ever since leaving Kentucky and by the time I got into Nicholas county I had to roll my windows up because it was so cold. Just before reaching Richwood I stopped to take a leak by the Cherry River and nearly froze to death during the short period that I was out of the truck. Again, this was July!

Once making it to my parent's house I pulled in and went inside. I was greeted with smiles and hugs from both my mother and father. I had carried in the bag of corn I had bought in Indiana and when I handed it to my father our brief reunion was forgotten as he rushed to the kitchen to cook the corn as if I had been there for a while and had not just returned form a nearly 7,000 mile journey across America and back. I had expected questions about the Rockies or New Orleans but all my dad could focus on was that corn. Oh if only Amanda was here. She would have gotten a kick out of this.

37

The evening I got to my parents house I went out and ran an easy three miles at a slow pace. My father warned that I should save my energy for the next day's race but I had to stretch my legs. I had been driving over 300 miles a day for almost a month and it was uncomfortable to walk. After I ran, and again against my father's recommendation, I did 50 push ups and 50 sit ups. I knew I was not going to do too well in the race the next day anyway and my main focus was my upcoming basic training obligation which was now less than two weeks away.

That night I slept in a bed in a house for the first time in a month. It felt great and I slept like a rock. It felt like I had just gone to sleep when my father woke me up the next morning at 7:00 a.m. for the race which started at 8:30. I got out of bed, drank some of Regina's tea, had a few pancakes then went down town with my father to check in at the registration table of the race.

Richwood was not the same town that it had been when I was growing up. Most of the middle class population moved out during the 1980's and 1990's as technology replaced manpower across the state. There had never been an "upper class" in the town to speak of so all that seemed to remain where retirees and low income families. Whereas there was once a boisterous shopping plaza where we would cruise in circles and hang out on weekends as teenagers and a Main Street lined with active businesses, there was now a half empty plaza and a Main Street lined with empty, barren store fronts. However, much of the allure to the area for myself and many tourists were the rivers and forests and fortunately they were still here and being well cared for by the Parks and Recreations services and the forward thinking timber harvesters.

Going down to the race was much like a reunion of sorts. I was reacquainted with my high school track coach, Bill Hutchinson who was now the principal at Richwood High as well as my assistant track coach, cross country coach and former art teacher Rocco Milanese. My father's best friend and fellow lumber mill businessman Bill Glasscock was there as well as he had been a runner and a cyclist for many years.

I spent some time catching up with my old friends before the race. When we all finally toed the line for the start I was happy to see that there were nearly 100 contestants running. This was the largest turn out we had ever had for a road race in this small town.

As I figured would be the case, I was unable to find my old fluid stride from the old days. This was due mostly to the driving I'd been doing but I knew also it was due to my age and lack of conditioning. Though I tried to do my best for the day I went through the first mile in only 6:30 and was already in eighth place. There were several college runners in from both my alma matta Fairmont State and West Virginia Wesleyan college, my old college foe when I ran at Glenville State.

Wesleyan had always been a pricey, private school and whereas Glenville State was the cheapest school in the state and was usually able to draw most of the West Virginia State track and field champions to attend, Wesleyan did a great job recruiting out of state athletes that were usually not champions in their states but would have been had they been in West Virginia. The kids at Wesleyan often referred to Glenville as "Cow Tech" due to its location well off of the beaten path. We always took great pride in running around the track ringing cow bells though each year as we beat Wesleyan and the rest of the schools in our conference at the conference championships nearly every year.

As the race progressed I was able to take advantage of a long down hill grade in the second half of the out and back coarse but I still only finished in a time of 19:57, the slowest I had ever run for a 5k. I placed 7'th overall and 1'st in my age group. This latter fact more because I was the only one in my age group more than any other.

After the race I spent some more time catching up with some of my old friends. I had brought my camera from home and my dad took several pictures of me with my old friends. I then went home, ate an early lunch and took a very long and much needed nap.

When I woke up I called Maia and we talked for thirty minutes. I was looking forward to spending a couple of days with my parents and trotting through the mountains I had grown up in but at the same time I was anxious to get back and see Maia for a few days before I had to go to Fort Benning. I told her as much and though she was just as anxious to see me as well she encouraged me to enjoy my time while I was in Richwood.

"I'm not going anywhere," she insured me in that angelic voice of hers.

Even though both of us were spent from running in the race that morning my father and I went for a five mile walk through the Monongahelia National Forest that evening. We drove up Handle Factory Hollow which is located behind my parents house, and parked and hiked out a road that was created by logging in the mid 1980's. This road had been a favorite hunting spot of my father's and mine when I was growing up and I had lots of memories on it.

As we walked, our conversation revolved around timbering as it commonly does when I am in the woods with my father.

"Last year alone the Monongahelia had a positive growth rate of more than 72 million board feet," my father informed me.

"What exactly does that mean?" I asked.

"It means that in spite of all the timbering, it would still take six mills the size of ours running twenty four hours a day to cut just the growth from the forest. That is not even touching the existing timber," he informed me. "People complain that we're cutting down all the trees in this country and the fact is that there is no way we could do that if we tried. There are more trees in America now than there were when Christopher Columbus discovered the place and there will always be more in the future than there is in the present."

My father had told me this fact before. I did some research online at one point and found out that it was true. One of the misleading things about the number of trees in America is the fact that for some reason the census takers don't count trees that have been planted by timber companies with the intent of future harvesting in their numbers. I found this fact to be quite absurd myself. Does this mean that these trees don't exist? That would be like not counting the money in your checking account as part of your net worth because you have intentions of spending it. Going on the same practices as the timber census takers that would mean that the money in your checking account didn't exist.

"What a pretty clear cut," my father said as we reached the turn around point of our walk, which was located beneath a portion of the forest where the most recent loggers had cut practically everything in site and left it to lay.

My father explained that clear cutting is another much misunderstood practice in the timbering industry. Most people who look at a clear cut at face value believe the loggers had come in and simply cut down everything in site for no reason at all. Actually, there were several positives to clear cutting as my father saw it.

First of all, much of what is cut is unhealthy, scraggly trees and undergrowth. By removing such undesirable flora and fauna the sunlight is allowed to make its way back into these parts of the forests and the undesirable growth is generally replaced with the healthier, more dominate species in the area like oak, polar, and in the case of the mountains surrounding Richwood, black cherry. This provides for a healthier forest and the future prospects of harvesting quality timber to insure a flourishing economy in the industry.

Secondly, clear cutting provides a home for much of the wild life in the area. The cuts are too thick for man to walk through, yet the beasts of the forests can disappear into their centers with the grace of ballerinas. Clear cuts provide homes for deer, bears, and many wild birds, particularly the Ruffed Grouse.

Ruffed Grouse is a beautiful species of bird that was on the brink of extinction around the 1950's mostly because of new timbering regulations that were imposed at the time. When clear cutting became more heavily regulated the grouse did not have as many safe havens in which to nest and their population was nearly decimated by such predators as foxes, coyotes, and several different types of birds of prey. With the loosening of clear cutting regulations these wild birds have again found a safer refuge and their numbers have climbed back dramatically.

Thirdly, another benefit of clear cutting according to my father is that it helps prevent and maintain forest fires. Much of the old, unhealthy growth that is not clear cut simply dies off eventually, falls to the forest floor and provides the best fodder imaginable for forest fires. It is no coincidence that states such as California who have some of the toughest laws against clear cutting also have the highest rates of forest fires. Clear cuts may not be as pretty in the eyes of everyone such as my father but according to him they do serve a healthy purpose in our forests.

While we were walking back to the truck my father and I spotted two deer, one a buck and one a doe, and a sizable black bear. Black bear too were found in dwindling numbers during the mid part of the last century but had made a great come back in their population not unlike the Ruffed Grouse. This is another fact that can be attributed to clear cutting.

After our walk it was nearing dark. I took another shower and called my kids in Seattle. I told them about my performance in the race and about the walk I took with my father. Though my performance in the race had been poor in my eyes, I looked like a hero in the eyes of my children. One of the things I loved most about being a father was that it didn't matter what kind of day I had, how much I had failed in life or in the eyes of others; in my children's eyes I could do no wrong.

After talking to my kids I sat up with my mother and talked and watched television until 11:00 p.m. before going to bed. Again, I hate television but my mother loves it. She particularly likes old movies and the sitcom "House." I figured I could tolerate the boob tube for a while as it gave me an opportunity to spend time with my mother.

The next day I slept in till 9:00 a.m. I was really enjoying the luxury of an indoor bed.

When my father got home from church just after noon we decided to take another trip through the wilderness. This time however, I would run and he would ride his Trek mountain bike. My father, being a bigger guy at 6 feet tall and 220 pounds always seemed to prefer the bike to running as his large frame did not have to fight gravity as much on a bike but running was such a love of mine that I never gave cycling a fair shake. I had done well at it in triathlons years ago but running is where my heart was.

On this day we would do a nine mile loop that headed up the South Fork of the Cherry River, crossed the Fork Mountain, and then came back down to the house. Nine miles was quite a way to go in my current level of conditioning but due to the terrain it would be a slow run and I was willing to put up with any discomfort I might experience in the latter stages of the run in order to retrace the footsteps of my youth through this country. I used to do this run twice a week at nearly six minute mile pace and never think anything of it. The older I get it seems the better I was.

The first four miles or so of the run took us along side the Cherry River. My father would ride ahead of me and then wait up once he thought he had gotten too far ahead. He generally only had to wait two or three minutes before I caught up with him. He could not ride too fast due to the freshly laid fist sized gravels that were put on the road by the latest logging operation. Had these gravels not been laid, the 150,000 pound fully loaded log trucks would have dug trenches into the dirt road that even a four wheel drive truck could not make it through.

At one point while running along the river I stopped to view over the edge of the bank into one of my favorite childhood fishing holes. I watched as a Golden trout, which is actually a DNA mutation of a Rainbow trout, rose to the surface and grabbed a gnat and then carried him to the depths and his death below. Two smaller native brook trout watched from a safe distance in the hopes of grabbing some gnats for themselves while Goldie was preoccupied below.

I started running again, after wishing I had my fly rod with me, and rejoined my father just around the next bend where we would start ascending the steep grade that would take us for two miles to the top of the mountain.

"You don't have to wait up for me," my father said as we began our climb. Though he had had the advantage on the flat land I would have the advantage going up hill and he knew it. I had always been a good hill runner, refusing to slow down up hills but instead maintaining my pace by leaning forward into the hill to readjust my center of gravity and pumping my arms like two angry pistons. The combination allowed for gravity and my arms to carry me up the hill. This is a technique I had learned at the cross country camp I attended in Pennsylvania all those years ago.

As I plugged my way up the hill I saw a huge hawk of some sort fly from out of the woods to my right, let out a scream and then lit on a branch about forty yards behind me. About two minutes later I heard this hawk scream again and I assumed my father was passing him now.

When I finally made it to the top of the hill I decided to stop and both wait for my father and get a drink of water from the small stream that ran under the road here. This road was known as Showers Run due to the sudden ten to twenty feet drops this stream made off of cliffs as it made its way down the mountain and into the Cherry River.

As I stepped into the creek bed it felt as if the temperature dropped by ten degrees. The water from the stream was so clear and cold that it felt like it was cutting my lips when I drank it. As I came back up out of the creek bed my father was making it to the top of the hill winded and red in the face.

"Did you see the hawk?" I asked.

"Yeah," he said. "Did you see it too?"

"Yea, I saw it," I told him.

After my father took several long swigs from his water bottle we rounded a sharp left hand turn in the road and began another, shorter descent. Nearly half way to the top of this hill I noticed that there was a new logging road heading up into the woods to our right. This road had never been here when I frequented these parts when I was a youth and it appeared to go to Bob Smith's farm, a small, mountain top farm owned by our friend and long time Richwood resident and native Bob Smith. Bob had been a marine and actually took part in the invasion of Iwo Jima during WWII.

"I wonder if that road goes to Bob's farm?" I asked my dad as we began making our way past the new road.

"I don't know," he said. "Why don't you check it out and I'll meet you back at the house."

"Ok," I said before veering to the right to explore the new road as my father continued on the main road back to his house.

This new road was very steep as it made its way to the top of the mountain. I had my head down leaning into the hill and did not realize that it was actually turning to the right, heading away from Bob's farm. When I got to the top of the hill I looked up as two does who had been standing in the road ran into the woods. This is when I realized I had come to the sudden dead end of the road and that it had veered as far right as it had.

Not to worry. Though I was nearly a mile away from where I thought the road would take me I knew these woods better than the back of my hand. I figured the Fork Mountain trail to be just at the top of the ridge above the road and when I sought it out it was less than 100 yards away. I could take this trail back to Bob's farm and then travel the road off of the other side of the mountain for about two miles back to my parent's house.

As I made my way through the Fork Mountain trail I ran were I could but made sure to walk where the footing was not as safe due to rocks and roots. My legs felt like spaghetti at this point after yesterday's race and walk and the seven or more miles I had already traveled today. I would certainly pay for all of this weekend's activities over the next couple of days. Fortunately, Maia loved to give me massages and she had promised me a long one when I got back.

I made my way to a point in the trail that held a very dear (literally) memory to me as it was the place where I had killed my largest buck ever when I was a kid. I was a freshman in college and the deer was an 11 point buck that had antlers that spread for 18 inches in the center. The antlers were so thick at their base where they met the head that I could not wrap my hand around them.

One cold morning in November of 1992 my father and I were in these very woods deer hunting. We had split up like we usually did and I had made my way to this point.

I was being so very careful not to make any noise as I crept through the woods when I startled several deer that were traveling through here together. I watched as four does ran off but a much larger deer stood there staring at me. I had never seen a deer this big in my life. It looked like a small cow!

I held my gun up to peer at the animal through my 12 power scope and could not figure out why I could not see horns on a deer this big. As I dropped the scope from my eye I saw why I had not seen the horns. As the deer turned to join his lady friends I saw the horns flash by as his head turned to face the other direction. I had not seen them before because I was not looking out far enough from his head.

I was unable to get a shot off at the deer, as I had always refused to shoot an animal while it was running, knowing that even if I hit it I stood a greater chance of simply wounding it than killing it. Like Teddy Roosevelt, I never believed in causing an animal unneeded suffering. I only took clear shots at vital spots, like the neck or the heart and lungs right behind the front shoulder, that would kill the animal without them realizing they'd even been hit.

When I told my dad that day about the deer I had seen he hardly believed me. The next day I went back to the same spot alone as my dad had killed a nice 8 pointer the day before. I sat in the same spot, the very spot I had seen this beast, from 7:00 a.m. until it got dark at 5:00 that evening. During the day I passed up shots at two smaller bucks in anticipation of the big one returning.

The next morning I was back at the same spot by the time the sun rose above the hill at 7:00 a.m. I would not have to wait that long this day. At 8:15 I heard the crunching of leaves and the crackling of twigs as something big was making its way through the woods. I raised my gun to my shoulder so as not to risk being seen doing so once the creature making the noise came within site of me.

Finally, a very large 8 point buck made its way around a large oak tree and into my sight about 80 yards down the hill form me. This was the second biggest deer I had ever seen in my life, smaller only than the 11 pointer I had seen two days earlier. Taking a shot at this large beast was very tempting.

I clicked my .243 Remington off of safe and honed in on the kill zone just behind this buck's front left shoulder. However, just before I pulled the trigger I noticed that this buck had stopped walking and I could still hear crunching leaves and cracking twigs just ten yards or so behind it.

I would have to make a very important decision. The 8 pointer was two steps away from going over the hill and out of sight. Did I want the sure thing of this deer, which would have still been the biggest deer I had ever killed up until that point or should I wait to see if the big one was behind him? I chose the latter and the choice paid off as just as the buck in the front stepped out of site the large 11 pointer I had seen two days before stepped into view. I zeroed in on the kill zone and squeezed off a shot. My heart was beating just as hard as it ever had during any one mile race I had ever run.

After the shot I heard a loud thud, a squirmish in the leaves and then silence. I walked down the hill and saw that I had aimed true and killed not only the largest buck I had ever seen myself in the wild but one of the largest bucks I had ever known of anyone else killing either.

I gutted this deer and attempted to begin dragging it off of the mountain but it was so big I could not do it alone. I practically ran home and called my dad to come help me. I told him I had gotten the big one that I had seen when he and I were out two days before and he rushed home from the mill as quickly as he could.

When we had made our way up to the big buck my father was astonished to see that it was every bit as big as I had told him it was. I could sense his pride for me seething through his pores. We had a taxidermist mount the head of this deer and it still hangs in my father's office at the lumber mill to this day.

As I finally made my way down the Fork Mountain trail to Bob's farm my mind was filled with many more great memories. Many of these memories included the many times I had seen black bears at this location on uncountable occasions.

Bob's farm was nothing like one might imagine when they think of a farm. There we no fields of corn or wheat as the terrain and rocks in this part of the state does not allow for such. There is a simple clearing of about three quarters of an acre where an old two story house is located off to the far most edge. There is a small orchard of about a dozen apple trees in the center of the small field and the rest consists of grass.

There is a very steep road that runs to the top of a hill on the opposite side of the field that the Fork Mountain trail comes from. This field was once used for planting but it has been vacant for several decades.

Once, while hunting with my father he took me to a spot in the woods about twenty yards out from this top field and showed me where he had discovered about half a dozen old graves. The graves appeared as sunken holes about six feet long by three feet wide. Their heads and feet where marked with triangular rocks and the sunken holes where positioned to face east and west. I had asked Bob Smith about the origins of the graves once and he said that all he and his family who had owned this land for almost 100 years could figure was that they were those of the original settlers of the land but even they didn't know that for sure.

When I was a teenager I would often bring my compound bow up to the lower field and target practice in the apple orchard. I would usually collect a paper sack of apples and carry them to one of my numerous deer stands I had built out in the woods to try to lure in a buck much like the one I had killed at the top of the Fork Mountain trail.

One late summer afternoon I had bagged a sack of apples and then begun shooting my bow. After I had released all five of my arrows I laid my bow down beside the sack of apples and walked to my target which was only twenty yards away and began pulling my arrows. Just as I pulled out the first arrow a large black bear, weighting probably 250 pounds, walked out of the woods and strolled right past me, passing only ten yards away, and went to my sack of apples. I sat there nervously on one knee as he sniffed the contents of my paper bag and then went about eating apples that were laying on the ground beside it. I watched this bear do this for about ten minutes before the sound of my father's truck coming up the hill scared the bear off. It ran back into the woods from which it had come, again passing me by only ten yards. It never seemed to know that I was there.

One time, I saw a huge sow standing on her hind legs ripping off part of the edge of a small utility building that is located about forty yards from the house while her two cubs ate apples from the field. I was in a secure location about 80 yards away while I watched this. Once the bears left the field I went to the building and raised my hand to the mark where she had been ripping off the wooden edging. She was ripping the building at a height of about seven feet. This is one way bears mark their territory. Any other bear who comes along will compare their height of reach and if they cannot reach higher than the original bear's markings they know that it is best that they move on.

On this day I went over to that same small building and saw that there were fresh rips at about the same level that I had witnessed that bear make years ago. I doubted that it was the same bear because so much time had passed but I wondered if it may be those of one of her cubs.

I then began making my way off of the mountain traveling down the main road, which was nothing more than a four wheeler trail. It was challenging getting a four wheel drive truck up this road at times but interestingly Bob did not own a four wheel drive truck. He usually only came to this farm in the summer and drove an old station wagon up to it when he did. My father and I probably spent more time up here than Bob did. We never understood why he didn't have a truck.

Half way down the mountain I noticed a new four wheeler path heading through the woods that appeared to be a short cut leading to the main road of Handle Factory Hollow. I began heading down this trail in an attempt to shorten the amount of time it would take me to get home.

About 100 yards into the trail I noticed fresh bear tracks. I was in a spot where the trail was surrounded by black berry bushes bearing more fruit than a dozen bears could eat in one passing. As I continued down the trail, picking and eating black berries as I went, I heard the grunts from a bear coming from about fifty yards ahead of me.

Black bears are actually very docile creatures that are only dangerous under two conditions. The first condition is if you mess with their young in the spring and the second is if you startle them and they react more out of instinct than any sort of violent nature that they really don't possess. Not wanting to sneak up on this bear and startle it, I began whistling and remained where I was for a couple of minutes. This would let the bear know I was there and give it time to clear out, which it did. I heard it crashing through the woods and I continued on my way.

I finally made my way to the top of Handle Factory Hollow. There are about a dozen homes up here that would match the typical Appalachian stereotype.

Most of the homes were mobile homes that had had extensions built onto them at some point to accommodate more family members. However, whereas these homes where once considerably run down when I was a child, they were now fixed up quite nice. They had been painted with fresh coats and the yards, which sported many broken down cars and household appliances were being well maintained.

On this day it appeared as if all the families who populate this mountain hollow were all located in the yard of one household. They were pitching horseshoes, playing bad mitten and blasting Johnny Cash music as loud as they could. They were having a ton of fun which was evidenced by their laughter and all the cans of Old Milwaukee and bottles of Crown Royal that were laid out in sight.

I descended Handle Factory Hollow from this point and was home in ten minutes. When I arrived I saw that my dad had already been home long enough to shower and change and grill some burgers and chicken breasts on the grill in the back yard.

"What took ya so long?" he asked when I walked in the door.

"That road didn't go to Bob's," I informed him.

"Where did it go to?" he asked.

"It went to the top of the mountain just above where I killed the eleven pointer," I informed him. "I picked up the Fork Mountain trail from there and came down that way."

"Oh," my dad said. "Are you hungry?" he then asked.

"I'm famished!" I said.

I gobbled down two hamburgers and two chicken breasts and a bunch of baked beans and salad. It was the most I had eaten in a while but over the past two days I had burned more calories than I had in a while too. I had walked/run 8 miles yesterday and my run/walk today had ended up being closer to 10 miles since the road I took had gone a different direction than I had previously thought that it did.

After I ate I showered and hung out with my mother in front of the boob tube for a while. I then called my kids and told them about my journey and called Maia and talked to her for a while before going to bed. Tomorrow night I would be back in Maia's arms and I could hardly contain myself.

38

The next morning, a Monday, I awakened fresh but with sore legs from my previous two day's activities. People often have the tendency to do nothing on the days they are sore from working out but I learned years ago that the best thing to do is to do a light work out to work out the lactic acid buildup in your muscles and to drink lots of water to flush it, so this morning I decided to do an easy three mile run. My mother was out grocery shopping and my father was out of town on a business trip so I would not be losing out on any quality time spent with them before I headed back to Virginia.

I had heard from my father that an old friend of mine, Mary Jo Fletcher was now managing the assisted adult living facility in Richwood. Mary Jo had been a distance runner at Webster County High School the same time I was running for Richwood and we had developed a friendship through seeing each other at track meets. In the summers we would often go to the same road races around the state so we could see each other then as well. Though she was a very attractive blond with beautiful blue eyes we had never dated and I used to kick myself in the butt for it back when I was younger. Opportunities had been there but during those days I didn't think about girls too much because I was so focused on my running.

I very stiffly jogged the mile and a half down to the assisted living facility then made my way through the door once I got there. Mary Jo's office was right on the inside of the door and when I went in she was talking to one of her employees. Her back had been to me but when she turned around and saw me for the first time in nearly fifteen years she smiled and squealed and ran over and gave me a big hug even though I was somewhat sweaty.

"Oh my God, how are you?" she said loudly as we hugged.

"I'm great, how are you?" I asked in return.

Mary Jo had gotten married since I had seen her last and had two beautiful sons as was evidenced by their pictures that were littering her desk. She and her husband lived in Fayette county so she had quite a commute to get to work every day.

We talked like old friends for about ten minutes before her duties with work called her away. I let her know where I was living and that I too now had children. I let her know that unfortunately my marriage had not lasted but I did tell her how happy I was to have found Maia. Mary Jo admitted guiltily that she no longer ran but that she intended to get back into it.

Mary Jo and I parted with another hug and then I went back outside to run back home. My calves were killing me, which let me know I really needed to drink lots of water today. In spite of my tight muscles I was soon back to the neighborhood I had grown up in and I began to walk around the block to cool down.

As I passed a familiar house on Cherry Street, the next street over form my parent's home on Water Street I decided to stop by and see another old friend. I walked up the steps of an old, yet well kept two story white house and wrapped on the door. About twenty seconds later a little old lady in her late eighties answered the door.

"Do you know who I am?" I asked as she looked up at me.

"Well sure I do," she said as if I had been crazy for asking. "You're Kevin Lake. Come on in."

This lady was Ernie Barker. She had been my fourth grade teacher more than twenty years ago and I hadn't seen her since I was in high school. We walked into her enclosed porch and she sat down in what appeared to be her favorite sitting chair and I took a seat on a chair directly across from her.

"How did you remember me after all these years?" I asked her, seeing that her mind was still as sharp as it had ever been.

"Those big brown eyes!" she said. "I could never forget them."

"So how have you been?" I asked her.

"I've been fairly well," she said. "I had the flu for a while and I lost some weight because of it but I believe I have kicked it."

"I was in visiting for a couple of days," I began telling her. "I'm leaving today and I wanted to stop by and see you before I left."

"Well, I'm glad you did," she said.

I had actually attempted to stop by and see Mrs. Barker the last several times I had been in Richwood but I was never able to catch her at home. She is part of what Tom Brokaw has labeled "The Greatest Generation" and I knew that my chances of seeing her again were diminishing with each passing day. At this time there are several thousand of the WWII generation folks dying each day and I had learned to really appreciate them when I worked with them as a broker.

Mrs. Barker's husband had died about fifteen years ago and she had been living here alone ever since. She has two sons in the area, one of which is a teacher as well, and they and her grandchildren stop by to see her regularly. She also has a young lady who delivers meals on wheels to her and checks in on her as well.

Mrs. Barker was one of the great old school teachers that came form her generation. I was actually one of the last students fortunate enough to be taught by her as she retired only two years after she taught me and my class.

We talked for more than an hour. We caught up on old times and I got to find out a lot about her that I had never known previously. Mrs. Barker told me that she had actually taught for many years without a college education. It seems that you could do so up until about the 1970's at which point all the teachers who did not have a degree at the time where given ample time to obtain one. Mrs. Barker had gotten hers through Glenville State College.

Mrs. Barker had grown up on a farm on Hinkle Mountain, a small mountain community just outside of Richwood. Her farm had consisted of 75 acres, 50 of which is still in the family. I did not realize it at the time, but when I had her as a teacher she and her husband would spend from the spring through the fall at the farm and then live in their house here on Cherry Street through the winter. The snow was so fierce on Hinkle Mountain in the winter that she would not have been able to get off of the mountain and get to school had she stayed up there in the winter. I knew this fact first hand as I often ran across the top of Hinkle Mountain in the winters when I was growing up. There were times when it was sunny in Richwood and the snow would be blowing so hard when I crossed the top of Hinkle Mountain that I could hardly see.

Like so many in her generation, Mrs. Barker had been used to a two mile walk to school when she herself was a student. She told me of a faithful dog she had for many years that would make the trip to school with her each morning and then be there at the end of the day to walk her home. Those were certainly simpler times when a little girl could walk that distance twice a day with no threats of being picked up by a child predator.

I had always wondered why Mrs. Barker bore the first name of a man. I asked her about this and she laughed, telling me that her parents had had nothing but boys before her and thought she would be a boy as well so they had picked out the name "Ernie" for her before she was born. When they saw that she was a girl, they didn't bother picking a new name. As with Harry "S" Truman's parents, I guess people of old never put too much stock into names.

I sat back and listened as Mrs. Barker reminisced about the early days with her husband. It seems that Mr. Barker had been a friend of one of her older brothers and when the kids would all hang out together Mrs. Barker would tag along and this is how she and Mr. Barker got to know each other. He was several years older than her and when he had grown up and left Richwood they had stayed in touch. Once, while on a trip back home he asked her to marry him, which she did.

"I'd like to ask you a question about the current state of the public school system," I broke in when she took a pause in one of her stories.

"What is that?" she asked.

"What is your take on this apparent epidemic of A.D.H.D. and the use of such drugs as Ritalin to control it?"

"Well," she began. "I really don't understand it or know too much about it so maybe I just shouldn't comment on it."

I was crushed at her response. Here was one of the great old school teachers from days gone by and I had hoped to get her opinion on this big, modern issue but she seemed reluctant to give one. Sensing my disappointment in her lack of an answer she began to speak again.

"I remember this one time though," she started as I sat back up in joy, knowing I was about to receive a hidden message.

"I had a class of twenty four students one year and twenty of them were boys," she continued. "I could tell on the first day that these two boys in particular were going to be trouble."

"The second day of class," she went on, "I told those two boys to move their desks up beside mine and sit on opposite sides of me. I told them that I had a very important job for them. Their eyes got big and their jaws dropped and they couldn't wait to find out what I had in store for them."

"I told them that I had a bad habit of misplacing things and that it would be their job to keep an eye on everything I did. They needed to watch and see where I laid down my chalk, my stapler, my grade book and anything else I touched because I could never remember where I put things."

"I would intentionally act as if I couldn't find things several times a day and those boys would jump out of their seats and point out where I had placed them. I had them sit up there with me all through the fall and the winter and then moved them back in with the class in the spring. I never had a bit of a problem with those boys," she finished.

She told me that she followed the progress of these two boys throughout the rest of their school days and that they were never a problem for any other teacher and that they graduated in the top of their class.

I remember a chilling statistic I had heard in one of my education classes when in college. Supposedly children that drop out of school make their minds up to do so by the time they are only in the third grade. I had to wonder if these two boys had made that decision or where heading toward that decision when they walked into Mrs. Barker's class that first day of the school year and if her actions had reversed that decision. She had handled their behavior in such a way that is unheard of these days. In essence this story of hers let me know exactly where she stood in her opinion of A.D.H.D.

I spent a little more time with Mrs. Barker on her porch but my stomach was calling. I hadn't eaten any breakfast before my run and I was now quite hungry in spite of all the calories I had taken in the night before. I said my goodbyes to Mrs. Barker, gave her a tender hug and then returned to my parents house to eat and pack my stuff to leave. Mrs. Barker truly was one of the greatest from the greatest generation.

39

On my way back to Virginia I would be traveling through one of my most favorite places on earth; Pocahontas County West Virginia. Pocahontas was the second largest county in the state and was mostly part of the Monongahela National Forest. Ronald Reagan had set most of this land aside as National Forest during his presidency of the 1980's at the request of long time West Virginia Senator Robert C. Byrd.

I made my way through Pocahontas county past several of my favorite trout streams and hunting spots. I eventually entered the small town of Marlinton. I could have avoided this town and taken a much shorter route that headed directly to the interstate but I had missed these mountains so much that I chose to take old state route 39 all the way to Lexington, Virginia where I would complete my 7,000 mile loop across the country before cutting back over into Charlottesville on Interstate 64.

As beautiful as Pocahontas county is though it had an ominous tone overshadowing it in the 1980's due to an infamous murder known as the "Rainbow Murders" that had taken place in 1980 at a remote location in the county known as Briery Knob.

The forks of the Williams River in the center of Pocahontas County is the meeting place for a large number of hippies known as the "Rainbow People" every ten years. When this group meets there are literally thousands of peace loving, tree hugging societal misfits that gather for about a month to frolic, use drugs in excess and be merry.

On June 25'th, 1980, two young women on their way to attend this gathering, 19 year old Nancy Santomero and 26 year old Vickie Durian were picked up by a local man while hitchhiking. There is argument weather they were picked up by one man or several men. At any rate, they never made it to the Rainbow gathering as they were shot and murdered and their bodies later found at Briery Knob.

A local man at the time of the murder, Jacob Beard was convicted of the murders in 1993 and sentenced to two life sentences. Beard had long since moved to Florida where he was managing a local automobile dealership.

Some time after Beard's conviction however, serial killer Joseph Franklin, the man responsible for shooting Hustler Icon Larry Flint in 1978 confessed to the Rainbow murders. Franklin, a white supremacist on death row in Tennessee claimed that he murdered the two young women due to their views on interracial relationships and he claimed to finally be admitting to the murders because he did not want Beard to get the credit for his work. Supposedly he described parts of the crime that only the true killer would have been knowledgeable of and Beard was reluctantly granted a new trial. In 1999 Beard was released on bond five years after he was first incarcerated.

In spite of the real life horror story that had been carried out in Pocahontas County its natural beauty is hard to be rivaled by any land in this country. I had been as far north as Maine and as far south as you could go, Key West Florida. On my current trip I had driven from coast to coast, taking in the Rocky Mountains and the rolling plains of the mid-west, yet still I had not seen any place as beautiful as the county that was only a hop, skip and a jump from my parent's house in Richwood.

I don't know how many times I had fantasized about one day returning to Pocahontas County, grabbing some cheap land off the well beaten path, throwing up an inexpensive log home or a Yurt and living happily ever after. Unfortunately at this stage in my life, with three kids to raise, there is no economy to speak of in this beautiful county that would allow me to be able to handle my financial responsibilities. It is sad that this is the case for much of the state.

As it neared dark I crossed back into my current home state of Virginia. I made it to Lexington and stopped for a bite to eat. I would be meeting Maia at her restaurant at 10:30 when she got off from work so I had some time to kill. I ate slowly and then got back on the road and continued east.

When I got back to Charlottesville I noticed that the mood had changed, at least for me. When I had left, I was overburdened with negative emotions and feelings due to all that had happened in the past couple of years; my divorce, losing my home and sending my kids off to Seattle. However, as I made my way back into town I felt as if these negative feelings had been lifted. What had happened to me over the past couple of years was simply a phenomena called "life." I realized through many of the experiences of my trip that hard times come the way of anyone who attempts to live as opposed to simply exist.

I thought of a young man who had great ambitions in the automobile world years ago and upon trying to find employment in the industry was handed a wrench and thrown into a grease pit. That young man, Walter P. Chrysler would have a huge impact on the auto industry forever.

I thought of a young man who was born poor and spent many years in a dirt floor cabin and who had gone through unbearable hardships yet in spite of these humble beginnings and tough times Abraham Lincoln would effect American history in a way no one else ever had.

I thought also of a man who had taken from him the ability to stand and walk on his own two feet and how Franklin D. Roosevelt would exemplify the strength of any ten men and lead our nation through a great depression and a world war in a way no other human could have conceived possible. I realized while looking back on my own hardships, which paled in comparison to the hardships of so many others, including the folks I had met in New Orleans, that hard times are not sent by an unjust God to punish and crush, but to challenge! Difficult times in life are not hurdles set in place to trip us up but rather are opportunities put before us to allow us to grow and become better.

These were my thoughts as I pulled into the shopping center at Forest Lakes, the part of town where Maia's restaurant was located. I parked my truck and then walked inside to lay eyes on the most beautiful woman I had ever known for the first time in a month.

After I had walked in the door I stood by the greeter's station for just a minute. I quickly spotted Maia waiting on a customer. When she turned around and saw me she almost ran straight to me. When she got to me we just stared at each other with big smiles on our faces.

"You know how hard it is for me to keep from hugging and kissing you right now?" Maia asked, knowing she had to keep her composure in the work place.

"Not as hard as it is for me to do the same," I told her.

It felt like an eternity while I sat at an empty table slurping on ice water waiting for Maia to finish work. I tried reading to pass the time but I didn't pay much attention to the book, I can't even remember which one it was, because all of my attention was focused on Maia. She moved with such elegant grace as she pranced around the dining room floor carrying out her simple tasks. She made them look artful though, not simple. She too was having difficulties focusing on her tasks as she kept looking over at me, mouthing the words "I love you."

When Maia finally did get finished she clocked out and we left the restaurant. We didn't make it half way across the road heading toward the parking lot before she said, "Kevin?"

"Yes," I said, turning toward her.

At this point, she wrapped her arms around me in a giant bear hug and laid a lip lock on me so tightly I could hardly breathe. I didn't much mind though as the breath of her essence was enough to sustain me. I reciprocated the kiss and we stood there, blocking traffic as we kissed.

"I told you I'd wait," she said as our lips finally parted and we continued to the parking lot and allowed traffic to continue flowing.

"I told you I'd return," I said.

Maia and I went back to her place on the farm in Orange county and were in each other's arms making passionate love in just minutes after entering her home. Though we went at it for over an hour it seemed as if only a few minutes had passed. We stayed up all night talking, making love and cuddling. This was the greatest reward at the end of my journey that I could have imagined.

Unfortunately Maia and I only had a few days to spend together before I had to leave to go to basic training at Fort Benning. Other than when she had to work we spent every waking hour of our time together. I told her of all the things I had seen and done while on my trip across America during the day and at night we stayed intertwined in each other's bodies, physically acting on the passion we had for each other in our hearts, minds and souls.

On the morning I had to leave to report for basic training we did not make love. Frankly, we were both too worn out from all the love we had made since I got back from my trip. Instead, we laid in bed and stared into each other's eyes and barely spoke a word. We both knew what our minds were thinking. We were madly in love and life was good.

After I loaded my belongings in my truck, Maia walked me out to the drive way to see me off.

"I'll wait for you," she said, just as she had before I went on my trip across America.

"I'll return," I said, giving her the same response I had before.

As much as I hated to do so I then pulled out of her drive after sharing one last passionate kiss. I watched in the rear view mirror as Maia stood there, not taking her eyes off of my truck until I was out of sight.

As I drove through the Virginia country side I thought ahead of what laid in store for me. I was off to Fort Benning, Georgia, the home of the infantry and I knew not what challenges I would face once I got there. I knew though that I was going with a greater sense of appreciation for what it was I was fighting for; America. I had now seen our great country in person and was convinced even more so than before that I had made a wise decision to roll my sleeves up and offer to do my part in protecting what such greats as George Washington, Andrew Jackson, Abraham Lincoln, Harry S. Truman and others had worked so hard to build.

I had another thought as I looked back on the great journey I had just completed. I don't know if the realization had come to me while I was driving across the plains of Texas or if it was when I was gazing out across the New Mexico desert. I don't know if it occurred to me while I was having my "baptismal" experience in the Colorado River in Utah or while I was bathing in the Yellowstone of Montana. Wherever I was when it came though, I realized that during my trip I had never been homeless at all, because no matter where I was, everywhere in America I was home.

978-0-595-50397-
0-595-50397-7

Lightning Source UK Ltd.
Milton Keynes UK
UKOW03f1147290914

239350UK00001B/270/P